Great Ad!
Low-Cost Do-It-Yourself Advertising for Your Small Business

Carol Wilkie Wallace

LIBERTY HALL
PRESS™

To my Father
ROBERT E. WILKIE
With Love and Remembrance

LIBERTY HALL PRESS books are published by LIBERTY HALL PRESS, an imprint of TAB BOOKS. Its trademark, consisting of the words "LIBERTY HALL PRESS" and the portrayal of Benjamin Franklin, is registered in the United States Patent and Trademark Office.

First Edition
First Printing

© 1990 by TAB BOOKS
TAB BOOKS is a division of McGraw-Hill, Inc.

Library of Congress Cataloging-in-Publication Data

Wallace, Carol Wilkie.
    Great ad! : low-cost, do-it-yourself advertising for your small business / by Carol Wilkie Wallace.
      p.   cm.
    ISBN 0-8306-8467-0   ISBN 0-8306-3467-3 (pbk.)
    1. Advertising. 2. Small business. I. Title.
HF5823.W412   1990
659.1—dc20   90-6681
                                                CIP

TAB BOOKS offers software for sale.
For information and a catalog, please contact:

TAB Software Department
Blue Ridge Summit, PA 17294-0850

Questions regarding the content of this book
should be addressed to:

Reader Inquiry Branch
TAB BOOKS
Blue Ridge Summit, PA 17294-0214

Acquisitions Editor: David J. Conti
Book Editor: Susan L. Rockwell
Book Design: Jaclyn J. Boone
Production: Katherine G. Brown

Contents

Introduction

ADVERTISING IS AN ART, NOT A SCIENCE. THERE ARE NO MIRACLES AND NO GUARantees for success, even for the business with a multimillion dollar budget. Large businesses have advertising agencies, filled with people who have training in the art of advertising, to help them get their message to the public.

You, as a small businessperson, have no such luxury. You have a small budget and a small staff. You might have already looked into the idea of using an agency, only to find that they won't help you, because they can't make any profit from you. So you're left on your own to muddle along as best you can.

Poor advertising is one of those factors that contribute to the high failure rate for small businesses in this country. The very people who need help the most can't get it. You could have a great service or a dynamite selection of goods to sell, but if you lack the know-how for communicating this to the public, you might not stay open long. If you've got a business to run, how do you get time to acquire this mysterious expertise that keeps the customers flocking to your door?

The answer is right here. There's no big mystery to advertising. It's mostly common sense. The trick is to figure out where the people are who want what you have to offer. Why do they want your service or product? What do they get out of it? Where will they be likely to see your message, telling them that you have what they're looking for? That's what this book is about—to help you find the answers to these questions, and to use them to develop a successful advertising campaign.

Your first goal, as an advertiser, is to think like the customer. Once you get into this mode of thinking, the rest will follow. Your choice of media depends on where and when your customer is available and receptive to your message. Your choice of advertising message depends on what your customer wants to hear when they are choosing products or services like yours.

To think like the customer, you need to begin with research. The first section of this book explains how to size up several factors that influence your advertising: your own business and its appeal to the public, your customers, and your competition.

You will learn how to set objectives for advertising, so that you can develop ads to solve specific problems and reach specific goals. You will also learn how to size up your competition and to set yourself apart from your competitors so you can lure customers from their place to yours. Finally, you will learn to take an objective look at your customers—both those you already have and those you want to attract.

You will find a series of checklists incorporated into each chapter. If you follow these carefully, at the end of the first six chapters you will have developed a profile of your business, customers, and competition that will give you a sound basis for your advertising decisions.

Once you know what you have to say in your ads, and to whom you want to say it, you need to know where you want to say it. The second part of this book deals with media planning.

There are hundreds of ways to broadcast your message. Radio, newspapers, and television are the first things that pop to mind when we speak of advertising. The small budget business might not be able to use these media often enough to make an impact. There are other, less expensive media that can communicate effectively within the limits of your budget. The section on media planning will take a look at media, from newspapers through balloons, examining the advantages and disadvantages of each. If you follow the checklists in this section, you should emerge with a media plan ideally suited to your budget, your audience, and your goals.

Once you know where you will be advertising, you can begin to develop ads to fit those particular media. This is the area where most small businesses fail. They might turn out some great ads—but they lack the one ingredient that earmarks a professional ad campaign—consistency. The third section of this book begins by explaining the difference between merely creating ads, and developing a consistent campaign. You will then learn how to develop ads that all have common characteristics for different media—a particular look and sound that people will learn to associate with your business.

Don't worry if you're not an artist, or feel that you lack writing talent. In this book you'll find sources for artwork. Checklists will lead you through, step by step, until you have put together creative ads with professional-sounding copy. In the end, you'll have created advertising that you can be proud of.

From experience, I know that you might be tempted to skip some of the steps in this book. Many businesspeople feel that they already know enough about their business and their customers that they can jump right in and start making ads. Unfortunately, this just isn't true. Good advertising is based on research and sound planning. If you follow the checklists in this book, you will have that foundation. You will also have an advertising plan that will guide you through the entire year. Your ads will appear when you need them, and where you need them—and they will contain messages that will help you to achieve your goals for the year.

There's one other way to get your name before the public, and that's publicity. Knowing what is newsworthy about your business, and what interests both press and public can help you to get free coverage on newspaper and TV. Chapter 16 will introduce you to the publicity process, and help you to sort out the newsworthy elements of your own small business.

Finally, there are legal problems that confront even the most well-intentioned advertiser. Pay attention to the warnings in chapter 17 to avoid unnecessary headaches with your ads.

One additional warning: Even the best advertising campaign can't help you unless you can back up your promises with real products and services. So take a good hard look at your business. What can you do that will honestly benefit your customer? What real promises can you make? Where might you need to make adjustments?

Small businesses are what this country is all about. Advertising is only one ingredient in the mix that helps to make a business successful. But it's an important ingredient. As long as you follow the guidelines in this book, you will increase your chances for success. Who knows—by next year at this time, you could be one of those lucky entrepreneurs who can afford to use an advertising agency.

1

Making Your
Business Advertisable

JAKE ADMIRED HIS NEW SIGN—BLACK WITH GILT SCRIPT LETTERS. NOW THAT IT
was finished, his new restaurant, Jake's Place, could open.

"Very elegant," he said to the workers. "How do you like my card?"

"Nice," said the painter, "but it doesn't look much like the sign."

Jake ordered his business cards early. The printer designed them—red ink
on white, with a cute little cartoon of a chef in the corner. The sign painter was
right. They looked totally different from the sign. And, if we stepped inside the
newly completed restaurant, we would see that neither of these looked anything
like the trendy Eurostyle interior in apricot, gray and purple.

Poor Jake is in trouble before he even opens his doors. He doesn't have a
consistent logo, and he has three different color schemes. If it weren't for the
generic chef on his business card, we might even have trouble understanding
what his business is all about. "Jake's Place" doesn't convey much about the
style, ambiance, or cuisine of his restaurant.

Your name, logo—the way you present that name—and colors are three primary aspects of your business identity. These can make or break an advertising
campaign because they convey to the public your identity, personality, and even
price range. Before you start buying ads, get the basics down. It will save you
time and money.

If you are a business that offers the public a product or service they want or
need, then you are advertisable. You have at least one, natural message to send

1

out to people—"You can find it here." To advertise effectively, however, you need to have all the right elements working for you before you even talk to a media salesperson. Problems can pop up to create advertising difficulties where you least expect them. Sometimes, as in Jake's case, the very name of the business will be a problem if it doesn't inform people about exactly who you are and what you do. Too often, the problem is that the advertising, which you've already done, lacks consistency.

Often, taking a scatter gun approach to ordering your invoices, stationery, bags, and business cards leaves you with no consistent logo or image to convey to the public. Sometimes you can be the victim of too many good ideas and too many images to make a clear impression on your public. This chapter will examine these aspects—your name, logo, and company colors—to see how to turn them into advertising assets. Take a quick look at your competition, because these aspects can also give you an edge over them.

MAKING YOUR COMPANY NAME WORK FOR YOU

There are a lot of theories on how to name a business. If you first talked to the people at the phone book, you would look for a name that begins with A, or better still, AA, or AAA. The idea here is that you will get the first listing in your category, and people will call you first as they run their fingers down the columns.

This idea does have merit if you are selling aardvarks, or if yours is a business where most of the competition is settling for fine print listings. But a first listing is usually helpful only if no one is using the bigger and more expensive display ads that the Yellow Pages user always goes to first. If that AA name doesn't convey something about the business, then it's making trouble for you everywhere but in the phone directory.

Another theory claims that, if your business depends a lot upon personal credibility, it's best simply to give your business your own name. This, too, works fine, if you're in a one-horse town where everyone knows your name— and if you are very, very credible. But your name, like the name "Jake's Place," doesn't tell strangers or newcomers much about what you do and how you operate. If they don't know these basics, they will very likely do business with someone whose name does convey these messages.

There are a lot of other theories—far too many to go into. Instead, let's just say that a good business name will convey to the general public, as quickly as possible, what you're all about. It should also say something about the kind of business you are, and the image you want to convey. Make sure the name is not too limiting, or your ads will have to spend time explaining who you are. If you're on a small budget, you can't afford to waste space on this. So get the name right—now!

Names That Are Too Limiting

A former client of mine asked for help in advertising her shop, called Hearth Heaven. When the business opened, the name was perfect. She sold fireplace accessories and lovely fireplace mantels. A few years ago, however, she expanded to include a whole line of brass and pewter accessories for the entire home. The fireplace line attracted one-time purchases (after all, how many log baskets can you use?). The real meat of her business was in limited edition pewter sculptures.

The customers she already had knew about this. The average person skimming the newspaper ads would never think to look for sculptures at a place called Hearth Heaven. Since the owner had already paid to register the fictitious name and had built a costly sign reading ''Hearth Heaven,'' she was reluctant to change the name. She did, however, add a tag line to her ads, proclaiming ''Accessories for Your Hearth and Home.''

Names That Are Misleading

Another client named his business Alternative Telephones. He meant that he was providing an alternative to having the phone company come in to install your phones. Most of the people who were attracted to his ad read it because they thought he was selling French phones, wooden crank models, and speaker phones—alternatives to the standard Ma Bell models. They turned away from the ad disappointed. He needed a name that conveyed service. He, too, was reluctant to change after going through the whole process of registering the name. He went out of business quickly. (Not that the name was the whole problem—but it didn't help.)

Names That Are Hard to Spell

Colossal Cards was a company that rented out life-sized plywood greetings. These could be erected on your lawn to announce special occasions. For instance, new parents could order a giant stork telling the world about their new baby. Most people we surveyed, upon seeing the name, assumed that Colossal Cards were oversized, mailable greeting cards. (Another problem with this name—no one could spell colossal. This spells trouble for a business whose clientele will probably go to the phone book for information.) This client did agree to change his name to Greetings in the Grass. It helped.

Names That Don't Mean Anything

GRE Insurance had a different problem. The owner had a good reputation, and her clients gave her good word-of-mouth referrals. They didn't help, because no one could remember the correct initials. To most people, GRE didn't stand for anything. A few students associated the initials with the Graduate Record Exam. Not until we created ads that featured the owner, Gretchen Rae Evans, did the name stick in their minds.

Names Too Similar to the Competition

Finally, there is the name that gets confused with the competition—perhaps the worst fate of all. A barber in Iowa City called his establishment Headquarters. Another was Hairquarters. Then there was the Hairliner, the Hairport, Headliners—you get the picture. One of them was recommended to me as a place for a great cut—but when I got to the phone book to call and make an appointment I was hopelessly confused. So, I went to the Hawkeye Barber Shop.

Names That Can Mislead the Customer

Country Antiques was so named because it was located way out in the country. The owner tells me that customers are forever disappointed by the lack of rustic oak, baskets, and duck decoys in the shop. His stock of Georgian, Victorian, and Chippendale in no way suits the implication of the name. On the other hand, Turn of the Century Antiques delivers exactly what it promises: memorabilia from the turn of the century. Golden Thimble specializes in gold antique jewelry. What you expect when you see the name is exactly what you get.

Solutions to Problem Names

If you have a problem name, you might want to consider changing it. If you have been in business a long time and have already established a reputation and a decent clientele, then at least consider adding a tag line that explains who you are to the name, for the sake of attracting new business.

If you have a burglar alarm company, and your business name is ''H. Smith,'' add a tag line like ''The Theft Protectors.'' Then people will have some idea of who and what you are. You don't even have to be that clever. H. Smith Burglar Alarms will communicate all you need to say.

Checklist for Determining Whether Your Name Works for You

- Would the average person, upon hearing your name, know exactly what your company does or sells?
- Would the average person, upon hearing your company name, know everything that you sell and do—or only a limited part of it?
- Does your business name convey the image and personality that you would like your business to have?

- If you have answered no to any of the preceding questions, have you developed a tag line (slogan) to help convey your business approach and image? Will this, combined with your business name, convey an accurate message to your desired customers? (If you need help in creating a tag line, the checklists in chapter 12 will be helpful.)
- Is your business name easy to spell? To pronounce?

YOUR LOGO: Name Plus Personality

Once you have your name, the next thing you need is a recognizable way of presenting it to the public. Your name needs a look and style that will show anyone who sees your ads, or passes your store sign, a definite image of your business personality—and maybe even your price range.

One of the major problems I've noticed with small businesses is their tendency to leave their print advertising to the guy at the newspaper. This person often sets up the ad in what is called standard ad type—so that your name comes out looking like everything else. (So does your ad, by the way, but we'll get to that later.) See Fig. 1-1 for examples of standard newspaper type, where the advertiser has left no input.

Fig. 1-1. These ads tend to blend into each other because they all use the same typeface—a common fate for those advertisers who leave the choices up to the newspaper. Notice how the one ad that uses a logo (even with a fairly common typeface) stands out?

Requirements for a Good Logo

Your logo is a way of presenting your name to the public so that it not only conveys who you are and what you do, but what image you are trying to convey. It must have personality—a personality that matches your business. It must be everywhere—in every print ad you run, on your sales slips, business cards, stationery, bags, signs—anywhere your name goes. Figure 1-2 shows several logos that give the business in question a definite personality, as well as a clue as to what the business does.

Take a good look at a big company with a professional agency doing its advertising. For instance, the name and golden arches of McDonald's are on everything—the signs, the bags, the place mats, the rubber floor mats, and even the straw papers and salt packets. That logo is in every ad you see. I'm surprised that it's not baked into the sesame seed buns. You know that symbol. You can't even look at the St. Louis archway without thinking of a Big Mac. That's how powerful the McDonald's logo has become. It works as a mini-ad, a reminder, whenever you see it. Your logo needs to do this for you.

Your logo can be simply a particular way of writing your name. It can be script, block letters, or even a picture. If your name is Hook, use a giant fish hook instead of words. If your business is manufacturing rubber stamps, make your name look like it's been rubber stamped. If you want to convey dignity, you will need a rather formal style of type. On the other hand, a place that thinks of itself as fun and lively can use typefaces that have that look. There are hundreds of type styles, and one is bound to suit the image you want to convey.

Creating a Logo

One way to get a good idea of what styles are available is to go to your local art supply store and ask for a catalog of press-on letters. For an investment of about $7.50, you can browse through an entire spectrum of letters, from plain block to calligraphy, and from the dignified to the psychedelic. Sheets of these letters can be purchased for a nominal fee. Sometimes the lettering style you choose will be distinctive enough in itself to make a good logo. Other times you will need to add some pictorial or graphic elements.

The above is the quick and inexpensive way to a stylish logo. If you're not sure of your artistic sense or if (like me) you're simply not neat enough to do a decent job of concocting a logo from little pieces, you might want to consider consulting a graphic artist. The fee will seem expensive—anywhere from $250 to $1000—but when you consider that this artist is, in a sense, creating your public identity for you, it's worth it. This should be a one-time expense, that will serve you well for many years to come.

For that reason, don't get too faddish. Choose a logo style that will wear well. Choose one that is easy to read. Make sure that the style fits yours. If you are a very elegant catering firm, you might want an elegant script. If you are a

Fig. 1-2. Logos function most effectively if they suggest the nature of the business. All three of these logos use both type and pictures to suggest their image and function. The top logo, incorporating a "K" into the wheel of the bicycle, is a rough design for a new business, Kober's Bicycle Shop, designed by hopeful owner Rick Kober. The ad for Waco Gunnery uses customized letters; the general shape is from a typeface called "Rodeo," but the artist, Patrick Quinn, woodgrained the letters by hand. In the bottom logo, Steve Sillner turned the final "s" in the family's business name into the handle of a frosty beer mug. No question here about what Sillner's serves.

Fig. 1-3. Logos must be easy to read. People won't spend time trying to decipher your message. This logo symbol for Victory Exterminators looks, at first glance, more like a melting ice-cream cone than a dying bug. Plus, the graphic almost hides the "V" for Victory. (Clip art from Carol Belanger Grafton, *Ready-to-Use Decorative Letters.* Courtesy of Dover Books)

chic and trendy disco, you'll want some sharp and trendy letters. If you want to be known as a no-nonsense place, for heaven's sake avoid letters with curlycues, no matter how much you like them. Figure 1-3 and 1-4 show two logos that are too ornate to be readable.

A word of warning—even if you use a graphic artist, mistakes can happen. One client I took over in midstream did everything right in the beginning, getting a professionally designed logo and introductory multimedia campaign. The logo, which showed a drawing of the client's off-the-beaten-track building, was a great idea during the introductory phase when they were running quarter-page newspaper ads. By the time it got reduced for letterhead and stationery, the drawing could have been almost any three-story place in the city. When the first big media blitz was over, and we started running 4-column inch ads (2 columns wide by 2 inches deep) no one could tell what the drawing was.

Fortunately, another professional had designed the sign on the side of the building using the same type as the logo, but adding an artistic banner to the letters. We used the building sign as logo in the next print ads and billboards, to much better effect. Since that banner is the single most identifiable feature on the building (painted at least 20 feet high) and since that is the symbol that anyone who drives by will associate with the business, it is also the best logo for the business to use in its advertising.

The lesson? Your sign is one of your best ads. Make sure that you start using your logo there—and then make sure that same logo goes on every other

Fig. 1-4. Logos need to be clear and readable. This logo for Hubbard Monument Company tries to communicate with a pictorial "H," which employs stonework—but only ends up being confusing and hard to decipher. (From Carol Belanger Grafton, *Ready-to-Use Decorative Letters* [Mineola: Dover Publications, 1986])

advertising vehicle you use. Another lesson: when choosing a logo, especially one that includes a picture, imagine how it will look when you reduce it to fit on your business card. If it is still clear and recognizable, you might be on to something.

Checklist for Determining a Good Logo Design

- Is the typeface that you have chosen for your logo easy to read?
- Is that typeface different from styles used by your closest competitors?
- Does your chosen typeface convey the personality that you would like your business to have?
- Does your typeface convey the price image you want for your business?
- If you have chosen a pictorial symbol as part of your logo, can it be reduced to business card size, and look equally well enlarged to billboard size?
- Does the sign on your place of business use your logo? How about your business cards? Stationery? Shopping bags? Your name on any cars or trucks used for business?
- Are you certain that your logo appears in all advertising that you do?
- Are there any places where your company name appears in a style other than that of your logo? Are these things that the public sees? If so, can you change them without undue expense? Replace as soon as possible?

CHOOSING COMPANY COLORS THAT WORK

Another way we convey our message to the public is through color. Take McDonald's again. When we think of gold and red, we tend to think of them. A certain combination of red and white screams Coca Cola. My husband and I had great qualms about doing our foyer in black, white, and mauve because we were afraid it would look like a Good 'n' Plenty. Color communicates.

As a small business, most of your ads will probably be in black and white—in the newspaper. Few of us can afford four-color ads. However, you will have stationery, and business cards, a sign for your business, perhaps a delivery car or truck. You might decide to advertise on billboards. Like your logo, the color you use on these needs to be consistent.

Choose two colors. Make sure that you like them, and make sure that they are visible—because you're going to have to live with them, and they need to work for you.

This is no place to go into the psychology of color. But do make sure that you choose colors that are consistent with your image. Black, for instance, looks sophisticated. Day-glo pink is funky. Brown is subdued. If you're not sure what colors suit the image you want to convey, take a trip to the local record store and study the record jackets. The albums aimed at the sophisticate look very different from those aimed at the teenage rebel. Or, take a look at the packages that people in your target audience are attracted to in the supermarket. Do they gravitate toward the bright packages or choose subdued ones? When you visit the homes of people who are typical of your good customers, what colors do they use for decoration? What about their clothing? Choose colors that appeal to your audience.

Don't get too trendy. Maybe the Color Institute is telling us that purple and chartreuse are in this year—but that doesn't mean that they won't look silly next year. Look at how dated your old avocado refrigerator looks today. Stick to something more stable.

Make sure your colors are visible. When your delivery truck, with its pale blue letters on dove gray, goes whipping through town, no one will be able to read the name. When your lemon-yellow billboard goes up, inscribed with a bright white greeting, most people will get tired eyes, instead of a message. The trick, then, is to choose two colors that can be used for both small print work like business cards and for large billboards, and to make these your own. A good place to start is with your friendly neighborhood printer. Ask what ink and paper stocks are readily available. If you can create your company colors using these, you will save money. If you choose special colors of paper and exotic shades of ink, the printer might have to place special orders before he can do your print jobs. You will face a surcharge every time you have work done, because the presses will have to be cleaned and set up especially for your too-unique ink choices. So, if you can create an identity with readily available colors, you're money ahead. If the printer's stock is just too limited for your image, then special order your paper, rather than your ink. Not only will you have more choices, but you will also get less hassle at press time.

Once you have these three elements—your name, your logo, and the company colors—use them consistently, everywhere. They are the bare bones of a consistent, effective campaign. With this in mind, let's take a look at the advertising you might have already done.

Checklist for Choosing Company Colors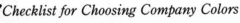

- Are your colors visible when seen from a distance? Do they have enough contrast to be seen clearly even on a very sunny day?
- Do your colors convey the image that you want people to have of your business?
- Are your colors ones that are likely to be attractive to the type of customer you are trying to reach?
- Are your colors different from those of your primary competitors?

- If your budget is very small, have you chosen colors that are readily available from your regular printer?
- Have you used those chosen colors everywhere possible—business cards, your sign, decor, stationery, company cars?

HOW PAST ADVERTISING AFFECTS YOU

The trouble with advertising that you've already done is that, even if you're unhappy with it, you're more or less stuck with it. Even if your past ads haven't been a smashing success, they have attracted some people who are used to your former style of advertising (or lack of style). You don't want to lose these people. Therefore, you need to retain the best parts of your old ads so they will still be recognizable to your present clients.

This means that, if you have been using a logo in your print ads, and you are keeping that logo—continue to use it. If you have been in the practice of offering a weekly special, continue to do so. If you have been using a certain radio voice to do your ads, continue to use him or her. If you have used a certain style of music, and it suits your business style—keep it. Save whatever is good. Then, start over with the rest.

Where have you been advertising? Have you done all print advertising? Take careful note of which newspapers, and in what sections. Can you in any way pinpoint which ads were more successful than others? What radio stations have you used? Did any ads work? Some better than others? How about TV?

Try to inventory your past ads—especially the recent past. Account for the successful ads—where they appeared, when they appeared, and what you said. Then, do the same for the ones that did not seem to produce results. Many things can account for the success or failure of your past advertising.

The Medium. If you were trying to reach teenagers in the newspaper, for instance, you probably did not have much success. Younger people tend to use broadcast media, and ignore the daily paper. The older and more educated your audience, the more likely they are to read the newspaper.

The Particular Medium. You might run a fantastic ad—but on a radio station or in a paper that your most likely customer doesn't pay much attention to. An ad for acne cream won't garner you much business on an all-news station, which tends to draw an older audience. Your bargain basement cut-rate special on Taiwan Ginsu knives might not be attractive to the upper-income and higher education levels of the classical music station listener.

The Timing. Some products and services are better presented in the morning, others in the evening. If you are selling expensive furniture, for instance, it might be better for your ad to appear in the evening paper, so that a husband and wife will see it when they are both at home with time to discuss such a major purchase. If you run a luncheonette, it will take a pretty spectacular ad to remain in the reader's memory until the next noon. You'd be better off in a morning paper, so that your name is implanted in the reader's mind when he or she begins to feel hunger pangs.

Timing is even more crucial in the broadcast media. If you're trying to reach housewives, and have been running ads on the radio at 7:30 a.m.—think again. That's exactly when Mom is wiping noses and packing lunches and looking for lost books. She'll never hear your ad. But a lot of commuters, caught in traffic on their way to work, will. If they're also in your market, at least you haven't totally wasted your advertising dollar. If you're running an ad for denture cream on late night TV because the rates are so cheap, better ask how many senior citizens are tuned in to "The Mummy's Curse." I know you'll find a lot of young people here.

Bad Ad. The timing could be right, the medium perfect—but the ad could fail to make a significant promise to the potential customer. This is the sort of failure that will be addressed fully in a later chapter—but let me offer one example. Your upper-middle class florist shop runs an ad on the 6 o'clock news on the area's most popular television station. You are reaching a large audience, and a great portion of this audience is your potential market. You offer them, if they mention that they saw your TV ad, $15 off on a $75 silk flower arrangement. Only one person responds.

Why? First, consider your audience. These people like to think of themselves as having achieved a certain dignity in life. They are not likely to want to bounce into some shop announcing that they were spending their evening watching TV (no one with any pretensions to dignity likes others to think they watch TV). Nor do they want to appear to be hungry to save money. Even if they were—think about your offer. Fifteen dollars off is a hefty discount—but in order to take advantage of it, your potential customer has to stir from his comfortable couch and drive to your place to see if what you're offering might be worth shelling out $60 that he hadn't planned to spend in the first place.

Bad Timing. There are some times when even the best ad will fail. Run a great ad during a blizzard, or in the dog days of summer when no one wants to stir from their air-conditioned rooms, and you might get dismal results. Don't get discouraged. It happens to everyone. But be careful of using this excuse too often. I've seen businesses who blame the failure of almost every ad they run on either good weather, bad weather, or the fact that it's either a holiday or not a holiday so people are busy. It's a convenient way to create false security—but it is false.

Take a good, objective look at your ads. Read through the rest of this book, then look again. Have you any better idea of what worked, and why? Of why the failures failed? Good. Then you know what to make permanent—and what it's time to change.

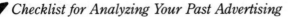

Checklist for Analyzing Your Past Advertising

- Have you used any elements in your past ads that would be consistently recognizable to your customers, such as a logo, tag line, border shape, picture, etc.? If so, are these elements consistent with any recent changes in logo, etc., that you might have made? Can you keep any of these elements for future ads?

- Did your past newspaper advertising appear in sections of the paper which the audience you are trying to reach is most likely to read?

- Did past radio advertising appear on stations whose audiences are mostly members of your potential and present customer group?

- Did your radio ads run at times of day when that audience was likely to be listening?

- Did the sales that you ran or special offers that you made offer customers savings on items that they were very likely to be in the market for whether or not you ran your offer?

- Did your past advertising offer your customers a benefit—a promise that you could do something meaningful for them? Or does it merely brag about all the great things that you have?

- Which ads worked well for you? Can you credit their success with the promises that they made? The media on which you placed them? The timing of the ads? Have you made note of these, so that you can use these ideas again?

HOW COMPETITION AFFECTS YOUR ADS

Before you change your name, logo, colors, or any portion of your past ads, take a good look at your competitors. You want to set yourself apart from them. If the plumber down the block is your closest competitor, and he's running around town in a red and white truck, advertising on a red and white billboard, and handing out business cards printed in red and white, then you want to avoid these colors. If your rival florist uses script for her name, you'll need to choose something else. If there's already a dress shop called Glad Rags, you definitely need a new name.

The point is, you need to set yourself apart from your competitors from the very beginning. You and the guy down the street might do exactly the same thing. You might even carry exactly the same merchandise or offer duplicate services. Or, you might have differences, which are too small for the buying public to perceive.

Unless you're one of the fortunate few whose product or service is different from anything else the world has ever seen, you need to create at least a perceptual difference in the minds of your target audience. If your competitor's name is cute, and yours is dignified, that makes people think differently about you, no matter how similar you might be. If she uses somber colors, and you use clear, bright ones, that creates another apparent difference. If your logo has a classical elegance, and theirs is crisp and contemporary, once again, you've set yourself apart.

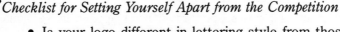

Checklist for Setting Yourself Apart from the Competition

- Is your logo different in lettering style from those of your competitors? Does it convey a different image?
- Are your colors different enough from your competitors to make you stand out as someone distinct?
- Do your colors and logos combine to create an image different from your competitors, but still appealing to the customers that you are trying to reach?
- Is your name distinctive enough that it won't be confused with that of one of your competitors?
- Does your advertising make a promise that is meaningful to your prospective customers, but different from what your competition is promising? (There will be help with this in chapter 11.)

SUMMARY

Remember—people tend to read ads and patronize businesses that match a certain image that they hold of themselves. Even if your business, in concrete terms, offers nothing that the competition can't offer, your psychological approach—your look and personality—can. Choose a name, a logo, and colors that appeal to your ideal customer and are different from those of your competition. You have a good foundation, with these, for beginning an effective advertising campaign.

2

Setting Your Advertising Objectives

ELIZABETH WAS OVERWHELMED BY ALL THE DETAILS THAT NEEDED ATTENTION before opening day. When the newspaper salesman showed up at her door, she made short work of him.

"Yes—I know I need to advertise—but I haven't got time right now. Just print a copy of this." She gave him one of her business cards. After all, it had her business name, her name, address and phone, didn't it? It did say "Catering" up in the corner.

Elizabeth knew that she should advertise her new business—but never thought about why. As a new business, she needs to set goals for her advertising.

A goal for most new businesses is establishing visibility—letting the public know who you are and what you do. Other goals include establishing a business image, and informing your target audience about all the benefits that you offer. Each of these goals requires certain kinds of advertising, which are different from the ads that established businesses should run.

Established businesses might need ads that seek to increase their market, change their image, or appeal to new target audiences. Once again, each of these ads requires different information, and different strategies. They might even require different media.

What about those special occasions—your sales, grand openings, and anniversaries? Don't each of these have a specific, short-range goal?

Every ad that you write should be designed to achieve a specific objective. Knowing what each ad must accomplish will help you to write better, more pointed ads. Knowing your objectives will also help you to assess the success of your efforts.

This chapter will discuss typical objectives for small business advertising, both long and short range, and the types of approaches that best achieve these goals. Finally, it will help you to set your advertising budget to a figure that, while affordable, should help you to achieve these goals effectively.

WHY ADVERTISE?

Unfortunately, many small businesses are frightened by the idea of spending what seems like huge amounts of money on advertising. True—it's difficult to dump large amounts of money into something so intangible. You can't stock it on your shelves, or enter any concrete returns in your books. Too often, I hear my small business clients ask me to ''just do a little something, for as little money as possible. All I want to do is get some word-of-mouth started.''

Look at your own business. Can you honestly expect to do the minimum in advertising and promotion, and yet still draw enough customers to make a profit? Some businesses can. Some businesses, because of location, type of service, or product, never spend a cent on advertising, but flourish. Chances are, yours is not one.

Why? Something has to get the word-of-mouth going. Some people are lucky that way. They build a better mouse trap or bake a better brownie. They never even intend to make it public. But it's so special that a friend wants one and tells someone else, who tells a neighbor—and soon everyone is beating a path to that mouse trap.

Few things, in this age of mass production, are that special or different that people will seek you out without some kind of enticement. In an age where there is so much that's new, even if you are special or different, people might not realize it—unless you educate them.

WHO NEEDS TO ADVERTISE

Word-of-mouth has to start somewhere. You need to build a reputation and a backlog of satisfied customers. You need to achieve a good initial level of awareness before word-of-mouth alone can keep you in the black. The easiest way to do this is to advertise.

This is not true for everyone. Professionals, such as doctors, lawyers, and even morticians only need a minimum level of initial awareness. People usually rely on the recommendations of others or their personal knowledge when choosing these very personal (and expensive) services. Artists and craftspeople can also do well without the media because they are, by their very nature, designed to appeal to the individual rather than the masses. These are not mass production people and could not accommodate the kind of business a mass ad campaign would bring in. They, too, can rely on the clientele who seek them out because "I saw one of your drawings in my partner's office, and wondered if. . . ."

If your product or service is very personal and/or very expensive; if it is extremely individualistic; if it relies more on reputation and personal recommendation than mass appeal, then all you need to do is some quiet advertising to introduce people to your business. This can be done through letters, personal introductions, community involvement, or through participation in professional organizations. Craftspeople often do shows, or offer demonstrations to interested audiences to acquaint people with their skills.

If, however, you are like most people and are trying to attract the general public (or at least a significant portion of it) to your doorstep, you will probably have to rely on advertising to start the rush. That means spending money.

Checklist to See if You Need a Major Ad Campaign

- Does your product appeal to a very specialized audience?
- Is your personal reputation more important than your actual product or service?
- Can you produce enough of your product or perform your service for a mass audience? Or can you only handle a limited number of customers at a time?
- Do you already have a good network of contacts who can refer you to other potential customers?
- Is there enough of a natural demand for your work product that these contacts can provide you with enough work to make your business profitable?
- Is the quality of your work product high enough that you can be assured that your present customers will continue to spread favorable word-of-mouth? If so: you might not need a full-fledged advertising campaign. But, consider the following.
- Does your product or service appeal to a mass market?
- Do you have competition for your target audience? Do you need to take business away from those competitors in order to survive?
- Do you need a high volume of business to make a profit?
- Are you offering a product or service that the public is not already familiar with? Or is your familiar product or service being offered in a way that is new to your public?
- Does your product or service appeal to people from a large geographic area?

- Is your product or service one for which people might comparison shop?
- Can you handle a larger volume of business than you are now doing? Do you have the feeling that you would do more business if only people knew more about who you are and what you do?

If so, then you need to advertise. Before plunging in, consider very carefully exactly what you want your ads to accomplish, and how much you should budget in order to accomplish these goals.

SETTING THE BUDGET

One of the first (and most frightening) steps in beginning your advertising campaign is to determine your budget. Too often, businesspeople rely on placing ads "When we feel like we need them—when we're running a special or something." There's a kind of silent budget in their minds—but no real plan. This approach is costing them money.

Plan Ahead

Determine how much you plan to spend on advertising in the coming year. Do it now, and stop making excuses. A planned budget will allow you to take advantage of the frequency and bulk space discounts offered by many media. This gives you more advertising for less.

How do you determine how much to spend? There are several methods, some of them so sophisticated that only the most experienced agencies and marketers can apply them. For a small businessperson, the simplest method is one based on a percentage of your sales.

The basic idea of this method is to allocate a fixed percentage of your gross income to advertising. You don't want to use only the percentage of profits unless you are heading for bankruptcy—because using net instead of gross figures could result in an advertising budget so small that it accomplishes nothing but a waste of money. (Yes—too little advertising is worse than none at all. It achieves very little, but costs you a lot of money, which you might as well just toss out the window.)

The fixed percent of your gross sales should be calculated on a yearly figure. This will give you a lump yearly sum that becomes your total advertising budget.

Determining the Industry Average

What percentage? That depends on your business. Some businesses can afford to allocate as little as one percent, others as much as nine percent. The percentage you allocate should be based on industry averages for your type of business.

Industry averages are published in many places. If there is a Small Business Development Center in your area, the staff there can help to advise you. Census reports and IRS reports also contain these figures, as do most trade journals. Check out the trade journals for your type of business, and make sure that your budgeting practices are competitive. Otherwise, you're behind before you even start.

Determining Your Own Budget

If you are already behind—if you're a new business going up against a powerful competitor—knowing the average percentage spent can help you to gain an edge. You'll need to spend a higher percentage than the other guy if you don't want him to keep all the customers. This might cut into your short-term profits for a while, but (and I don't want to sound heartless) you have to spend money to make money.

Which sales—or gross figures do I use? That depends. Many businesses base their budget on last year's sales. This is sound practice if your business is well-established, and has experienced no major surges or depressions. If, however, your business is in flux, you would be wise to take a percentage of average sales in the past few years.

If you are a new business, you should base your figures on an estimate of future sales. Try not to be too optimistic—but don't fall into the easy trap of being overly pessimistic and allocating a pittance to ads. If no one knows you're out there, your gloomy prophecies will prove all too true.

Finally, if you have a past sales record but sense that business is beginning to boom, make your estimates based on an average of both past and projected future sales. Be hard-headed about it—but not stingy. The increase in budget that this method allows will help you to reach more potential customers and make that boom a reality.

Once you have an annual budget, take time to explore two other options: co-op advertising and trade-outs.

Co-op Advertising

Co-op advertising is advertising financed jointly between a distributor or manufacturer and a retail or service outlet. The larger company will pay for a portion of the ad, if the small business features its products in that ad. If you carry a recognizable and desirable brand name product, or routinely use a reputable brand name product in your service work, then advertising that fact can be an added inducement for the public to do business with you. Even more important, advertising that brand can noticeably enlarge your advertising budget—if the brand's company will do cooperative advertising. Many companies demand that you place a minimum order with them before they will furnish co-op funds, so check with your distributors to see if you qualify. If you do, find out what terms the company will offer you—and add this to your budget. Make sure that you mark your calendar to ensure that you run the agreed upon ads at the most beneficial times.

Sometimes, companies which offer cooperative advertising plans will also offer to furnish you with a sign bearing your business name and their logo. Given the high cost of signs, this seems like a tempting offer. Be careful. It's your name and your logo that you want the world to see—not RC Cola's or Budweiser.

Trade-Outs

A second way to enhance your advertising budget is through trade-outs. Many newspapers, radio, and TV stations are willing to trade their time and space for products and services. A restaurant, for instance, can offer a radio station 30 lunches, in return for ten radio spots. The station can use these lunches to wine and dine prospective advertisers, to feed the help on busy days—whatever they want. Meanwhile, you get air time.

Does your business offer any products or services that your local media might find useful? If so, when you begin to talk to the media sales reps, try to negotiate some trade-outs. If not—all is not lost. You can often make a sort of barter trade. Assume that you're an electrician. The local radio station cannot foresee any need for your services, since they have their own engineering staff. The local restaurant, however, needs your help in installing the 20 Tiffany lamps that they bought for the cocktail lounge. You can arrange to install those lamps in return for the restaurant's 30 lunches—which you then trade out to the radio station in return for air time. This might seem like a roundabout way to get things done—but it happens all the time.

Maximizing your budget might take a bit of wheeling and dealing, but it can be done. And, if your budget is as small as that of most small businesses, you would be well advised to grab every advantage you can.

The section of this book on media planning will tell you more about exactly how to allocate your budget to maximize your advertising dollar. For now, however, simply knowing whether you have $3000 to spend this year or $30,000 will help you to be more realistic about setting your advertising objectives.

Checklist for Setting Your Budget

- Determine last year's gross.
- Check this gross against previous years. If there is a lot of fluctuation, take an average. If you anticipate a large upward trend, average last year's gross with next year.
- If you are a new business, estimate your projected gross.

- Find out the average percentage of gross allocated to advertising for your type of business.

- Divide this into your gross estimate to find out your advertising budget.

- Now check with your suppliers to see what (if any) cooperative advertising funds you might qualify for. Add these to your total, making careful note of any conditions the company might impose.

- Finally, think carefully about the possibility of trading out your products or services in return for advertising.

SETTING LONG-RANGE GOALS

The first thing you need to decide, in planning your advertising campaign, is what you want your advertising to do for you in the coming year. What do you need to accomplish? What would you like to have happen to your business and its reputation? Having a clear, concise long-range goal will play a large part in determining what your ads need to say, where, and to whom.

The objectives of your advertising campaign are affected by many things. Are you a new business, or an established one? Have you made any major changes in the past year? Does your business seem to be on the decline? Have you suddenly come up against stiff competition? Depending on where you are in the business cycle, and what problems you have encountered, your long-range goals could range from establishing visibility to building an image, to increasing store traffic, or simply informing the public that you're new and improved.

Establishing Visibility

If you are a new business or an older one that few people seem to have heard of, then your major goal should be to let the public know who and what you are. You will need to spend your money in a concentrated effort to reach all your potential customers with an appealing message that "I'm here—and I do all the things you've been looking for."

Visibility ads are largely informative. People have to be introduced to your business. They need facts rather than a lot of cutesy creativity. And, unless you have a highly specialized product or service, your ads need to reach a lot of people at this stage. You might get more shoppers than buyers at first—but your aim is to get people through the door. If your business is solid, they'll keep coming back or at least spread the word about you to people who *are* interested customers.

If visibility is your goal, then your ads must tell people about the main services that you offer, or products that you carry. They should establish an image and price category for your business and define any new products or services with which the public might be unfamiliar.

Building an Image

Once people know about what you are, you must be more selective with your advertising. You want to reach people who really fit your business approach. If yours is a new, trendy restaurant, you'll want to concentrate your advertising efforts on communicating that message to the public. If your insurance business relies heavily on trust and customer confidence, your ads for the year should spend the bulk of their time communicating that. Therefore, every ad you place during your campaign should aim at conveying your desired image (as long as you can live up to it).

Of course, even your initial, visibility ads should convey something about your image. But once that visibility has been established, you can drop a lot of your purely factual information, and begin to concentrate on style and on special features of your business that are especially attractive to your desired customers.

This doesn't mean that you avoid facts in your ads. A lot of image can be conveyed by the look and sound of your ad, the typeface you use, or the music. We'll deal with that in the creative section. Just be aware, at this stage, that image making is a long-range goal. It signals your target audience by presenting them with advertising messages that fit their own self-images. These ads signal to your customers that "this is my kind of place."

Changing an Image

Perhaps your business has changed. You might be under new management, or have redecorated, or perhaps the product you've been selling, formerly considered stodgy, has suddenly become the "in" thing. Your main aim, then, should be to tell the public about the new and improved you. In the first place, people like anything new—they might come through the doors out of simple curiosity. In the second, the new and improved you should appeal to a new, and hopefully larger segment of the population than before. You'll want everybody to know about that appeal.

Changing people's minds about an image is not easy—you have to lure them through the doors to see for themselves that things have improved. But image-change advertising lends itself perfectly to one of the most tried and true methods of advertising—ads that use words like "New," "Improved," "Announcing," and "At Last!" Used with a promotion designed to draw in the crowds, image-changing ads can be very effective.

Increasing Store Traffic

There's nothing new, and you're already visible to the public at large. But you still want more customers. Your ads, then, should work at giving people more reasons to come in. Your total campaign might be based on a series of sales, promotions, special events. Or you might choose to start using new media, aimed at audiences you might not have been reaching before. The general theme of your campaign this year will be "1000 reasons (or one good reason) to come to us."

Decide whether you want the same people to come in more often—or to get more people to come in. Then, look for reasons why they should. You can increase store traffic both by creating ads designed to appeal to new audiences, and by placing your ads in the media that these new audiences are likely to use.

Explaining a Complicated Idea or Product

Maybe you have a new product or service that people don't know much about. Maybe people know about it, but want assurance that they are dealing with an expert. If the public has questions, your main objective should be to answer them.

You can do this in several ways. You can run a whole series of ads, each conveying new facets of your product and/or service. Or, you can run *answer-man* types of ads—"Dear Bob the Plumber, my P-trap won't fit, what should I do?" "Dear Dr. Tooth, my gums have purple spots." Sure—all your competitors can hopefully answer the questions as well as you. But you're the one whose name gets associated with answers. So, you become the expert.

With this objective, you need to have a very clear idea about the people who are your best prospects. Your ads must signal this audience very clearly, and promise that your product or service can solve a very specific problem for them, or fulfill a definite need. Include a phone number, or a coupon encouraging people to seek more information. Strongly consider using direct mail. Mail advertising is one medium where the length of your message doesn't really affect the cost of the ad. So direct mail gives you a chance to explain yourself fully.

Complicated ideas also benefit from publicity. Try to interest the local media in doing a story on your business. If your product or service is really new and different, it is also newsworthy. Chapter 16 will provide you with help in getting publicity for your business.

Keeping the Name Visible

Everybody knows your name. Your business is steady. So why should you continue to dump money into advertising? Why does IBM do it? Why do Coke and Pepsi? Because, if you don't, the competition will be more visible than you are—and get your business.

The happy thing about this campaign objective, however, is that you can spend less time informing people about what you do, and more on creating happy images of yourself and your satisfied customers. You just want to remind people that you're still there, still doing a great job, and still satisfying people.

You can only do visibility advertising like this if your business is well established, well-known to the public, and has a good reputation. If you fit these criteria, you can have a lot of fun with your advertising. Image advertising is the kind that pops to mind when we think of creativity in advertising. Lots of graphic impact, off-the-wall messages, a lot of laughs or emotions, but not much real information. You don't need it if the public already knows who you are.

Your long-range goals will determine the basic look, sound, and theme for your advertising. However, from time to time during the campaign, you might have some smaller, more immediate tasks that need to be accomplished through advertising. These short-range goals can still be accomplished, as long as they fit into the over-all framework your long-range goals have established.

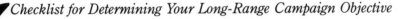

Checklist for Determining Your Long-Range Campaign Objective

- Your goal is establishing visibility if:
  —You are a new business.
  —Your research (see chapter 6) shows that few people have heard of you.
  —You are an established business, but are opening a new store in a new area.
- Your goal is building an image if:
  —You already have good visibility among your target areas.
  —Most people in your target market are already aware of who you are and what you do.
  —You want to refine your advertising in order to attract a specific type of customer.
- Your goal is changing an image if:
  —Your research tells you that people have a wrong idea about your prices, style, clientele, etc.
  —You have made changes designed to upgrade your store, or reduce prices, etc.
  —You have taken steps to correct previous image problems and need to communicate that change.
  —Your target market is changing, and you need to communicate an image that appeals to that changing market.
- Your goal is increasing store traffic if:
  —Business has leveled off, and you feel that it can be made to increase.
  —Changes in your business now allow you to handle more volume.
  —Changes in your business will appeal to new and different target markets.
  —Because of changes in the market, you feel that people can now be made to buy your product or use it more often.

- Your goal is explaining complicated ideas or products if:
  —No one else offers the type of product or service that you have.
  —Your product or service is something entirely new.
  —Your product or service solves a specific problem, but people need to be made aware that the problem needs to be solved.
  —Your product or service requires a lot of technical expertise.
  —Your target market is relatively unsophisticated, with no prior knowledge of your product or service.
- Your goal is keeping the name visible if:
  —Your business is well established, and most people know who you are and what you do.
  —You already have a definite (and positive) business image.
  —You are satisfied with the volume of business that you are now doing, and only want to maintain that level.
  —You have no new competitors who threaten to cut into the market that you have captured.

SHORT-RANGE GOALS

Short-range goals are exactly that—objectives that need to be accomplished in a matter of a few weeks or days. If your major objective is to establish a sophisticated image for yourself—to which end you have been running very classy, stark ads—but this week you are running a clearance sale, you must remain in your "classy image" framework. Your ad must have the same basic look or sound, but convey specific information rather than the more general copy that your normal advertising uses.

Your short-range goals might include introducing the public to new products or services you are carrying, or promoting a special event. You might want to acquaint your customers with a new employee, or run a sale. You might even want to capitalize on current events that affect your business.

For instance, a local deli has made a good business based on a humorous, fun image, and a promise to deliver their lunches anywhere, hot and in under fifteen minutes. Their print ads feature a cartoon character, on wheels, spinning down the road with sandwich bag in hand. Their radio ads use a voice that sounds like it could belong to this character. Their long-range goal for the year is to establish an image of their place as a fun but efficient place to get take-out food.

Last winter we had a terrible blizzard. Most of the radio stations devoted their day to announcing cancellations of schools and businesses. Deli-Quick was open—and on the air with the short-range goal of capitalizing on the fact that most folks were snowed in. They used the Quicky-Man's voice to tell listeners that he was riding the snow plow straight to the doors of all hungry snow-bound people. The image was the same. Only the short-term goal had changed, just for the occasion.

The point is that establishing long-range goals does not keep you from advertising special events, or addressing special needs that might arise during your campaign. Instead, they give you a framework within which to work, so that you maintain a consistent image, and the public receives a consistent message. This helps to build recognition for all your ads, which in turn increases their impact and effectiveness.

USING YOUR GOALS TO BEGIN CAMPAIGN PLANNING

Once you know what your objectives for advertising are, you have taken the first step toward planning your advertising campaign. You have the budget that will allow you to work toward that objective, and you have an idea about the ideas that your ads must convey.

Your next step is to create a campaign calendar. Buy yourself one of those calendars with large spaces for writing beside each date. You might want to photocopy this a few times, to allow you to experiment and to make mistakes.

The first thing you want to do with this calendar is to mark in the months when your business is high and low. Go to your past sales records to determine what percentage of your business you do in each month. If this percentage varies from year to year, take an average of the past few years.

Now, take your total advertising budget figure, and break this down in accordance with sales. In other words, if you do 12 percent of your business in January, then take 12 percent of your total advertising budget, and allocate that to January. Go on to February, on through the year.

This allocation makes many businesspeople uncomfortable. They question spending a lot on advertising when business is already good, and doing less during slow months when business needs improving. But there's a logic to this plan that works for most businesses. The theory is that there are natural months for business, when people are both in the mood and in the market for your product or service. This is when your name needs to be visible. There are also months when people are not inclined to patronize your type of business without a very special incentive—a major sale, perhaps. Since you are not likely to change their natural habits and inclinations, it is better to spend when the customers are available. That's when your competition will be advertising—and you don't want to lose out to them.

When you have allocated your rough budget, go back and mark in any holiday, sale, or event that will require special advertising. If you are using cooperative advertising, mark in those times when you would most logically advertise the products you have agreed to feature. When planning your media calendar, you might find that you need to borrow money from adjacent months to accomplish this advertising—but for now, you are only making a rough estimate.

Now, look at your advertising goals. If you are a new business, then you will have allocated your advertising dollars according to industry averages. Your major goal for this year will be to establish visibility. Let's say that your grand opening will be in June—but that your allocation only gives you $800 for that month. Common sense will tell you that this will not allow you to buy enough advertising to establish much visibility. So you begin to reapportion dollars.

If you are an established business, but know that you will be remodeling in March, then you know that you will need extra advertising dollars to communicate your new image to the public. Once again, you might have to shuffle your monthly allocations to allow you to accomplish this.

Until you have looked at the different media, you might have difficulty in determining how much advertising you will need, and how much you need to spend in order to accomplish your objectives. Nevertheless, having a firm idea about your objectives will aid you in setting a workable budget that will help you to accomplish your business goals.

Checklist for Establishing a Basic Media Calendar

- Buy a 12-month calendar with large spaces for writing.
- Look up your past sales records, and determine what percentage of the year's business you typically do in each month.
- If you are a new business, find out the industry averages for business per month in your type of business.
- Divide the percentage per month into your total ad budget to determine how much of that budget should be allocated each month.
- On your calendar, make note of any special occasions—anniversaries, sales, or grand openings that will require extra advertising expenditures.
- Check your advertising goal for the year. Does this in any way suggest times when you will need to advertise more heavily? Note this on your calendar.
- Write the amount allocated to each month on the appropriate page of the calendar. Do this in pencil.
- Check to see if the amounts allocated to special event months seem to be sufficient. If not, borrow from the other months to give you a better balance.
- Now write in the final monthly budget on the appropriate calendar page. (Note: this is only written in ink, not etched in stone. When you have looked at media rates, you might still want to do some budget adjustments.)

SUMMARY

Knowing your objectives will also determine the content of your ads—information or image advertising? Heavy persuasion or a gentle nudge? It's good to make these decisions early in the planning process.

Knowing your objectives might also determine what media you will have to use. Visibility advertising, for instance, means trying to reach a large enough number of people to attract an initial base of customers and to narrow down later advertising to a specialized target group. Therefore, you will initially need to advertise in media that reach a wide portion of the population, such as newspaper, TV, or billboards. However, increasing the use of your store by people who already shop there means that you only have to reach the customers you already have—you might want to design ads meant to be mailed directly to your clients.

Once your yearly budget has been determined, you will know to some extent, just how far-reaching your advertising goals for the year can be. This should help you to set up realistic, long-range objectives. These long-range objectives should be the guiding principle for any advertising you do until that specific goal has been accomplished. These objectives will determine the overall theme of your ads and should be flexible enough to accommodate any specific messages that you might need to communicate to your public.

3

Using Advertising to Help Solve Problems

WHEN RICHARD JOINED THE LIONS CLUB, HE WAS DEVASTATED TO LEARN THAT most of his fellow members bought their plants from the corner variety store rather than his own nursery. Most of them admitted that they had only middling success with variety store plants—but they always assumed that the variety store had a bigger selection and better quality than Richard's business.

Richard's plants were crowded and jumbled—finding the flower of choice was a lot like searching for buried treasure. Richard had such a big stock, and spent so much time keeping his plants strong and healthy that he had no time left for fancy display. So, he was losing business.

Richard suffers from perception problems—something that his advertising can solve. Now that he knows what the trouble is, he can begin to concentrate on ad messages that communicate his wide selection and the superior health of his nursery stock. If he feels brave, he can even compare the survival rate of his plants to that of his chief competitor.

Often, advertising is the only way to overcome your business problems. If you have a bad image, or a powerful competitor, or if you have a business function that no one really understands, then you need to communicate the truth to the public. Your advertising objectives must now aim at problem solving.

One warning: advertising can only work if your business can back up your promises. If you have a terrible location, and don't offer the customer benefits that make it worth the drive, then advertising can't help you. If your problems are largely in the mind of the public, rather than in the weakness of your business, then advertising can work!

This chapter will help you to identify possible problem areas in your business and point you toward advertising strategies aimed at solving those problems. Particularly if you are pitting yourself against a strong competitor, this chapter will help you to discover strategies that work to give you a competitive edge.

PHYSICAL PROBLEMS

If we expect the customer to come to us to do business, then a good location is crucial. Unfortunately, there are only just so many "good" locations, and too many of them cost more than a small businessperson can afford. The trick, then, is to make the best of a less-than-desirable location.

This is crucial. When prospective customers read your ad or hear it on the radio, they might be intrigued. They might even say "Gee—I'll have to try that place sometime." But, resistant as we all are to persuasion, the old inertia principle soon takes over. Our minds immediately start throwing up objections about why we should avoid doing what you want us to do. The easiest objection in the world for that inert mind to make is "But I don't know exactly where it is. . . ."

In a print ad, this is a fairly easy problem to overcome. You'll need to include a small map. If possible, include a time estimate of how far you are from someplace that people will drive to, such as "Just two minutes from the stadium." If you are down the block or across the street from some place that is well known, use that as a landmark for indicating your location. All these tactics will remove that niggling question from the minds of your prospects. Be careful of the landmark you use, though. I had one client whose best identifying building was the county jail—a rather negative association. Another had to be stopped from identifying his close but more well-known competitor as the landmark of choice. If you have these problems, settle for naming recognizable cross streets.

Your other objective, here, is to convince people that it is worth their while to make that extra effort. If location is your primary problem, then a set of ads aimed at helping locate your business is a crucial first step in your campaign.

On the other hand, you might be findable, but people still avoid you because you have no place to park. Having almost no ability to parallel park, I often find myself going two or three miles out of my way to patronize a place with a parking lot, rather than risking one where I might have to play chicken for a space on the street. Experience tells me I'm not alone.

In this case, one of the primary objectives of your next bunch of ads is to minimize that difficulty in the minds of your potential customer. This could involve something other than advertising. Make a deal with some nearby business that does have a lot, so that your ads can promise nearby parking. Initiate a delivery service. Or, make your business sound so irresistible that it's worth the inconvenience.

In the last 20 surveys my class did for small business clients, the respondents rated "parking" as one of the most important factors that helped them to decide what business to patronize. So, if you have problems here, it's crucial that you aim some of your ads at making people aware that you're worth the walk.

Checklist for Determining Possible Physical Problems

- Is your place of business located close to the area where most of your customers live?
- Are other businesses in your area catering to people with the same general income and lifestyles?
- Is your business located in a high traffic area?
- Are there any recognizable landmarks which make your location easy to locate in people's minds?
- Do you have a parking lot, or do your customers have easy access to a parking structure or lot?
- If you do not have a lot, is your business located within easy walking distance from the area in which most of your customers live or work?

If you answered no to any of these questions, then your business might have a physical problem.

PERCEPTUAL PROBLEMS

Sometimes, determining what people think about your business can be tough. After all, for the most part, you only talk to your friends, and to your present customers. They know who you are and what you do, and so their perceptions are likely to be accurate. However, if you have inherited an image from a former owner, or if the research you've done suggests that there's trouble, your advertising must be aimed at correcting that trouble.

Perceptual problems deal with images, prices, services, and selection—or simply the atmosphere that your business conveys.

Determining the Best Image

You want people to have a good image of your business. However, like beauty, a good image is in the mind of the beholder. Your best image is the one that your most likely customer will respond to positively. Your best image reflects, to a degree, the image that your most likely customers have of themselves.

The image of you created through advertising, however, has to be one that you can live up to, and one that suits your business. A lawyer, for instance, might want to attract a lively, swinging ''yuppie'' crowd—but lively, swinging lawyer ads are more likely to repel than to attract. If you happen to be the gregarious, bouncy type, then don't advertise in an extremely dignified, subdued fashion, because that image will be dispelled as soon as your customer walks through the door.

The average small business is in competition with a lot of other small and somewhat similar businesses. The average customer, without the aid of well-written, pointed ads, is likely to perceive all these businesses as having no real and important differences that make one preferable to the other.

If we had the chance to shop around at every small dress shop, or book-store, or hardware store in town, we would most likely settle for one because it suits our image of ourselves. This one offers good value for our money—and we like to think of ourselves as wise shoppers. That one is a bit more expensive, but it carries a lot of unusual equipment—and we like to take on unusual projects. Another's stock is nothing special, but the atmosphere is upbeat and lively, and the help is young, perky, and knowledgeable. Just like we'd like to think we are. All of them will provide us with what we want, but one will suit our self-image better.

Dealing with a Poor Image

Since the average consumer doesn't have time to try out every business in town, you must rely on your ads to convey that image. If the people you could please with your current business practices have the wrong idea of you, then they will stay away in droves. Those who see your ad, which conveys a cut rate image, will go away disillusioned, if you don't live up to that image. So your ads, your business, and your target audience must be well matched.

I once had a client who had just taken over a drugstore. The former owner was more interested in a book-making operation in the back room than he was in pharmaceuticals. The place was dingy and depressing. Not surprisingly, only the desperate brought their prescriptions in to be filled. The new owner knew he had image problems to overcome.

He began with the physical. He cleaned up the place, making sure everything sparkled. He used lots of white, and bright colors. He sorted stock into attractive displays.

Then he began to advertise. He made sure the ads looked as bright and clean as the newly redone store. He emphasized personal, professional service. Before long, the neighborhood forgot the old, dingy image. Both the new ads and the remodeling conveyed the image that people wanted in a pharmacy.

If people keep murmuring to you ''Oh, I always thought you were really expensive. . . .'' or ''Gee, I never realized what a good selection you have,'' you have an image problem. The objective of your advertising must be to correct that wrong impression.

Some perceptual problems can only be discovered through outside research (see chapter 6). However, pay attention to the customers who do come in, and you might gather some clues about how you are perceived.

Checklist for Determining Possible Perceptual Problems

- Do people often seem surprised about your quality, selection, size, prices, etc.?
- Take an honest look around your business, inside and out. Can you think of five negative words that people might apply to your business? Can any of these be overcome by advertising, or do you need to make physical or personnel changes?
- Do you offer services that no one ever seems to ask for? Could this be because no one is aware of them?
- Make a list of five positive words that you would like your customers to use when describing you. Now listen to your customers carefully. Do you think they would describe you the way you want? If not, can you change their ideas through advertising? Or must you make some changes in the business? Or perhaps you aren't attracting the right type of customer.

DEALING WITH LIFE CYCLE PROBLEMS

Not all advertising objectives are aimed at correcting problems that are in the consumer mind. A few of your problems are natural ones, that arise from the natural progress that a business makes in its life cycle.

A lot of your advertising decisions will be based on your stage in the life cycle. There are four basic stages: introduction, growth, maturity, and decline. Each stage requires a different approach to advertising.

Introduction

If you are a new business, or if you have changed your image drastically, or if you have, up till now, been largely invisible in the marketplace, then your business can be placed in the introductory cycle. You will use advertising to introduce yourself to the public. Very few people know who you are, or what you do; your ads need to tell them.

Growth

Once you have achieved a basic level of awareness in your area, you have moved into the growth stage. In this stage, you have presumably achieved enough business strength to expand—to get in new lines of merchandise, to add to your stock, to feature new services or more expert help. This is what your advertising needs to communicate—you are not just a stodgy little business that remains at a standstill, but rather a progressive company that keeps changing with the times.

Maturity

The next stage is maturity. This is that enviable time in the life of a business when everyone knows your name, and everyone knows what you do. At this point, your ads only need to keep reminding the public about your fine qualities and good image. (You may ask, if everyone already knows about you, why keep spending money on advertising? The answer is quite simple: the public is fickle. If they don't see your ads, you slip out of consciousness, and they begin to do business with those people whose names do appear in ads each week.) This advertising does not, however, require a lot of facts. Your name, your tag line, a graphic that conveys your image—plus, of course your address and store hours— is enough to keep your name current.

Decline

Then there's that sad stage called decline. The customers have started to go elsewhere. Other stores seem more up-to-date and in tune with the new fads and fancies. Your main products seem passe. Do you fold up your tent and steal silently into the night? No! You change your advertising. You try to help people to find new uses for your product or service. You initiate changes in the business that bring you up to the level of your more successful competitors. Or, you advertise to new markets who still use and enjoy the types of things your business has to offer. The important thing to do at this stage is communicate to the public about any aspects of your business they still can benefit from.

The Life Cycle of One Business: Case History

Let's assume that you are opening a brand new service business. It's called a "Wish Registry," and operates much like a bridal registry, but for nonbrides. The average shopper can register with you for items that he or she has seen and would like to receive as gifts. Your service consists of keeping track of these items and prices, and the dates of the shopper's birthday and anniversary. When these dates approach, you will send a card to the shopper's spouse, children, or friends, telling them that you can help them find a gift that is exactly what their birthday person wants. The idea is new in town; no one knows exactly what it is. Your ads, then, must somehow explain this to the shopper, convincing them to sign up with you and make their special occasions perfect.

Now, assume that you have managed to introduce this service so well that most people in your market know exactly what the Wish Registry is. You still don't have enough customers to satisfy you. Re-explaining things would be a waste of ad money at this stage; people have already been introduced to you, and know who you are and what you do. You have entered the growth stage, where you want to expand your market.

At this point, you need to either seek new markets, and introduce yourself to them, or you need to improve yourself to encourage more people in the present market to make use of your service. (Yes—it's time to become the new and improved Wish Registry.) You add services, like actually buying and sending that special gift in order to save time for the busy executive. (This ensures that the wife will get what she wants, because it gives extra added insurance that the husband will take advantage of the information she has registered with you.)

This goes over very big. The Wish Registry becomes the new way to shop, and you are doing a good, steady business, with a hired staff, a nice, efficient office building, and a fleet of limousines for gift delivery. You are at your maturity stage in the life cycle. Lucky you. You no longer have to sweat over new ways to inform the public about who you are and what you do. Instead, your ads only need to remind people that you're still here doing business as usual. Coca Cola has been in this position for a long time now. Their ads don't even have to tell the public that their beverages taste good. If we keep seeing images of healthy young people drinking Coke, we'll remember the name.

But, doomsday eventually comes. The age of computer shopping arrives, and now every husband can just sit at his PC, tap into a database program, order whatever his wife's heart desires, and make an electronic payment. You've almost gone the way of the dinosaur. It's time for new ideas. It's time to tell the people about your personal touch in this cold technological age. It's time to create new needs for your service that people might not have thought of in a while. Or, it's time for you to computerize your Wish Registry. When you hit the decline stage, you either advertise to show that you can keep up with the times and deliver—or go under.

Black and white television had to do this, as soon as color TV caught on. Nobody wanted to look at gray people when they could afford a color TV set. So, set manufacturers represented the black and white models as inexpensive alternatives that would allow each member of the household his or her own private TV. Then they began to miniaturize the sets to make them more convenient and portable than the color models. These moves added several years to the life cycle of black and white TVs.

In review, the introductory stage is the time to give the public new information about you and your business. The growth stage adds new information, and perhaps new products and/or services that make you better than you were in public perception. This stage can also reach out to new audiences in order to make that growth possible. The maturity stage only needs to remind people that you're still here, and still doing a great job at answering public needs and wants. And the decline stage advertises and institutes changes to keep up with the times.

THE COMPETITION

So far, we've looked at your business in isolation. But, in order to do an effective job of advertising that business, there's one outside factor that you need to take a hard look at. The competitor. The guy who lures customers away from you and into his own lair. The one who, to a point, determines how much you have to spend on advertising in order to keep up with him and when you have to place those ads. What you need to do to keep up with or beat the competition could greatly affect your advertising objectives.

Understanding Who the Competitor Is

If you ask any small business person, they will immediately tell you that they know exactly who their competition is. It's that other guy across town or down the block (depending on your area of trade) whose business is a lot like yours. Right?

Well, maybe. A lot depends on public perception. Let's say your job is refinishing furniture. There's another shop across town that also refinishes by hand stripping, hand sanding, and hand finishing. He might be your primary competition to a lot of people. Then, there's that place down the street that dip strips furniture in a large vat. You know that this isn't good for the furniture—but does the average guy on the street? Especially when the dip-stripper only charges half what you do? So chalk up another competitor. Then, what about your friendly neighborhood hardware store? They don't actually do refinishing, but they have an endless array of wood strippers, varnish and lacquer solvents, sandpaper, stains, and finishes. Which means that a lot of people aren't bringing their heirlooms to you because they're doing it themselves.

So now you have three distinct advertising approaches. One is to try to convince the public that you are superior in some way to the guy across town who does things like you. A second is to try to convince the public that your superior service is a more sensible alternative to what the dip-stripper does—if they care for their furniture. Your last job is to convince the do-it-yourselfers that there is some advantage in coming to you. Unless you have a huge budget, you can't do all three. So you'll need to determine which of these three types of competition is taking away the most business from you, and which customers for these three types of competitors are most likely to be convinced that you are the best alternative.

Another example. You own a bakery, so it seems logical to assume that you're competing against other bakeries in the area. Think again. The real question that determines the competition is this: If I want baked goods (or wood refinishing, or medical care, or computer supplies, or help with my plumbing) where can I conveniently go to get these? With the bakery, it could be that the choice is between you, the grocery store, or Grandma's baking. If you sell automobiles, it's not just other Chevy dealers, it's also Buick dealers, and Datsun dealers, and the want ads, and notices posted in the supermarket. Even for your current customers, you have competition. Ask yourself, "If I were closed, who would my current customer go to instead?"

How a Customer Determines Your Competition

While the identity of your competitor is limited by your area of trade, to an extent, it is not limited to the obvious things like type of business, or even necessarily price range. The next time you go out to eat, try to remember why you chose that restaurant. First, decide things like "Do I want to get dressed up?" and "Do I feel like driving far?" Both of these limit the choice of competitors from "all eating places" to ones with a certain dress code, in a certain area of trade. Then, we narrow things down further by checking the wallet. The competition is now among moderate-priced establishments within five miles of home that allow casual dress. Next, "What do I feel like eating." This could eliminate seafood places and move Italian to the forefront—this time. Next time you'll want something hot and spicy. So, the competition is different. Next time, it might be pay day, and the whole agenda will change. If you think determining your competition is easy, just keep this exercise in mind. The consumer mind operates this way in almost every case—unless you're the only game in town.

Even if you are the only game in town, be careful. There are still, to many minds, ways of avoiding you. If you operate the only miniature golf course in town, don't assume that you can sit back because people will have to come to you. You still have competition—the movies, sand-lot baseball, the driving range, the TV set. Very few businesses can truly say that they have no competition. Most businesses would be wise to identify that competition carefully because this is where you begin to develop your advertising strategy. You get new business by being a superior alternative to that competitor. You're more fun than the TV set and healthier than the movies. You achieve higher quality work than the dip-stripper, you're more convenient and faster than baking a cake at home. (Plus, yours are prettier.)

You've got to convince the buying public that you are their best alternative, out of all the choices that may come to their minds.

Checklist for Determining Competition

- Do I know who my competition is?
- Do I know how their business compares with mine?
- Do I have an understanding of what advantages the public might see in my competitor's business?
- Do I have a grasp of those advantages I have over my competitors?
- Do I understand what meaningful distinctions I can make between my business and that of my competition when advertising?

How Is My Competition Different from Me?

Once you know who you're competing against, your next job is to find out in what areas you are competing. How might they be considered better than you are in the minds of your potential customer? In what ways might you have the leading edge?

If possible, visit your competitors. You can't exactly walk into the home of the do-it-yourselfer, but you can talk to a few, and find out why they prefer that method of getting service. You can often, however, walk right into the competing business and check things out for yourself. Try to put yourself in your potential customer's shoes, and see what differences they might find between you and your competitor. If you can't go yourself, send a spy. Make them take along the following checklist.

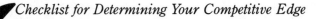

Checklist for Determining Your Competitive Edge

- Location:
  a. Is the business convenient to get to?
  b. Do they have better parking facilities than I do?
  c. Is the shop located near enough to other stores to make this a good, one-stop shopping place?
  d. Is the place easier to find than mine?

- Appearance:
  a. Is the store front attractive?
  b. Does the shop appear to present a different image than mine does?
  c. Does the inside layout offer convenient shopping?
  d. Is the place clean and attractive inside?
  e. Does it have a distinctive personality? How does that differ from my business's personality?
  f. Do they play music? Do I? Do we play the same kinds?

- Service:
  a. Does my competitor have competent staff members?
  b. Are these people pleasant and courteous?
  c. Are they more knowledgeable than my staff?
  d. Are there enough staff members to handle business?
  e. Does my competition offer any services that I don't (delivery, credit, repairs, guarantees, alterations, instructions, etc.)?

- Price:
  a. How do we compare price-wise?
  b. If his or her prices are lower, is there any easily detectable loss in quality to account for this?
  c. If his prices are higher, is there enough increase in quality to account for this?

- Selection:
  a. Do we carry the same selection? Who has more?
  b. Who has the "better" brands? Who has the more popular brands? In looking at the competitor's layout, does the difference in selection seem apparent?
- Reputation:
  a. Do you know what kind of business reputation your competitor has?
  b. Do you know what your own reputation is? How do they compare?

Once you have answered these (and probably many more) questions to your own satisfaction, you can begin to draw some distinctions.

Distinguishing Yourself from Competitors

Take a look at your customer—the one that you are trying to keep away from the competition. You've tried to see the competition as that customer is likely to view it. Now take a look at how you compare in that hypothetical customer's mind.

Where does your competitor have the advantage over you? Some things you won't be able to change. If you've got the poorer location and a definite parking shortage, then these are problems that need to be addressed in your advertising. If you find that the competing store is brighter than yours, a coat or two of paint might help. Try to equalize the differences between you, when you can. What's left? The disadvantages that you can deal with in your ads. If you're hard to find, hold a treasure hunt. You're the treasure. If it's impossible to find a parking space, try to make your customer feel like it's a privilege to try and compete for those few available spots. If the other guy's advantage is that he's been around for 35 years while you're the new kid on the block, how can you turn that to your advantage? Perhaps by emphasizing your freshness and innovation. The key thing to remember when advertising anything is: never promise anything that you can't deliver. That doesn't mean that you can't try to make lemonade out of lemons and turn your deficits into pluses. Remember, L'Oreal had great success telling customers that "It costs a bit more—but I'm worth it."

Distinctions that Customers Care About

As for your advantages—those are your competitive edge. As long as the advantages that you have over your competition are important to the consumer, then these are key advertising points that you can use to lure that consumer through your door. (And if the competition is also reading this book, and slinks around to spy on you—fine. Competition is healthy. It will keep both of you on your toes, always trying to improve things. That's what free enterprise is all about.)

One key phrase in the above paragraph that should not escape your attention is "advantages that are important to the consumer." If you own a supermarket, and your stock clerk knows more about aluminum cans than anyone in town, this is a probable difference that you have over your competition. But, few of your customers will care. While it will allow you to advertise yourself as the "more knowledgeable grocery," your knowledge is not very significant in the customer's decision-making process. Therefore, it won't give you a good competitive edge. If, however, your check-out clerks are all great cooks who can help your customers learn new ways to prepare all the exciting new items you've been stocking, then this meaningful bonus might attract people to your store if your customers are adventurous cooks who like to try new foods.

The big question for you, in looking both at the customers that you have and at the ones you want to attract is "Why do they go where they go?" Let's take two antique shops, both on the same street. One is clean, bright, and all the antiques are placed in beautiful room settings so that the customer can see exactly how things were used. Every piece is either in perfect original condition or has been beautifully restored. Everyday, several BMWs and Mercedes line up in front of this shop, while ladies in designer clothes drop in to browse and buy. Down the street, we have a little, cluttered shop with treasure piled upon treasure and no attempt at rhyme or reason. Many of the antiques are just as rare and fine as those in the place up the street, but they are dust-covered and have not been repaired. Yet everyday, a line of BMWs and Mercedes pull up outside to drop off ladies in designer jeans who come to browse and buy. As the spy from the first shop, checking out the little dusty place—wouldn't you begin to wonder?

This is why knowing your customer is so important. The two shops are not really competitors. One appeals to the shopper who is looking for instant class and history—one who looks at a fine piece of furniture and knows that she can instantly move it into her home and possess proudly. She has taste and money, and she is willing to spend that money on quality goods. She is not willing to play guessing games about whether a treasure lurks under those five coats of beige paint. The shopper in the dusty shop, however, is a gambler. She views the antique quest as a treasure hunt and is willing to wait for either her own labor or that of the local furniture refinisher to see what sort of investment she has made. This lady also has taste and likes quality—she's just more of an adventurer. The first, beautiful shop, made life too easy. Plus, it's more fun to brag about the great chair you snagged for $10 because it was covered in paint than to simply present a nice, $300 chair that everyone could always see was great. (Another thing about these two shoppers. One of them—the first—paid cold hard cash for her BMW. The second one bought hers on time. The first lady was born wealthy. The second is one of those infamous Yuppies—in search of quality, but not yet able to waltz right in and pay top dollar.)

So you see, there are three keys to knowing your competition; knowing how your target customer perceives them, knowing how they differ from you, and knowing in what ways these differences are important to your ideal customer. As a corollary to these: make sure that the competition is really the competition.

Even if they appear to be in the same type of business, they are not competitive with you if they attract customers who would not be attracted to you, and vice versa.

How Does My Competition Advertise?

Before you can do an effective job of advertising against your competition, you need to do some background work. You already have familiarized yourself with their actual operations and customer types. Now you need to look at the face they are presenting to the media-reading public. Where are they advertising, to whom, and what promises are they making?

Some of your competitions' advertising will be easier to locate than others. Start by checking the phone directory to see what type of ad they have placed there. Many companies place display ads that are very similar to their normal print media advertising. If your chamber of commerce puts out a directory, check the ads in there.

Next, scan your local newspapers. You might need to check for several weeks because most small businesses cannot and do not advertise every day. Clip all ads that you see for businesses with whom you might be competing. Note the day that they advertise, the page, and, if possible, the ad's position on the page. You will find this helpful when you are placing your own advertising.

Notice, in every ad that you clip, what promises the advertiser makes to his potential customers. Is the emphasis on price, style, service? Or do the ads use an emotional appeal, trying to instill fear, guilt, adventure, or maybe a sense of status in the reader? Some of the ads you clip, especially if you are in the retail business, will be special event ads that stress sales and special promotions. Others will be ads aimed at building consumer recognition.

What type of promises are your competitors making? What is your competitor giving the public as the chief reason they should respond to his or her ad? Can you make a similar promise? Perhaps, but you probably won't want to.

One of the aims of advertising is to set yourself apart from the competition. That means that you want your ads to make meaningful promises about what you can do for the customer that are both different from and more attractive than what the competition is offering. (If you've done your homework and paid attention to what your customers are saying, you've got a jump on the gun here.)

Different from the competition can present a problem. Let's assume that you own a service station, with two gas pumps, a service bay, and a very knowledgeable mechanic. So does the man a mile down the road. He got there first, and is advertising "you can trust us to make your car better." Since gas pumps are gas pumps, and a service bay is only as good as the mechanic in it, your competitor seems to have stolen the one claim that you can make to attract customers. With this edge, he also seems to be stealing away a lot of your potential customers. So you advertise that "Our mechanic is the spark-plug gapping champion of 1986.'' You're both making the same claim—that you have reliable mechanics. But you're making the claim in different ways. What happens when he comes back with ''Our mechanic won the National Engine Rebuilding Contest of the year?'' How can you top that?

This game of one-upmanship could get ridiculous. So it's time to regroup. You can either say that your mechanic is both skilled and fast—so that we save on labor charges—or you can switch tactics altogether and attempt to establish your significant difference along some other line, such as emergency road service.

The rule of thumb here is: when there are no important differences, you can make the same claim as your competitor—as long as it sounds different. You are much better off, however, to set yourself apart completely so the public doesn't get confused. Sometimes this means offering an emotional, rather than a real difference. You could claim that your gas station is the one preferred by BMW and Rolls Royce owners—the station with class. Put the pump attendant on roller skates and advertise that yours is a fun station to come to. Hire a singing mechanic, to make that dismal wait in the service bay more fun. Make yourself the focus of the ad—the face we can trust our cars to: Honest Ed. Promise them anything—but not what the competition is promising.

In most businesses, there are several approaches to even the most factual ad. If you are selling men's clothing, for instance, you will have customers who come in because they like the service, others who like your selection, several because of your pricing strategy, and a few because you have snob appeal.

Now, a good ad can only make one main point before it loses the interest of the reader or listener. So, if your competitor has a good ad, he is probably only making one of the above points—that he has a great selection, terrific service, or bargain prices. You can choose any of the other meaningful claims—or maybe two. (Great quality at bargain prices, for instance, is a popular—maybe over-popular—claim.) Then you will have distinguished yourself from the competition. Your competition might come to be known as the place with great prices, while the public comes to associate you with style.

So far, we have only looked at a few of your competitors' ads—those in directories, and those in newspaper. These are good starting places, particularly for retailers, since newspaper, especially, is the retailer's favorite medium.

If the competition knows how to advertise well, you already know what you need to know about the promises he is making. A good ad campaign makes only one consistent promise—and then makes it everywhere, in every type of ad, in every medium. Don't stop there. Listen carefully, and see what TV and radio stations your competitor uses. What time slots do they appear in? Drive around and try to spot their billboards. If they are doing well, you want to try to benefit from their success. If they are bombing, you'll want some clues about what to avoid. Keep a careful record of all your competitor's activities. When it comes time to establish your own objectives, and begin to establish your own niche in the marketplace, you will need this information. Knowing where your competitors are advertising, and how often, will help you to establish both your advertising budget and your media plan.

SUMMARY

Setting your objectives means sitting back, before you begin to advertise, and figuring out exactly what you need to tell people. A small business usually has a small budget, which means small ads. Therefore, your ads must be to the point and aimed at tackling your most important business needs quickly and clearly.

Many businesspeople, wise in the ways of their own field, but inexperienced in advertising, simply place ads in a scattergun fashion or whenever a media salesperson is especially persuasive. The smart person, however, has a plan. He knows what his ads have to say and why. She knows that people need to be persuaded to drive a bit out of their way—or that the parking hassle will be worth it because of the great service provided. They know that people have the wrong impression of who they are, and that their ads need to correct it. They know what the competition is doing and how to set themselves apart.

Only by sitting down and carefully taking stock of yourself, your business pluses and problems, and the strengths and weaknesses of your competition can you hope to achieve an effective advertising campaign.

4

Finding and Knowing
Your Best Customers

"I WANT MY AD TO APPEAL TO EVERYBODY," SAID MARTY. "I MEAN, EVERYBODY has to eat, right? So why should I limit my appeal?"

His wife sighed and licked her pencil. "But Marty—if I put in that you've got low prices, you'll scare away the people who like a fancy lunch. If I say you've got homestyle cooking, the gourmets won't come. And if I put that you offer a leisurely lunch hour, you'll scare away the secretaries who don't have much time. I just can't write an ad that will please everybody!"

That's true for almost any business. You have natural customers—those people who already want what you have. These will form the basis of your primary target audience—the people you advertise to when you're starting out. Write your ads specifically for that target audience, featuring the benefits that mean most to them. Place your ads in the media that these people are most likely to see and hear. Try any other approach, and you will waste valuable time and money.

Targeting your advertising means identifying the primary group or groups of people who are likely prospects for your business. This chapter will explain how to identify your target audiences and to determine their relative importance in your business and advertising efforts. How do you apportion your budget to fit your target audience? How do you determine which target audience is most important? Finally, where do you find these target audiences, and how can you make them grow?

THE ADVANTAGES OF TARGETING

Because of many factors—the type of business you have, the selection you carry, your location, your own personality, or the image that people hold of you—some people are more likely to buy from you than others. While it might be disappointing to realize that you cannot get the whole world to flock regularly to your door, there are advantages to choosing a target market.

Saving Money

Targeting your advertising to your most likely customers saves you money. Once you know who these people are, you can also make some very educated guesses about the media they use and the times during which they use them. This narrows down the field considerably when it comes to choosing and buying advertising space and time.

Refining Messages

Targeting your audience creates more effective messages. If you know who you're talking to, then you have a clear idea of what you should say to them. Teens respond to different messages and promises than do senior citizens or mothers of five; wealthy people have different response patterns to sales than does the middle class.

Refining Your Business

Knowing your target audience can even help you to refine your business. If you discover that your most likely customer is a 28-year-old female Yuppie, on the rise in her career, and valuing quality over quantity, then you can remove all the impulse items and anything made of plastic or polyester from your inventory. And you certainly won't feature items like these in your ads.

Targeting at Work: A Case History

Let me give you an example of how targeting works.

You have a sandwich shop located half a block from an urban college campus. Most of the retail stores are two to three blocks away, but there are office buildings in the area. Given your menu—fast food in a sit-down atmosphere—you discover that the bulk of your business is done with three groups: college students, college professors, and businesspeople from the immediate six block area.

Knowing this can save you a lot of money. You will not want to buy TV time, because this will reach thousands (maybe millions) of people who will never even be in your neighborhood. You are charged, in TV, radio, newspaper—any medium—according to the number of people that medium reaches.

Radio, too, could be a waste of money, unless you buy ads on the low-powered campus radio station. With campus radio, you will reach your primary audience—the students—for a very reasonable cost. You will waste very little of your money in reaching people not in your geographic and demographic market. The school newspaper is also a good buy, because, again for very low rates, you can reach two of your primary target audiences—students and professors.

You could buy the morning newspaper to reach that third audience—the local businesspeople. This will remind them about your daily specials before they decide where to eat lunch. It will also reach thousands of people who don't care—another waste of money. So you choose a small, downtown business journal, and then send direct-mail fliers of your menu and delivery service to all the secretaries in the downtown area.

Knowing your limitations has also helped you to refine both your message and your business. Knowing that businesspeople will rarely travel more than a block or two for anything less than a power lunch, you have initiated lunch-time deliveries. Knowing that students and professors often have to eat on the fly, you also begin to advertise the QuickService—phone in advance, and we'll have a hot lunch ready and waiting. You can also feature your quiet backroom, for more leisurely study lunches.

If you hadn't known your best target audiences, you might have wasted hundreds or even thousands of dollars advertising to people who will never be your customers. You might also have wasted time and effort trying to set yourself apart from other downtown lunch places that you are not really in competition with. You would have had a much harder time trying to figure out which features of your business would be most attractive to the people who do come in and appreciate you, or who are most likely to be lured by those promises. See? Targeting pays off.

PRIMARY AND SECONDARY TARGETS

If you're worried about unduly limiting your potential by targeting, take heart. Most businesses have more than one target audience. Usually, there is a primary target group—the one with which you do the bulk of your business, because they most naturally are attracted to what you have to offer. In the above example, college students were probably the primary target audience, simply because there are so many more of them than of professors or accessible businesspeople. However, you would not want to ignore these other two groups.

You might decide that you already have a good business from students without devoting much effort and advertising toward attracting them. They might be less important to your total plan than the businesspeople. Directing your primary efforts to attracting this group might result in a substantial increase in business. In that case, they would be your primary target—the group on which you spend the largest portion of your advertising budget and efforts.

The Object of Targeting

The object, in defining your primary target groups, is to take a careful look at who you want to attract and who you are likely to be able to attract. Divide these people into two or three identifiable groups. Then, decide how important each of these groups of customers are to your total business plan. By this I mean that you should estimate the relative importance of each group to your success. Out of 100 percent, how much business comes (or should come) from each group that you have identified? In the above example, you may have decided that, with advertising, you could increase traffic among businesspeople to make up about 50 percent of your business. This means that you want to devote about 50 percent of your budget to advertising to this particular target group. You might prefer an older crowd of customers. Assign 30 percent of your effort to attracting the college professors and university administrators. The remaining 20 percent of your advertising budget and efforts continues to encourage students to have lunch with you.

Refining Your Target Market

Should you later discover that business and university people simply don't mix well, you might want to adjust these percentages. If you decide to become a college hangout, you might want to spend 60 percent of your budget reaching students, and 40 percent at faculty and administrators.

Whenever you make changes in your business, or whenever there are shifts in population that affect your business, you could find that your target markets will also change. At that point, you must carefully calculate the importance of each new group to your business. This will also change your media buys and your media budget. But, to fail to make these adjustments could mean to fail in your business. The point, in determining your best advertising plan, is to identify your target audiences, and then stay flexible.

THINGS TO CONSIDER BEFORE COMMITTING YOUR BUDGET

Before you decide who to spend your budget money on, you should carefully assess the characteristics of your present customers, their value to your business, and the potential value of other potential target markets.

Who Is My Present Customer?

Take a good look at the people who come through your door. If at all possible, try to take a door count to note demographic or psychographic characteristics. Try to arrive at some generalizations about the kind of people who are your best and most usual customers. What age level do they tend to fall into? What income level? Who is a buyer, and who is a browser? Do they spend freely or look for bargains? Do they seem well educated? Interested only in *Hustler*? Do they tend to dress well and care about appearances? What kinds of interests do they seem to have?

Normally, you'll have more than one type of average customer. You might have a large percentage of men shopping in your corner hardware store, most of them associated in some way with the building trade. You might have an even larger percentage of do-it-yourselfers, who spend less but shop often. You'll find a surprisingly large percentage of women, especially in the paint, stain, cabinet hardware, and houseware departments. Try to estimate what proportion of each make up the bulk of your trade.

Many businesses have seasonal target markets. At holidays for instance, businesses traditionally aimed at women, such as lingerie stores, perfumeries, jewelry shops, etc., will notice a large influx of men looking for gifts. Gyms and exercise classes might have largely adult populations except during summer, when school is out and teens are getting ready for beaches and bikinis. A smart advertiser is aware of this and runs ads that feature appeals to these seasonal audiences. This means that in normal months, your budget is divided among your normal target audiences, but during these seasonal surges, a greater portion of your monthly expenditure should go toward attracting your more transient audiences.

Is This Who I Want?

You've got customers. Maybe even enough customers to keep the business going in a decent enough fashion. Are they the customers you want?

A former client of mine had a gourmet shop in a small mall near a major university. He did a brisk business there, selling cheese and candy to the university crowd—occasionally even attracting some of the faculty wives who fancied themselves gourmet cooks. The college clientele always made the shop seem full so he appeared to be a success. But this crowd did not care about triple-creme Brie, or raspberry vinegars, and the little cans of truffles Martin kept under lock and key. The people who wanted these, however, tended to be put off by the crowd of college freshmen who always seemed to be hanging around nibbling Lindt chocolates.

The solution? Well, it wasn't all advertising. Martin had to do some price and stock adjustments, phasing out the cheaper impulse items that made the young nonspenders so prolific. He also had to change his advertising. He had to create an expensive and tasteful look for his ads; he had to learn to feature some of his more exotic items—the ones designed to appeal to the culinarily wise. He had to cut out those bargain ads in the college newspaper, and place ads on the adult-oriented radio station and in the city magazine. Not wanting to alienate the faculty wives, he bought space in the alumnae magazine. He even tried a billboard, way off campus. With the new, more exclusive image and the more careful media plan, Martin increased his target audience among the affluent gourmets, while gently discouraging the young people who were scaring the prime audience away.

The lesson that Martin learned the hard way was to think very hard about the kind of clientele you want to attract. What are their likes and dislikes? What are their spending habits? What kind of places do they like to patronize? What kind of people do they like to associate with? Where are they most likely to be found?

No business is ever going to please 100 percent of the population. Trying to accommodate everyone will only mean that you'll partially (but not meaningfully) please some. So take a good look at the type of customer you want to see coming through that door. Then concentrate on attracting them, both with the type of business you run and the way in which you present that business to the world.

Is This My Only Possible Customer?

Maybe you like the clientele you're attracting. If that clientele gives you enough business to keep you happy, fine. Stick with them. If not, take stock again. Who else might find your type of business appealing? There are many places to go to increase your clientele.

Geographically. Perhaps you can increase your business among the kind of people you are now attracting by simply advertising in a wider area to attract people from further away.

By Gender. Perhaps your business largely appeals to the female shopper. You can attract men, at least seasonally, by proving through advertising that you're the ideal place for feminine gifts. Perfumes do this with great success. During the year, they concentrate on telling women how much sexier, alluring, prettier they will feel by using a particular scent. But at Christmas and Valentine's day, most perfume ads do some variation on ''Promise Her Anything, but Give Her Arpege.''

By Type of User. A local plumbing supply shop did a brisk business with the contractors, but not much with the retail trade until they began advertising a hot line that would answer all questions for the do-it-yourselfer. Suddenly it became a favorite place for anyone in need of plumbing. A beauty shop that begins to feature a male in the ''after'' picture for its ''$12.95 Permanent Special'' suddenly seems ''OK'' for guys who previously thought of it as a female stronghold.

By Age. Be careful here. If you attract a young, loud type of crowd, your advertising might lure the older, sedate types in once—but never again. But, if you see that your business can naturally attract a slightly younger or older crowd without making any major adjustments, go for it. For example, your dress shop might be doing a brisk business with the polyester pantsuit crowd—and yet at the same time carries a sedate line of business clothes. This business line attracts your current customer, but could also be ideal for the younger female executive. Let your ads say so—feature these clothes in your window. Make it obvious. Then change the music in your radio ads from Lawrence Welk to something a bit more up-tempo and current. People will get the message.

By Income. If you carry a line of products that is a bit high priced, but of lasting quality, you will appeal to the higher end of the income scale. By pointing out that your product's quality and classic styling are a smart shopping move because they'll last so long they're actually more economical, you may make some inroads into the lower-income levels some of the time. On the other hand, inexpensive but well-designed items that are typically bought by the lower-income group can be promoted to those with more disposable income as splurge, fun items to be used then tossed aside.

Within the Existing Audience. If you're content with the type of customer you have but would like more business, then you want to encourage the people you already have to buy more or use more of your services. Advertising that promotes new uses for products or creates more need for existing products and services can help this problem. If you sell seafood, try using recipe ads, so that the people who like fresh fish have more reasons to buy. If you style hair, start promoting cuts that require more frequent trims. If you're a caterer, write ads that give people more reasons to give catered parties.

Checklist for Determining Your Target Market

Customers You Already Have

Take a rough inventory of your customers during the next two weeks. Take notes about their age, sex, the type of person they are, and type of things they buy. Then answer the following questions.

- What percentage of your customers are male?
- What percentage are female?
- What age group do most of your male customers fall into?
- What age group do most of your females fall into?
- Do your most typical customers fall into any describable groups?
- How important is each group to your business? Assign a percentage to each group.
- Can you add any information about your groups of typical customers: income, level of education, interests, motivations for buying? Who looks versus who buys?

- Do your products or services fall into any recognizable seasonal pattern, when your customer percentages might change? During what months do you need to be aware of these changes? How important are these seasonal customers to your total business?

Customers You Want But Do Not Have

- Does your business offer any features that could be attractive to a group of customers other than those with whom you are already doing business?
- If not, can you attract a different group of customers without having to make changes that might alienate your present customers?
- If you can attract a new group of customers, from where do you hope to attract them?
  —From a different age group?
  —From the opposite sex?
  —From a slightly different income group?
  —From a different geographic area?
  —By appealing to a different type of user?
- Can you increase your business by advertising ways for your present customers to use your services or buy your products more often?
- By what percentage do you hope to increase business by appealing to this new group?
- What importance do you give this group in your advertising budget plan?

To Determine Your Advertising Budget per Target Group

Describe each target group that you either do a large percentage of your business with or hope to appeal to in terms of demographics. (See chapter 5.) Determine the percentage of importance that each group has to your total business plan. Now, look at any seasonal audiences you might appeal to. During these seasons, approximately what percentage of your business would you like to do with this group?

Take your media calendar. On each page you should have a dollar figure—the amount of your budget that you will be spending that month on advertising. Divide that amount according to target audiences. Go month-by-month, so that you remember to include seasonal customers in the appropriate months.

For example: In January, 70 percent of your business is done with middle-income females, ages 35 – 65 who buy flowers for their home. Thirty percent of your business is done with male executives, ages 45 – 65 who send flowers for business purposes. In February, 50 percent of your business is with that same group of females, 15 percent with the businessmen, and the remaining 35 percent are younger males 25 – 40 who buy flowers at Valentine's day.

In January, your advertising budget is $600. You spend 70 percent of that ($420) on ads in the women's section of the newspaper to encourage your females to continue beautifying their homes with flowers. The rest of the budget buys $180 worth of ads in the local business journal.

In February, because it is a busy season, your budget jumps to $1,000. Fifty percent of that budget remains directed at your regular female customers, and 15 percent with the businessmen. You spend $350 (35 percent of your February budget) on radio spots and newspaper ads directed toward the young men who form your seasonal audience. These ads, of course, all cluster around Valentine's day.

Do this for each month, until your entire budget has been allocated. There's no need to worry yet about what media you are buying, or what your ads will say. For now, what you have accomplished is a sound budget plan, where your media spending will be based on the importance of each type of customer to your business. Figure 4-1 shows a typical calendar for one month.

YOUR AREA OF TRADE

Suppose, as we did in the preceding section, that you are located in a lower-income section of town. Does this mean that your typical customer will be a lower-income shopper?

It depends on your type of business. Every type of business has a typical area of trade—the area comprising the distances which people will travel in order to patronize you. Knowing your average area of trade is important to you because it strongly affects the choice of media that will reach your market cost-efficiently.

Small Areas of Trade

There are some businesses that people simply will not travel to. Very few customers will drive miles out of their way to patronize a particular picture-developer. Instead, we tend to drop our rolls of film off at the first convenient place we come to—the drugstore or supermarket. Therefore, if you have a photo-developing service, you had better be located very conveniently to large numbers of people. Second, you want to spend your advertising dollar wisely so your ads are not traveling to amateur photographers in the next county. This same principle holds true for many businesses: drug stores, mom and pop markets, or any type of operation that provides goods or services that tend to fall into the convenience category, such as gas stations and fast food outlets.

Medium-Sized Areas of Trade

Other businesses have a wider area of trade. Businesses which fall into the ''shopping'' classification attract people from a wider geographic area and need

February 1989

BUDGET $600

70% ($420) FEMALES 35-65

30% MALE EXECUTIVES ($180)

TIMES ADS - $12.50 COL. INCH

JOURNAL ADS - $2.00 COL. INCH

SUN	MON	TUE	WED	THU	FRI	SAT
			1 BUSINESS JOURNAL 3×5"	**2**	**3**	**4**
5 2×2" WOMENS SECTION, TIMES	**6**	**7**	**8** BUSINESS JOURNAL 4×8"	**9**	**10** 2×2" WOMENS SECTION, TIMES	**11** 2×2" WOMENS SECTION, TIMES
12 2×2" WOMENS SECTION, TIMES	**13** 2×2" WOMENS SECTION, TIMES	**14** 2×2" WOMENS SECTION, TIMES VALENTINES DAY	**15** BUSINESS JOURNAL 3×5"	**16**	**17**	**18**
19 2×2" WOMENS SECTION, TIMES	**20**	**21**	**22** BUSINESS JOURNAL 3×5"	**23**	**24**	**25**
26 2×2" WOMENS SECTION, TIMES	**27**	**28**				

Fig. 4-1. Once you have figured out your monthly budget, your calendar will help you to determine when and where your ads will run. In this example, the business journal was an inexpensive weekly. Because there were only four issues, the advertiser applied the savings to purchasing an additional ad for her primary target audience.

to buy advertising media with a wider circulation. Many people, for instance, will travel 5 – 10 miles for a good haircut or a good meal. They will go far out of their way for a doctor they trust or a hardware store that carries the unusual supplies they require. If your business falls into this category, then you will have a more difficult time categorizing your typical customer since you will tend to draw a variety not particularly typical of the neighborhood in which you are located.

Large Areas of Trade

Finally, there are a few businesses with extremely large areas of trade to which people will spend hours driving, if necessary. Stores that carry specialty goods that are not generally available, such as fine antiques, special brands of furniture, exclusive label clothing, or foreign cars, need advertising that reaches a wide geographic area.

Areas of Trade for Service Businesses

Then there are services. Not every business operation requires that the customer come to you. Many service operations go to the customer. If you are a roofer, a plumber, a tree surgeon, or an upholsterer, the area of trade is, to a certain extent, up to you. How great is the potential need for your service in the immediate area? How much business are you equipped to handle? If you want to be the friendly, neighborhood appliance repairman, then concentrate your advertising efforts on small, local circulation media. If you want a larger slice of the pie, be prepared to buy more mass media and to advertise competitively.

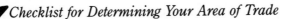

Checklist for Determining Your Area of Trade

- Find out how far the typical customer in your primary target audience travels to do business with you.
- Find out how far your typical secondary target customer travels to do business with you.
- Do this for all main target audiences, including seasonal.
- Get a map, and draw out the travel area (area of trade) for each of your target audiences. Code these, so you know which area of trade belongs to which customer group.
- Save this map. When you begin to buy ads, this will help you to determine which media will best reach which target audience most efficiently.

SUMMARY

In order to maximize your advertising effectiveness, you need to target your advertising to those consumers most likely to want what you have to offer. Audiences are targeted by location, gender, age, perhaps by education, income, or even religion. They are also recognized by their psychographics, or lifestyle and personality characteristics. All these factors not only affect the percentage of your budget that you must spend to reach your audiences, but also the messages you need to convey and the media that you will buy to convey them.

The next chapter will describe demographic and psychographic characteristics of audiences, what these say about your customer, and how these characteristics will affect your advertising.

5

Knowing What Makes the Customer Tick: Demographics and Psychographics

PETER GESTURED AT THE PEOPLE BROWSING IN HIS SHOWROOM. "FUNNY thing" he said, "but I can almost tell what each of these people will end up with. Take that couple there—strong traditionalists. They'll want a sofa with classic lines, well built, in a subdued fabric. But those people by the Memphis display— they just hit the big time, and they'll go for something contemporary—trendy even—and splashy. Yuppies—well, they want the money they spent to show. They care about quality, but trade things in for a newer style every few years anyway. Then there's that lady with the six kids. Her husband's a doctor, you know—makes good money—but with all those kids, she'll go for medium price, sturdy, with a print that hides stains. If you know your customer, you can almost predict what will appeal to them."

Know thy customer. That's the cardinal rule in business and in advertising. Your customers might seem to come in all shapes and sizes, and of course, they're all individuals with different quirks and qualities. But they do have certain things in common—the things that attract them to you. These commonalities can usually be broken down into demographic and psychographic factors.

Demographics describe your customer according to age, sex, level of education, income, family size, and several other factors which will allow you to draw certain conclusions about your target market as a group. In this chapter we will take a look at some generalities that apply to different demographic groups in the marketplace. Even within these groups, there are differences that you must account for.

Psychographics, which look at people in terms of whether they are leaders, followers, status seekers, individualists, etc., can help you to draw a more rounded picture of your typical customer. When you know your customers demographically and psychographically, you can better identify the messages that will motivate them to respond to your advertising.

Many people have fundamental objections to describing people in terms of demographics and psychographics. Demographics describe groups in terms of their vital statistics. Psychographics take into account personality characteristics and lifestyle. To many of us, this seems to rob our customers of their individuality. But when we advertise, we are dealing with large groups of people that we hope to attract rather than to the individuals we know and love. Therefore, demographics and psychographics are necessary evils that allow us to cope with the necessity of communicating with large audiences.

While knowing someone's age will not necessarily tell you his or her general outlook on life, there are statistical trends that tell us most people in certain age groups are predisposed to view life in a certain way. This will not, of course, hold true for every individual in that category, but it will hold generally true. The same goes for income levels, education, etc. Advertising, by its very nature, deals with generalizations about audiences. Therefore, a little knowledge about what demographics and psychographics can tell us is a valuable thing.

DEMOGRAPHICS

Demographic descriptions of audiences include their age, income, sex, geographic location, social class, occupation, family life cycle, religion, and ethnicity. While not all these statistics might be relevant to your advertising, many of them are. Therefore, all are worth investigating.

Age

Knowing the average age category for your typical desired customer is important. For one thing, many radio and TV stations sell their time slots according to ratings. Ratings tend to describe the typical age groups who watch or listen to a program at a given hour. Therefore, knowing the average age of your target audience helps you to make wise media selections.

Age and Audience Response. Age affects the ways in which we typically respond to advertising messages. For instance, at the risk of insulting many people, let me say that, as a group, the very young and the very old tend to be somewhat self-centered. They look at things and make decisions based on whether something will make their life happier, easier, or more fun. Their first question in responding to an ad is "What will it do for me?"

Young people do this because they have not yet had to shoulder much responsibility; they have yet to discover that they are not the center of the universe. Older people do this because they have shouldered responsibility for so long. They are now sitting in empty nests with leisure time on their hands, less income, and a lot less security. They worry about how a purchase will affect that security, will help to keep them independent, and will make them comfortable. Older people often look for advertising messages that reassure them.

Age and Message Style. Age also affects the style of message we respond to. If, at the grand old age of 40, I am flipping through the newspaper, I tend to ignore all the ads with psychedelic lettering. I know from experience that those are "young people ads." Nor, at this age, am I very worried about huge popularity or a date for the prom. I am also less likely to respond to ads that ask me to take risks or promise that I can change the world. The reason for that is statistical, but also common sense. When we are very young, most of us believe that we can make a difference in things—that somehow we can change the world. The idea is very attractive. Unfortunately, the older we get, the more pessimistic we get, and therefore, the more cautious.

Sex

Women's Lib has changed some things about advertising. We're now almost afraid to advertise a cleaning product with a woman using it unless she's in a business suit and has her briefcase in the other hand.

Sex and Message Styles. Other things, however, have not changed. Women are still, for instance, more open to an emotional advertising appeal, or a humanitarian one, than men. This is not to say that men are hard, unfeeling creatures. Men have been socialized to be the rational, unemotional (or less emotional) of the sexes. While a male might, psychologically, respond as powerfully as the female to a portrayal of a cute kitten or a crying baby, he does not feel as though he should admit it. He therefore searches out the factual portions of ads to justify his emotional response. So does the woman, especially as her level of education rises. Women simply aren't as embarrassed to admit that they also involve their feelings in a purchase.

Sex and Advertising Spokespersons. Knowing whether your primary audience is male or female is important for another reason. As ad consumers, we have been conditioned to respond to certain ads because something in their sound or appearance signals to us, almost unconsciously, "This one's for me." As a rule, when women see another woman in an ad, they check it out, assuming that it has a female-oriented message. Males do the same. There are many exceptions, of course, but when my students have tested audience response patterns to ads, males tended to respond instinctively to male voices and pictures, and females to women.

However, there are times when a male will not listen to another male, and a female won't trust a female spokesperson. Let's say you have a small perfume boutique. It's holiday time, and you want to advertise to all those men who are looking for feminine gifts. Should you use a man in your ads? Probably not. A male spouting rapturously about essence of jasmine is likely to be suspect. A woman enchanted with a scent is more convincing to the male buyer. During the rest of the year, though, when women primarily replenish their own perfume supply, they are less likely to respond to a radio ad where a woman tells us how good something smells than she is to a man reacting to the scent "his woman" wears (remember "Wind Song stays on my mind?"). A lot depends on why your customer is making the purchase and whether a man or a woman is most likely to be the authority on it. These last factors are things that your preliminary research should have told you.

Sex and Media Choices. Knowing the sex of your primary target also affects the media you buy. Some newspapers still have women's pages—primarily because in those areas there are a lot of traditional women. Sports pages are good places to reach men. At certain times of day, more women than men listen to the radio and vice versa. Certain TV programs are preferred by one sex over the other. (I was always amazed to discover that *Charley's Angels*—a show I thought was the male fantasy personified—was most avidly watched by women and was an ideal place to advertise perfume, women's clothing, etc.)

Income

There is no doubt about it. The price of your service or the price range of your store affects the way prospective (and current) clients perceive you.

There are two facets to this perception. One is how expensive your product or service actually is. The other is how expensive people perceive it to be. Being expensive or middle-priced or even dirt cheap is never a problem—as long as you have a potential audience willing to pay your price and are communicating the correct price expectations to that public. If your image is confusing to people, however, beware.

Price Classifications and Customer Perception. The average customer will tend to view your business as one of three kinds: convenience, shopping goods, or luxury. *Convenience stores* are those which tend to carry a large selection of goods that are bought by a large segment of the population with no great brand preference involved. These include drugstores, small groceries and mini-marts, bargain outlets, and sundry stores. The person who patronizes a convenience store expects to pay a bit more for his or her bread, milk, or batteries and light bulbs, because of the convenience. They do not, however, expect to pay luxury prices because none of the products carried are distinctive.

Shopping goods stores, on the other hand, carry products that come in many styles and brands. The average shopper does not expect to walk into any single store and find everything he or she wants. Instead, they assume that they will shop around, do a bit of comparison pricing and make a final decision based on many things including price, style, service, perhaps brand name, and maybe even some psychic satisfaction that could come from buying at a certain type of store. This category is a bit trickier than the convenience store. Some shoppers make their decisions based on low price and quality. Some don't care about quality, but buy low priced items because then they can buy more of them. Some people buy mainly by style and appearance. Some buy certain brand names, either because they trust them or because they have a reputation that makes the buyer feel good. A few buy higher priced items because high price equates to them with quality. Some shoppers buy mid-priced items, except when it comes to gift-giving, when quality and a higher price are more desirable. That's why it pays to know your typical shopper. Price, brand name, the purpose of the purchase—all these help determine where someone shops and what they buy.

The final category, *luxury stores*, is a bit simpler. Here, the big draw is mainly image. Brand name or reputation become much more important than actual price. Women long for Joy perfume simply because it is "the world's costliest." Scotch drinkers feel more secure when they offer their friends Chivas Regal. Some people save for years so they can finally be seen driving a Cadillac, or a BMW. The satisfaction is mainly emotional, and it's hard to put a price tag on emotions. Plus, you're dealing here with the great American myth that "You get what you pay for." To many, price equates with quality. Using expensive items and services implies that you have "the best." Also, many Americans have a great longing for possessions that seem to give us status. A local clothing store that sells Ralph Lauren's Polo line claims that many customers refuse to buy an item of clothing unless it has the Polo logo prominently displayed on it. As the customers say, when they pay all that money for a brand name they want people to know what they've got. That, too, gives us great emotional satisfaction.

A word to the wise: a big price tag does not necessarily put your product in the luxury category. The potential purchaser for a small truck expects to hand over a small bundle and wants a lot of good, hard facts to help him or her to justify that purchase. Therefore, the truck belongs in the shopping goods category. You'll need to advertise cost and logical reasons to purchase. On the other hand, the luxury item, like the Cadillac, exerts more of an emotional pull. Ads for luxury items tend to emphasize feelings and emotions, style, and status over facts. When the price tag rises especially high, you might need to deal with facts to take the sting of guilt out of self-indulgence. But you still need to talk more to the emotions than to the mind.

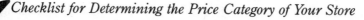

Checklist for Determining the Price Category of Your Store

Your business falls into the convenience category if:

- You carry goods for which few people have a strong brand preference.
- Your goods and/or services are inexpensive enough that expertise and quality have little bearing on customer selection.
- People will choose your goods or services without first shopping around to compare prices and qualifications.

Your business falls into the shopping category if:

- There is a wide variation in style available for the type of goods you carry.
- The price for the generic category of your line of merchandise varies widely by brand.
- There is a large variation in quality within the general category of merchandise that you carry.
- If yours is a service business, you fall into the shopping classification if the public tends to perceive a difference in workmanship, types of services provided, and price.
- If there is some brand preference, but only among brands roughly competitive in price, style, and quality.

Your business falls into the luxury category if:

- The goods or services that you provide are perceived as being unique, or at least not products of mass production.
- The price of your goods or services is high, as is the quality.
- If people will travel a great distance to take advantage of your very special goods and/or services.
- If there is a strong brand preference.

The Importance of Correct Classification. The important thing to derive from this is that you must be very sure what category your store falls into in your customer's perception. If people perceive you as a shopping store, and you try to sell your product as though it were a luxury, you will miss the boat with most people. If customers perceive you as shopping, and you try to offer convenience prices and services, people might think your quality is slipping.

One of my clients learned this lesson the hard way. He worked hard to set up a very posh hair-styling salon, complete with clothing boutique (and out-of-sight clothing prices). Then he advertised "No appointment necessary. Haircuts $9."

The reaction? Confusion. People who wanted a $9 haircut were not people who bought luxury clothing. The people who wanted luxury clothing would never trust their heads to a stylist who could be bought for a mere $9. Moreover, the "first come-first served" approach took away the luxury of choice and personal preference that the "class" customer wanted. So people stayed away in droves until the stylist raised his prices.

This businessman, too, was confronted with the strong feeling among members of the general public that "You get what you pay for." If an item is low priced to start with, people tend to equate this with low quality. If the item is normally high priced, however, and can be bought for some reason at a reduced price (year-end sale, manufacturer's overstock, special anniversary celebration, etc.) this seems to reassure people about quality.

How Price Perception Changes with Lifestyle. Beware of labeling an item "expensive" or "cheap" until you've really taken stock of your customer, their level of income, and their level of disposable income. What is expensive to one person is a mere pittance to another. When I was in graduate school, making a mere $6000 a year, I haunted antique shops in search of used furniture and accessories for my apartment. The $25 I once splurged on a cut glass compote seemed exorbitant to me and was truly the most expensive thing I bought during this period of my life (even though I might have shelled out $50 for a blazer or $75 for a good, used couch). As a college professor (still not rich, by any means), I can look back at that price for cut glass and say it was phenomenally cheap. The same thing holds true for any group of people. If you are situated in a lower income neighborhood, then expensive becomes relative. Your $2 bouquet of cut flowers can be every bit as expensive to your customer as the $5 one is to the downtown florist's trade.

Income, however, is not the only factor that affects the buyer's perception of your pricing system. A person's lifestyle also changes his or her outlook on spending. The low-income family, with no immediate prospects for disposable income, becomes accustomed to shopping on the low end of the price scale, except, perhaps, for very special occasions. The low-income graduate student or temporarily unemployed person has been accustomed to higher prices and might bargain hunt for certain items (food, perhaps, and household staples) yet still spend a higher amount for clothing or certain familiar brand name items.

There is yet another confusion when it comes to associating the advertisement of price with your class of customers. The people who respond to so-called bargain shopping might not be the lower-middle income types you might expect. If you offer quality merchandise at low prices, don't be surprised if the people who come through your door are higher-income people. These are the smart shoppers, which is one reason they have a lot of disposable income. I worked as a checker in a gourmet grocery store during college where the Fords and the Fishers of Grosse Pointe shopped. They were the people who carefully clipped coupons and bought sale items. Those whose positions in life were less secure tended to buy more by brand than by price, as if to reassure themselves that they could afford a few of the same luxuries as the Fords and Fishers.

For this same reason, in certain depressed areas of the northeast, the upper-income families, secure in their status, tend to shop clothing outlets for brand names at discount prices. Those with less disposable income, paradoxically, shop the department stores and pay full price. This seems to be a sort of ego-pat for the spender, who can then tell himself or herself that they are not yet reduced to shopping the cut-rate stores. They will pay more to buy less, simply to reassure themselves that drastic economy measures are not a complete necessity. Pride is a powerful motivator for the buyer.

Geographic Location

Geographic location does not affect some types of businesses at all. Others must pay close attention. Your advertising, what you choose to feature and when, can be very strongly affected by the geographic location of your target audience. To be obvious, you would not expect to even start a successful air-conditioning shop in Nome, Alaska. In a four seasons climate, you can expect people to have less disposable income while they are paying the winter heat bills. How much business you do can be affected by extremes in heat, cold, ice, rain, etc. In these extremes, expect only those customers who are geographically close to you.

In other words, to a certain extent, geography affects seasons, which affect shopping and service habits. These, in turn, can affect both your actual volume of trade, and your message.

More important, however, is to determine how the geographic location of your target audience will affect your media buys. Your area of trade determines this. If your market is a large, widely scattered one, you will need to buy wide-reaching media like TV and newspapers. If it is a small one, which rarely travels more than 6 – 12 blocks, then you will probably confine yourself to circulars and fliers.

Being aware of the size of your area of trade will allow you to assume certain things about your audience and their perceptions of you. What can you assume if you know they will only travel six blocks for your kind of business? Twenty miles? (Hint: the preceding section on price perception, should provide you with a few answers.)

Level of Education

The more education the people in your target audience have the more likely they are to examine the facts in your ads, to tear apart your factual claims, and to question them. You need to be more rational than emotional. You need to back up your claims.

This is certainly true if your target audience consists largely of the college educated. Not only has college trained them to easily spot the flaws in any factual claims that you might make, but they are also more ego-involved in doing things that will make them appear to be as intelligent as their education implies.

This is not to say that the college-educated person is immune to the emotional appeal. They just want you to give them some logical reasons why they should gratify those emotional impulses.

This is also not to say that only those people with higher education are likely to spot spurious claims or to demand factual back-up. Education is not always a function of higher learning. If you are selling farm tools, the typical college grad is as clueless as the next guy. But the farmer, even with only an eighth grade education, will demand good information when he approaches you. He is educated to the land and knows very well what his machinery has to be able to do. "Keep up with Farmer Jones" simply will not sell this man unless your machine is truly faster and more efficient.

Level of education, then, is the degree of experience and expertise your typical customer is likely to have when confronted with your products and services. A high level of expertise demands factual and logical support for any emotional and image oriented claims you might make. The lower the level of education and/or expertise, the more you can depend on the purely emotional to sell. (Note: Emotional but truthful. I repeat once again that advertising claims that you cannot back up will only disillusion potential customers and keep them from coming back to you.)

Social Class

Social class does not necessarily equate with income. Just because a man makes $200,000 a year does not put him in the upper-class category. Many of the maintenance people at the university where I teach not only make as much money as I do but have more money in their savings accounts. Yet they live differently than I do, spend differently, and most people would consider them, generally, to be in a different social class. Class is a combination of many factors—income, education, heritage, and lifestyle.

You cannot attempt to define class by neighborhoods. Nor can you necessarily define it by looking at occupations. While it is possible to define it, according to a lot of complicated, sociological rules, we do not necessarily know it when we see it.

Nor does everyone, as prime time TV would have us believe, necessarily want to escape from the class they are in to move on up. Not everyone is motivated by upward mobility. Many are content right where they are. It would be a shame to disturb their peace of mind, as long as they are comfortable and happy. Not only would it be a shame, but if these people have no aspirations to a higher class, then ads that make this assumption will not motivate these people to buy.

What I am trying to say about class is—while you might have some ideas about the social class you are trying to appeal to, appeals based on those ideas are, at best, risky.

Family Life Cycle

Family life cycle describes the stage in familial development which your target audience has reached. This is a factor that weighs heavily not only on what motivations will move your hoped-for customers to act, but also on how much disposable income they might have. Just imagine the difference in lifestyle and buying pattern among the newlywed, the couple with their first baby, those with four kids in grade school, those who have one or two in college, and those who have suddenly found themselves with an empty nest. Let's take a hypothetical couple through the family life cycle.

Pete and Jill are newlyweds. They both have good jobs and, at 22, decide that a small home would be a good investment. They had the usual traditional wedding, and so have a supply of china, crystal, silver, etc. But they need furniture, linens, some of the more mundane cookware, and more. They are in the market for paints, basic tools, rugs, wallpaper, plants and appliances. They also look for decorative accessories—nothing too expensive and artsy, but pieces to to give the house a homey feel. They tend to spend a lot of time at places like K-Mart, purchasing mops, scrub buckets, and toilet bowl brushes. All the basics. They also buy lots of books, and go out to eat at fast food places and medium range restaurants. They see a movie a week, and buy lots of records, plus tape rentals for the wedding gift VCR.

Now, Pete and Jill have a baby. They eat out less, rent more tapes. Movie money is gone. They spend money on diaper services, baby clothes, and nursery furnishings. Some of their treasured accessories have to be put up on shelves to avoid baby's curious reach. Crystal is replaced by unbreakable plastic, the china by durable pottery. They entertain at home more (babysitters are tough to find, and expensive) and spend more on deli foods, beer, and wine than before.

When baby goes to school, there are suddenly tuition fees and school clothes to buy. Pete and Jill buy fewer clothes for themselves because they are budgeting madly for growing feet and limbs. They find they need a station wagon to accommodate themselves, baby, the brownie troop, and the cockapoo they bought for company. Pretty has been replaced by practical, for the most part. Therefore, luxury items tend to be saved for gift-giving occasions, and tend to be things that will be safe from careless kids—perfume, jewelry, and personal items. A few of Pete and Jill's cheap, early marriage furniture purchases are wearing out and need slipcovers. The dishwasher is on the blink, and appliance servicemen are getting to be first-name buddies.

Two babies later, Jill has had to stop work entirely. Peter, however, has moved up in the world and makes a good living wage. They have a larger house and need more furniture, of the sturdy, fingerproof kind. Practical is still the byword of the day. Toys, children's books, clothing, convenience foods, and household items made of child-proof fabrics head the shopping list. Jill has little time for books, but still buys records and tapes to play while dashing after the toddlers. Pete, however, now shops in better men's shops, and while Jill still wears jeans a lot around the house, she needs good dinner dresses for his business affairs. The china and crystal are trotted out for late business dinners, and new linens and table accessories, flowers, and gourmet cheeses become part of the shopping vocabulary—at least occasionally. Otherwise, the menu includes lots of hamburger, spaghetti, and casseroles.

Twelve years later, one child is married, and two are in college. Pete makes a better living than ever, and Jill has gone back to her former, high paying job. Tuition is high, however, as is room and board, so there is no more disposable income than before. A lot of what is left goes for college care packages. Appliances and foods that make for convenience are features on Jill's shopping list, since she still maintains a neat home and feeds Pete well. They eat out more, however, because they both work hard. The old furniture is getting shabby (slipcovers are a big item), and the wedding china is chipped and incomplete. Their tastes are changing a lot. They have developed an interest in antiques and sculpture. They buy china by the place setting, and small, inexpensive collectibles that express their developing interests.

They convert the married daughter's room to a guest room, using paint and elbow grease to accomplish miracles. The long distance phone bill skyrockets. Repairmen and maintenance people—painters, paperhangers, etc., are big items in the budget, as they try to make the house and car last until the tuition bills end. Some luxuries, however—decent clothing, a monthly touch-up to hide greying roots, a favorite brand of perfume, weekly Delmonico steaks, and a quarterly "big-bash" cocktail party, have become necessities. So has a new, smaller car.

Then, Pete and Jill look around and find that all the swallows have flown. The nest is empty. They can buy that luxury condo they've been eyeballing. Herculon furniture can finally be replaced with the velvets and brocades that their taste in antiques has demanded. Vacation and travel join the agenda. They can finally invest in some of the art they love. Except—daughter number one has a new baby. So, Grandma and Grandpa invest in plastic slipcovers and whatnot shelves to keep the breakables out of baby's reach. Instead of a condo in Florida they get a cottage at the Jersey Shore so the kids can visit. They maintain a cellar of finer wines, now, but are back to buying lots of beer and jug wine for family parties.

Jill buys jeans again so she can roughhouse with the kids. So does Peter. And the beat goes on.

Religion

Contrary to popular belief, you do not need to be a bible salesman before the religious make-up of your market has any effect on business. Religious holidays can have an effect on ad schedules. If your population is largely Jewish, for instance, you can avoid the normal Christmas blitz of ads. Religious holidays affect such variables as the opening and closing of businesses, gift-giving habits, entertaining, and the entertainment menu.

Religion especially affects dietary habits. If you are in a food-related business, you need to be very aware of the religious make-up of your target audience so you know when to stock up on seafood-related products and when to buy lots of matzoh.

Certain religious beliefs can strongly affect the ways in which people perceive your advertising. A strong Baptist population would frown on ads featuring dance music or frozen daiquiri mix as an enticer. Better to feature something else. A heavily Catholic population presumes a lot of very large families. A heavily religious population, period, assumes a lot of traditional values. If you are trying to reach a mass audience, your ads had better not violate these value systems in any way.

For example, I once had a client whose main products were soaps, bath salts, and other luxury items for personal cleanliness. We came up with a tag for his radio ads which extolled ''The Bath Shoppe—Where Your Fondest Fantasies Needn't be Dirty.'' The heavily traditional, church-going population of the little town where he did business only sniffed. We changed it to ''Good, Clean Fun.'' Business boomed.

Ethnicity

Some businesses are affected by the ethnic composition of their target markets. Bridal shops, for instance, need to take ethnic wedding customs into account before they can offer a successful, full-service line to their clients. The grocer with a heavily Italian population knows that he needs to stock up on a huge variety of seafood on Christmas eve and had better carry a line of pasta, good olive oil, and fresh basil year round. Ethnicity affects many things—color preferences, family customs and traditions, cooking equipment, decorative preference, etc.

Once again, we seem to be dealing with stereotypes here. If I claim that a Latino population will prefer bright colors in decor, you will say ''Aha! She's fallen for the stereotype. Why I know a Mexican lady, right down the street, and she's decorated her whole place in beige and brown. . . .'' Perhaps so. We are all individuals, which is why an ad, no matter how good, does not work perfectly on most of us. But we do tend to follow general response patterns. We do tend to go along with many of the generalizations that can be made about our referent groups.

If we don't respond perfectly, that is because of our individuality. Nevertheless, we recognize, instinctively, ads that aim at our general "type." Since we don't have time to read and absorb every advertising message that comes our way, we have learned to screen out all those messages that don't look or sound as though they are aimed at "our type."

Checklist for Determining Your Customer Demographic Profile

Answer the following questions for all of your target audiences:

- Does the sex of my target audience affect my advertising message? The spokesperson I will use when doing broadcast advertising? The types of promises I need to make in my ads?
- What is the income level of my typical customer in this target group? How much of this is disposable income? How will this affect the way that customer perceives my prices?
- Will my target audience perceive my goods and services as necessities? Luxuries? Occasional splurges?
- Where do my customers come from? Does this in any way affect my advertising message? How about the media I advertise in?
- How much education does my typical customer have? What is the level of expertise that my typical customer has about my goods and/or services? How does this affect my advertising message?
- Where is my typical customer located in the family life cycle? How does this affect their spending patterns and their disposable income?
- Will the religion of my typical customer affect my business, or the way in which I advertise? If so, how? How about their ethnic heritage?

Demographic segmenting is important in designing ads that appeal to the audience you want to reach. Appendix A gives a sample of a demographic profile as it applies to advertising. Another important factor to take into account is lifestyle.

PSYCHOGRAPHICS AND LIFESTYLE

Demographics can tell us a lot about groups of people in general, based on their vital statistics. Psychographics try to look more at individuals within those demographic groups, who vary according to their view of themselves and the world around them.

What Are Psychographics?

Psychographics are fine-tuners for demographics. Within any definable demographic group, we find a multitude of variable personality types. Take my high school class, for instance. Since I went to an all-girls, Catholic, private school, we were demographically, a very similar group—same level of education, same religion, same general social class, level of income, age, etc. But we were also very different. Some of us were shy. Some were very bold. Some were education-oriented, some home and marriage-oriented. Some were creative, some very practical. Some were gregarious, some retiring. A few loved to read, write, or draw, others preferred to party. Some of us were very ambitious. Others were content. At dances, a few lucky ones danced every dance, and a lot of us hid in the girl's powder room. Demographically the same, we were still a huge variety when it came to personalities, preferences, and perceptions of ourselves and the desirability of goals, possessions, and appearances. No matter how demographically similar your own target audience might be, they too are psychographically different—something your advertising will need to take into account.

What Psychographics Can Tell You

Psychographics and lifestyle research has become big business on Madison Avenue, because it allows advertisers to adjust their message to the hopes, fears, desires, and perceptions of their audience. If you are fascinated by this aspect of marketing, there are dozens of good books available on the subject, and I suggest you seek them out.

For practicality's sake, however, you can fine-tune your own advertising to the psychographics and lifestyle of your audience by doing a little soul searching. Ask yourself, first, "What is someone likely to get out of doing business with me?"

The answer might seem obvious. If they come to your shoe store, they will get a pair of shoes. If they call your plumbing service, they will get their leaky pipe repaired. But there is more to it than that.

Why do they come to your shoe store and not the one down the street? Down the street you can get cute shoes for $29.99. Yours are $70 and up. What kind of person buys $70 shoes? Why? What kind of concerns do they have? What do their shoes mean to them?

Possible answers: "Cheap shoes don't last well. They're not as comfortable. I care about my appearance. Good shoes show good taste. They show good grooming. They convey the message that I am professional and careful. I want to wear good, expensive shoes, so that people will realize that I have a good job and am doing well. They are necessary for my career, which is just starting to get off the ground—I need to look as successful and competent as possible. They are classic, and so they are good buys. I wouldn't want anyone to recognize those bargain basement special shoes and think they were the best I could afford.''

The customer for the inexpensive shop down the street might tell you ''I buy these shoes because I like variety in my wardrobe. I like to have things coordinate, and this way I can afford shoes to match most of my wardrobe. I don't care that much about shoes anyway, so I buy what's on sale that looks OK. I'd rather spend the money on great clothes—who looks at your feet? I'm hard on shoes anyway, so why spend a lot of money. The styles are up to the minute, and as long as they're cheap, I don't mind getting rid of them when they're outdated.''

What I'm getting at is that a customer's decision to purchase your product or use your service depends a lot on how they view themselves in relation to that product or service. This will affect the way you advertise. The $29 shoe man would not do well if he tried to advertise ''Investment dressing—for a Look that Lasts!'' You would not do well to advertise ''Fads and fashions! Try several.'' Your most likely customer will not respond or even recognize herself in that ad.

Yes, psychographics and lifestyles are, once again, typing people—this time not according to vital statistics, but according to personality and habits. The following are some of the ''types'' you might be appealing to:

The Leader

The leader is always the first on the block to try out a new style, or to have a new gadget. He or she is not afraid to be different, to stand out from the crowd, and to take chances. If you are offering new merchandise, or brand new services that the general public might resist, you will need to direct your ads at leaders, who will try your product or service and assure others that it's OK.

The Follower

These are the majority. They respond strongly to bandwagon appeals. Join the Pepsi generation. Everyone is turning 7-up. Preppy is in. These people are afraid of being too different, or of being thought odd. They respond to ads that promise that what they are doing is not only accepted, but the popular thing to do.

The Individualist

This person looks for things that other people will not have. If everyone else is doing it, they're not interested. They respond to ads that promise that they will be unique, that they are getting something one-of-a-kind, or that things will be customized. They are often do-it-yourselfers, because this assures individuality. When people start to copy them, they move on to something else. Do not promise these people that what you offer is unique—they have become very wary of that over-used word. Do promise them that they will not see themselves coming and going if they shop with you.

The Careful Shopper

No matter what the price category, this person needs to believe that he or she has gotten the best for their money. They respond to appeals to practicality—lasts longer, hides dirt, goes with everything. They shop sales, and seek out places where prices are better. They tend to believe that large businesses can buy in bulk, and so offer better price—but they scan ads carefully to find out where the sales are. Tell these people that your product or service is an investment, that it will help stretch the budget. Always include price. If they're not sure, they won't even come in.

The Traditionalist

These people don't care what's in style. They like classic, reliable, tried and trues. They buy Chanel perfume, and classic clothing and furniture. Quality is as important as looks. Fads are anathema, not because these people are individualists, but because they don't want to look dated. Understated, timeless, classic—these are all good words to use in appealing to this group. They want to please themselves. They tend to feel confident in their taste and don't worry about the opinion of others.

The Upward Bound

This group looks for ads that promise to help them look successful, efficient, and wise. While they like "classic," because it implies solidity and good investment potential, they also buy trendy items because they tell the world that they have disposable income and are making something of themselves. Conspicuous consumption is one of their watchwords—although they don't like to admit it to themselves. Instead, these people often make purchases based on their assessment of what their friends will say and think. If their purchases will make others think of these people as they would like to think of themselves, they feel good about things.

The Status Seeker

Closely related to the upward bound, the major difference with the status seeker is that they worry less about getting good value for their dollar. These are the people who are attracted to anything with a designer label on it. Anything that is currently supposed to be "in" might be on this person's shopping list. If *faux marbre* is more in vogue than real marble, you can bet they are looking for an artist to transform their woodwork. They probably redecorate frequently to keep up with styles, and buy lots of trendy clothes. They have to be restrained from resewing old Dior labels into new K-Mart dresses. If it was done last year, they are no longer interested. These people respond to "association appeals"— ads that associate a product or service with people who have a certain image or status that the audience wishes to achieve. "Hairdresser to the Stars" or "The wine the Vanderbilt's preferred" have inherent appeal for this group.

The Homebody

Comfort and efficiency. These people like timesavers, materials that can be used without fear of damage, tools for living that will allow them to enjoy their homes with a maximum of comfort and enjoyment. They like furniture, accessories and appliances that are no-nonsense, but attractive. Furniture you can put your feet up on. Work surfaces that clean easily. Products and services that promise to make the house more familial and homelike. They don't worry too much about what others think. Instead, they worry about practical house matters, and how these affect the quality of their life at home and with their family. Practical is a watchword here, but so is attractive, homey, warm, and inviting.

The Combination

In reality, this is all of us. Few people fall exclusively into one of the above categories. How we react to prices, things, and status symbols depends purely on what our interests and priorities are. For instance, I am both an individualist and a careful shopper when it comes to clothes—I shop factory outlets during sale time, but prefer good used clothing stores where I can pick up silks and well-made wools for a song. They don't have to be in style—they have to suit me. Furniture, however, is a major expense, and so I tend to be a traditionalist. This justifies the investment in my mind. My car is a major expense also, but one that I know I will have to replace eventually—here I am something of an upward bound person. Having researched good value and status, I bought a flashy sports car in a middle-price range, with every promise that it will become a classic and appreciate in value.

When it comes to services, my husband and I both tend to be individualists. We try to do it ourselves and enjoy coming up with creative solutions. If we can't manage the job—roofing or well drilling—we are followers, though, depending strongly on the lead of others before trusting an hourly skilled person with our work and money.

The trick, in defining the psychological characteristics of your audience, is to put yourself in their shoes and try to imagine what hopes, fears, and values would motivate them to buy your products, patronize your store, or use your service. We spend our money with more than practicality in mind. The psychographic profile in Appendix A gives an example of how this is done.

Checklist for Developing a Psychographic Profile of the Target Audience

- Does my typical customer have any good, logical reasons for shopping with me?
- Are there any possible emotional reasons why my typical customer does business with me?
- How do you think your typical customer would most like to be described if someone asked you what type of person/customer they were?

SUMMARY

By attempting to describe our target market in terms of demographics and psychological characteristics, we can form a clearer picture of how to talk to that audience. Demographics help us to draw generalizations about a group based on their vital statistics. Paying attention to their psychological characteristics allows us to fine-tune those generalizations to take into account personality types and motivations.

The clearer a picture we have of our market, the better a message we can send to that audience in advertising. As we will see, demographics and psychological characteristics also affect people's media use. Therefore, having a profile of our intended market will allow us to make logical and effective media buys for that advertising message.

6

Finding Out What the Public Thinks About You: Designing a Survey

THE TOP DRAWER SOLD EXCLUSIVE WOMEN'S CLOTHING, LINGERIE, AND ACCESsories at a very reasonable price. Marijene's only problem was her store front, which had very small windows—only two feet tall—nice for a jeweler, perhaps, but disastrous for displaying fashion ensembles. So Marijene's window displays showed what looked best—her intimate apparel and accessories. Even though she was on the main street of her small college town, business was slow.

"I don't understand," she lamented. "I stock what the students wear, and my prices are better than my competitors. Why don't they come in?"

Her regular customers were at a loss. They knew what a good selection Top Drawer had. They were no help at all. Then Marijene had the inspiration of asking the students at the college. An advertising class designed a survey for her and administered it.

The result? Students stayed away from Top Drawer because they didn't know what it sold. The window showed them lingerie of a type they didn't need and couldn't afford. The name suggested clothing that went into a drawer—once again, fine lingerie. So most students went to other stores that sold what they were after for their clothing.

As a business owner, you know your stock, and you know your price advantages. You know what your current customers like about you. You might not know what they dislike. And you have no way at all, short of overhearing a conversation, of finding out about the perceptions of the customers that you're not reaching. That's why research is sometimes essential to a successful ad campaign.

Chapter 6 will discuss business problems that your current customers and friends are unlikely to be able to help you with: lack of awareness among the larger population, lack of understanding about who you are and what you do, and any image problems you might have.

This chapter discusses ways to go about designing a survey to find out more about the wants, needs, and perceptions of the customers that you want to reach. Although it is advisable to have someone else—friends, employees, an outside research firm, or a college marketing or advertising class—do your research, this section includes helpful hints on how to do it yourself as a last resort.

AREAS OF CONCERN

Your major interest, in surveying the public, will be to find out why those people who have not patronized your business, haven't. Certain factors could already be obvious to you: parking, out-of-the-way location, past image problems, or the fact that people who don't come in are simply not part of your target market. Senior citizens, for example, almost never buy acne cream.

Other factors, however, will not be apparent to any business owner, because you can never know what the people whom you are not seeing in your place of business think or know about you. Their perceptions might be very different from those of your present customer. Certainly their level of knowledge differs.

Lack of Awareness

A common reason for not patronizing a particular business or service is that the public simply doesn't know about you. A second reason is that people know that you are there, but not exactly what it is that you do.

Awareness that You Are There. This might, at first, be difficult for you to believe since you work daily with customers who are aware of exactly who you are and what you do. They might have found you by accident because they were in the neighborhood or through word-of-mouth. There could be hundreds of people out there who would be glad to follow suit—if only they knew. This is where advertising comes in. Your primary goal in advertising will be to get the word out that you are open for business, and that you provide specific types of goods and/or services.

Awareness of the Nature of the Business. People might be aware of your existence but fuzzy about exactly what it is that you do, as was the problem with Top Drawer. People might know generally what you do but remain unaware of specific services that set you apart from the competition. To many people, a paint store is a paint store—you buy paint, brushes, rollers, etc. If yours will custom mix paint to match a Granny Smith apple or a stick of cold butter, or anything else a customer brings in and wants on his or her walls, this gives you an edge over the competition. How many people know that you do this? How many of your regular customers know that you have done it, but think this was a special favor to them rather than a regular service that you provide? If you aren't advertising it, even your regulars might be in doubt. You may be the only one who knows for sure.

Lack of Understanding

People might not understand what it is that you do. If only they knew about you, they might be glad to do business. For instance, I once had a client who advertised "Custom Furniture." On a hunch, I surveyed the area to find out what they thought custom furniture was. They generally replied that the merchant would take stock furniture and finish it according to the client's wishes. However, this man could create furniture from your original design. Our ad campaign had to explain this basic fact.

Even what seems obvious might not be. In a northern area of the U.S., with a heavily ethnic population, a Mexican restaurant owner was stunned to discover that few people knew the difference between a taco and a burrito. Most were afraid that all Mexican food was searingly hot and spicy. Not so. Once again, an explanatory campaign was the answer.

Especially with services, there is a great potential for public misunderstanding. Find out if people know what you're really about and be prepared to explain in your advertising if you find out they're wrong.

Image Problems

You know what image you would like to project. Your present customers know what image they have of you—but what about the person who has never come in? Your trendy-looking ads and slick storefront might say to them: "Too expensive!" Yet you might be very reasonably priced. Your small store footage might have said to a few who looked but didn't linger that your selection is small—but we all know that looks can be deceptive.

On occasion, businesses have misread their market. In Scranton, PA, for instance, most people tend to assume that, since Scranton is known to be a "depressed area," there is a huge market for mid-to-low range furniture—the type with glossy plastic finishes and Herculon upholstery. If the store-owner assumes that this is the best that the typical citizen can afford, he might also begin to advertise this as "good quality"—which it could be, in its price range. But even low-income people read the ads, visit other homes, window shop, and dream. They know that this is not Henredon or Ethan Allen. So the "quality" ad campaign might lead people to think of you as "cheap—slightly shady." Your perceptions must match those of your target audience, or you might appear to be dishonest.

Checklist of Things to Learn from the General Public

Depending on your business, you might want to find out several of the following from the general public:

- Where do you usually go for _____ (whatever it is you sell or do)? This helps you to determine the competition.
- Why do you go there? This should help you to determine what benefits they perceive your competitor as having.
- If that place were not available, where would you go as an alternative? This further helps you to refine your perceptions of the competition. It narrows things down to primary competitors.
- Is there anything you dislike about these places, or wish you could change? (Here's your chance to see if you have any edge over the competition—or to make business adjustments that could give you an edge.)
- How far will you travel or how long a drive are you willing to make to use this business? (This helps to determine area of trade.)
- Describe your feelings about the price of this establishment's products, service etc., in relation to what you get.
- Why do you use this product, service, shop etc.? (You are trying to get at motivation here, whether it be convenience, or type of people who go there, or price category, selection, status, etc.)
- Name five other places where you can get this. What do you know about these places? (If they haven't named you yet, you hope they do here, so you can get some idea of your image in relation to your competition's. If few people do name you, you know you have an awareness problem.)
- Who makes the decision to use this service, or buy this product or shop at this store? (You want to know your primary target audience here. Is it the wife? The kids?)
- What magazines do you subscribe to or read regularly? (This might sound like it's coming out of left field, but knowing this can be a big help in determining lifestyle, interests, level of education, and even income.)
- What do you (meaning your likely customer) like to do in your spare time? (Once again, this is a big help in determining your customer profile. The athlete is different from the TV watcher, who is different from the avid reader or the lady who refinishes furniture in her spare time, or knits.)

- Have you ever heard of _____? (Here, supply the name of your business, plus one of your main competitors. Never give only your own name, or people will suspect what you are trying to get at. Their tendency is to be polite and say nice things, even if they don't really know anything about you. Asking about a competitor too will not only get you more honest answers, but extra information.)

- What can you tell me about _____ and _____? What type of merchandise do they carry? What services do they offer? What is their price range? Do you think they are competitors, or would you choose one over the other? Why?

You can probably think of other things that you would like to know. Write them out in essay form, like the above questions. You want to have a very clear idea of what it is you don't know, so that you can begin to find out.

You will use these questions to conduct what is known as a *focus group*—a group gathered for the express purpose of focusing on the questions you have about your kind of business, what they expect from it, and what fears and problems they might have with it. A focus group supplies you with material upon which to base a questionnaire, so that you can do a more reliable, broader survey of the public.

The main reason for doing a focus group first is that the people in this group will, in their discussion, supply you with the forced choices you will need for a good questionnaire. If you tried to compose a quick questionnaire (one that can be answered in less than ten minutes by phone) on your own, you would be limited by your own perceptions about who your competition is, what people want from businesses like yours, and why they shop where they shop. By conducting a focus group, you are letting the real public tell you what's important. Their answers can be informative—and often surprising.

THE FOCUS GROUP

To determine what the general public out there wants from your type of business, you need to do research. Major ad agencies hire professional firms to do this. If you can afford to hire a research company, by all means do. The information you get will be invaluable, not only in fine-tuning your business, but in determining the best approach to take with your advertising.

Most small businesses, however, cannot afford to hire an outside company. Then you might want to check with your local colleges and universities. Many marketing and advertising classes are looking for businesses to use as projects—maybe you can get them to do the work for you. If not, take a long deep breath and be prepared to do it yourself, with a little help from your friends. The focus group is your first step.

What Is a Focus Group?

A focus group is a small gathering of people in your target audience, who all meet for an informal discussion about the likes, dislikes, fears, and motivations with which they approach businesses like yours. A hobby shop, then, would want to collect a small gathering of hobbyists, a plumber would want homeowners, a teen dress boutique will want to talk to teens—whoever is most likely to be your customer.

How to Conduct a Focus Group

It is best if you don't do the focus groups yourself. People like to be helpful and to tell you what they think you want to hear. Therefore, the answers you get when you ask people what they like about buying sports equipment are likely to be slanted if your focus group knows you own a sporting goods store. If you want honest answers, get a friend to conduct this session and tape it for you. Never let the people in the focus group know which business you are especially interested in, for the same reason. Simply tell them that you are doing some research about area restaurants, or plasterers, or whatever the general business type is.

When he or she has gathered eight or ten people together and relaxed them with coffee and donuts, or whatever, your ally should lead this group into a discussion by asking general questions about their habits in buying, shopping, or using your type of service or product. The list in the above section provides a guideline for the types of questions you might ask.

It's a good idea to have a careful list of the information you are seeking, so you are sure to cover all these questions during the session. However, the discussion leader should never try to prompt the participants or suggest possible answers. You want to know what people think. Likewise, the leader should never suggest his or her opinion of the answers given. You want people to be open and honest, and your approval or disapproval might cause people to adjust their answers.

Make sure you cover all the major questions but if the discussion takes off in some unexpected area, pay attention. Your focus group might be expressing concerns and motivations that might never have occurred to you. Probe, if you want more information. Make sure you understand what people are really trying to say. Once again, make sure you don't in any way try to lead them to discuss your particular business. This might seem frustrating since that's what you want to know about. Trust me—human nature being what it is, and the kinds of people who will participate in a focus group being who they are—this will only mislead you. These people will try to be helpful, and in the end this can only result in partial and misleading information.

Tape record your session, if possible, but also take careful notes about who said what. Do different types of people express different wants and concerns?

Don't be discouraged if your business is not mentioned too often during this focus group discussion. This simply tells you that you have an awareness problem. At least now you know who you are competing with for these people's attention, and what their advantages and problems are. You also have identified several wants and needs of your potential target markets.

Once you have your major questions answered, if you have heard little or nothing about your own business, you can finally ask—as long as you don't reveal that this is your main point of interest. Let's say that you now know everything you want to know about people's grocery shopping habits, where they go, why, and what they would ideally want in a grocer. Your name, sadly, never came up.

Bury it in a short list. Ask, very casually, if anyone in the group has ever heard of grocer a, b, or c. Have they ever gone there? Why or why not? Why don't they shop there now? Don't spend too much time on this but satisfy your need to know.

The reason you are gathering these people into a group is that it helps to free the discussion from the influence of the interviewer. When you ask ''Where do you buy your groceries,'' someone will say ''Cutrate,'' and another says ''Well, I go to Vilano's.'' The first person then says, ''Oh, yeah—I go there for my meats, but I buy my canned goods and dairy at Cutrate because it's cheaper.'' One participant might spark others to tell you things that might not have occurred to them on their own. The discussion leader can then sit back and take notes, throwing in a new major question whenever the old topic has exhausted. You get maximum mileage out of a focus group done this way.

Alternatives to a Focus Group

Unfortunately, it is not always possible to find a group of people who are in your target audience and are not fully aware of who you are. There is another way to get the information you need.

I hesitate to suggest this alternative method since it is not in any way scientific, is much more subject to interviewer influence, and doesn't yield as rich a supply of information as the group method. In a pinch, it will give you some information, and is better than nothing.

When I get student advertising teams who just don't know any local adults except faculty, I have to take these measures. Interviews with faculty will not necessarily give us useful results, if they are not the exclusive target audience of the business for which we are working. So we resort to the individual, telephone focus interview.

In this interview, we telephone a minimum of twelve people, recommended by friends, faculty, etc., who seem to be in the target market for the type of business we are investigating. After carefully explaining the purpose of the interview, these people are given the same questions that we would have asked in the focus group. On occasion, we are able to get two or three of these people to agree to meet in a group to discuss our questions. Usually, we have difficulty getting twelve people to agree to spend the necessary 30 minutes or so required for a good interview.

You need at least twelve interviews, however, because asking questions individually precludes the spontaneous discussions and suggestions that spring from group meetings. Your interview is severely limited by the immediate recall of your interviewee. If you want reliable material for your questionnaire, you cannot afford to rely on the answers of a few, isolated individuals.

The advantage to this individual telephone interview style, if you can get people to talk to you, is that you can do it yourself, as long as you don't tell people who you are and why you want the information.

Getting Interviewees to Cooperate

You need a good introduction for your phone call. First, give your name. People feel better if they are dealing with a named individual than with an anonymous voice. Having someone's name, in a sense, is power. If, however, people are likely to associate your name with your business, you might have to use an alias. Otherwise, you will get the same, skewed results that I warned about in the formal focus group. Tell the interviewee that you are doing a survey about local business in the area, and would like about 30 minutes of their time. Give them the name of the person who suggested that they might be willing to take part in the interview. This often helps to break down resistance. If they don't have the time now, but are willing to cooperate, arrange to contact them at a more convenient time. Assure them that you are not selling anything, and that the results are very important. Promise them that all answers will remain confidential. Don't be discouraged when a lot of people hang up on you—it has nothing to do with your personality. Hangups are the inevitable fate of the telephone surveyor, no matter how congenial, and if you plan to do a more sophisticated survey later, you might as well develop a thick skin now.

THE SURVEY

By now you should have collected a lot of good information from a few people. This is not enough to proceed on. The people in your focus group might or might not be representative of the larger population. You will need to survey a much larger group before you can feel sure of the accuracy of your information. Therefore, you need to formulate a survey.

Unlike the focus group, you will not be using essay questions on this survey. Essay questions, as you will have discovered, take a lot of time. Besides, they are difficult to tabulate in any significant way. Therefore, a good, easy survey will consist of forced choice questions: multiple choice, checklists, and ranking and rating questions.

Begin, once again, with a list of those things that you want to know from the general public. Your focus group should have helped you to narrow this list down to a few crucial items. Generally, you will want to know who is your biggest competition, why people go there, what they are dissatisfied with, what image you have vs. what image they have, and what products, services, etc., are important to those people in your market. You will also want to know about the lifestyles of your target audience, so that you know how to appeal to their emotions and needs in your ads. The trick is to formulate questions that will help you to uncover this information. The various forms of questions described below should enable you to get the information you need in an efficient manner.

The Multiple Choice Question

We have all had these in school. You ask a question, and then give the respondent several options from which to choose the answer. Only one answer—the one that the respondent considers to be the best—is allowed.

In formulating a multiple choice question, you want to give your respondents a long enough list of options to cover everything that is important, but a short enough one to allow them a meaningful choice. Use no more than six choices. If you need to supply more, to cover all possibilities, then you probably need a different type of question.

Don't Stack the Deck. Be careful of stacking the deck in this type of question. Don't word your choices so that some sound negative, and only one sounds positive. For example, in asking what image the respondent might have about shopping downtown, you might give five choices: a) great variety, b) convenient, c) unusual and appropriate merchandise, d) more fun than the mall, and e) too hard to park. That final choice sticks out like a sore thumb. It will confuse those who do like downtown shopping. Those that don't, since you have given them no other alternative, will tend to choose option e because it is the only negative choice. They might dislike the downtown because of the crowds, or they might simply prefer malls. You haven't allowed them that choice, so they give the only possible negative response. You then conclude that parking is a major deterrent, when, in fact, most people prefer to take the bus downtown anyway. You would get a more accurate response by evenly distributing the negatives with the positive options.

Define Your Terms. Sometimes, in creating a multiple choice question, you will need to define your terms. If people are unsure what you are talking about, you will get confused responses. For instance, you might ask which of the following is most important to the respondent when choosing a family style restaurant: price, location, children's menu, atmosphere or service. Now, there are several ways to define family style restaurant—from one that doesn't serve alcohol, to one that doesn't use tablecloths but uses a lot of formica, to one that serves family style—with big bowls in the middle of the table from which everyone helps themselves. If you want to know about one of these types, you will have to explain that to your respondents.

The rule is, if you are using an unfamiliar term, or one that has several meanings, define it. The second rule is, with multiple choice questions, you must be sure to specify that respondents choose only one option. A good idea, if you are unsure about covering all possibilities, is to allow an option of "Other—please specify _____.'' This avoids frustrating respondents who do not find a suitable option on your list, and also allows you to uncover information that you might not have discovered in the focus group.

Eliminate Obvious Answers. You will have discovered, in your focus group, that sometimes certain answers are so obvious that most respondents will tend to choose them. Therefore, when formulating answers, make sure that you exclude that alternative. For instance, if asked how they heard about their plumber, most people will tell you "word-of-mouth." So, when asking which of five factors were influential in helping them to choose a plumber, you exclude that option. ("Aside from word-of-mouth, which media was most useful in helping you to choose your present plumber?")

The Checklist

A checklist is useful if you have a long, long list of options from which you want people to choose. In a checklist, respondents might choose all the listed activities, services, places, or problems in which they are interested. For instance, a beautician might want to know what services are most likely to attract people to her salon. She could formulate a long checklist of everything from cuts and permanents to eyebrow waxing, manicures, fantasy coloring, etc. People could check every service they use. This allows her to get a feel for needed services in the area. People could also check a second column in the list "Things I would use if they were available." (Note: This is not as reliable as asking about actual behavior. What people say they would do and what they actually will do are often two very different things. Nevertheless, asking about wants might help you to decide about services you might provide but have not advertised. It can also help you to identify wants and needs not being met in your market.) You can also give respondents an opportunity to specify how often they would use things in your checklist. (Check all the services you would use. Specify if you would use these weekly, monthly, or for special occasions only.)

A good checklist should exhaust all the likely possibilities. Don't let it get longer than a typed, double-spaced page, though. Answering long, long, checklists tends to become fatiguing, and as fatigue increases, the sincerity of the response decreases.

Rating Questions

Rating questions allow you to determine exactly how well your respondent feels something measures up to their hypothetical standard of perfection. For example, as a specimen of feminine perfection, Dudley Moore rated Bo Derek a 10, on a scale of 1 – 10.

Getting the Most from a Rating. You might have discovered, through using a multiple choice question, that a respondent uses Brand X (or maybe even your brand). Now you want to find out what qualities in brand X your target market perceives as good, bad, or indifferent. You use a rating question for each attribute or quality you want to know about.

Let's say that you are surveying to find out, once again, about family style restaurants. Through a multiple choice question, you have allowed respondents to choose the one to which they go most often. Now you want to know exactly how your respondent rates that place's quality of food, prices, service, standards of cleanliness, and menu selection. You ask: "On a scale of one to five, with five being excellent, one being poor, rate the restaurant you go to on quality of food." Next question: "On the same scale, rate it on quality of service." And so on. From this, you not only learn the perceived strong and weak points of your competition, but you can also draw conclusions about what people will put up with if the food, price, or whatever, is perceived as being right. You will also learn a lot about how people who name your business perceive you.

Rules for Rating Questions. Three main points to remember: Make sure that you ask respondents to rate things with respect to some quality, be it price, service, atmosphere, etc. A general request to rate a place on a scale of one to five, without qualification, is meaningless. Second, make sure you specify what is the high end of the scale, and which is the low end. Some people, otherwise, might be giving an answer of "One," because they think number one is a high rating, when you are counting it as the low end of the scale. Finally, limit your rating scale to five. Anything more becomes difficult to handle, and somewhat meaningless.

Using Ratings to Discover Strength of Habits and Opinions. You can also use a forced-choice rating scale when you want to find out exactly how strongly someone agrees with a statement, or get a feel for the relative frequency of their behavior. Often, we want to ask whether people do some particular action, or agree with a particular statement. (Do you eat lunch out?) If you ask people to answer yes or no, your respondent will be in a quandary. He eats out about once a month—but does that count? He eats out, but only on payday. Is that enough to say yes to? To force a person to choose between yes or no is often frustrating, both to you and the respondent. So instead, you use a rating scale.

Do you eat lunch out?
1_____ never 2_____ rarely 3_____ sometimes 4_____ often 5_____ always

Although this still leaves some latitude for interpretation, you will get better answers with less frustration if you allow a scaled response.

Rating scales are also used to gauge the strength of an opinion. You might want to know if people perceive all lawyers as shysters. You would ask:

Lawyers are out to take your money
1_____ strongly agree 2_____ somewhat agree 3_____ unsure 4_____ disagree
5_____ strongly disagree.

Basic rules to follow when composing rating scales: Allow no more than five options. More than this, and distinctions become meaningless. Keep all rating scales together, in order to make the questionnaire easier to administer.

The Halo Effect. If you are handing this questionnaire out, beware of the halo effect. People have a tendency to fall into a set response pattern, especially with a long list of rating scales. As a teacher, for instance, I get student ratings every semester. Occasionally there is a student who "has it in for me," or even one who thinks I'm the greatest. Not reading the questions very carefully, these students automatically check the first or last responses on the page, assuming that these are the high and low ratings. The university, however, anticipating this halo effect, has cleverly switched the scales, that is, every few questions, the last option is the high, rather than the low end of the scale.

You will know, almost inevitably, if a respondent has checked the same response for every scale, that person has not carefully read the questions. You might as well throw away the questionnaire, for it will contain little significant information.

Rankings

In a ranking question, the respondent arranges a set of responses in order of preference. Ranking lists must usually be limited to about five choices, especially if you are doing a phone survey. Anything else becomes too cumbersome and hard to remember. You want to be able to do a phone survey quickly.

Uses of Ranking Questions. Ranking questions are useful when you want to know priorities. They will allow you to assess the relative importance of certain qualities in customer perception. They can also allow you to see how well you fare against the competition in the public eye.

Example: Rank the following services in relation to their importance in making you choose one realtor over another, with one being most important, five least: member of multilist, good reputation, is listed as realtor for house I want, located in neighborhood, advertising. Another example: Rank in order of importance the media that influence you to call one travel agent over another, with one being most influential, five least: radio, television, newspaper, direct mail, Yellow Pages.

Limitations for Ranking Questions. You don't want to ask too many of these questions on a phone survey, because they are difficult to answer quickly and easily. However, they are very useful in helping you to determine priorities. Sometimes, one or two ranking questions can take the place of a whole raft of multiple choices.

Dichotomous Questions

These are questions that only allow a response of yes or no, or agree, disagree. My usual rule with these is, don't ask them. As I explained with rating questions, they usually frustrate the respondent, and deprive you of valuable information. To the question, do you drive to work? a respondent might wish to say "Yes—unless it's snowing." The dichotomous question does not leave room for the unlesses. So, they are not very useful.

On occasion, however, there is no other possible alternative. If you are selling custom kitchen cabinetry, you might want to ask people, before involving them in a long, detailed, questionnaire, if they are homeowners. Since there are only two possible answers (yes and no) and only one that interests you—yes—you would be foolish to try to create a scale for this.

Use your judgment. If yes and no are the only possible answers, then go ahead and ask a dichotomous question. If there are any possible maybes, yes buts, or sometimes—choose another form.

PUTTING THE QUESTIONNAIRE TOGETHER

The first question students usually have, when I give this assignment, is "How long should it be?" The answer is: As long as it has to be to get all the information you need, but it should take no longer than ten minutes to administer. Five would be better.

Careful question arrangement can help to shorten the length of time it takes to administer a questionnaire, so your first task should be to make up a trial arrangement of every question you have put together, and time it.

The Effective Questionnaire Opening

Begin with a screening question, which will eliminate time wasted in questioning people not in your target group. For instance, if you are a roofer, you probably only want to interview people who either need a new roof soon, or have just had one put on. You might begin your questionnaire by asking if you are speaking to a homeowner, and then asking if they have either had a new roof in the past three years, or plan to get one in the next three. (This, of course, comes after you promise them that you are not selling anything. You are talking to past customers, who are undoubtedly not in your audience at all, because they can tell you a lot about competitors, qualms, etc.—plus what went into their decision to choose one roofer over another.)

Once you are past the screening question, you want to ask an easy question, to assure people that this questionnaire is not going to be a difficult ordeal. Beginning a questionnaire with checklists or multiple choices is a good idea, for this very reason.

The trick is, your initial easy question must also be an interesting one, which will make the respondent want to give an opinion and continue to cooperate. (This eliminates a lot of time you might otherwise waste persuading people not to hang up.) Opinion questions are usually more interesting than factual ones. Personal questions about income, age, etc., are to be avoided here at all costs. First, they are boring to the respondent, who already knows the answers. Second, and sadly, we worry about handing out this sort of information to strangers for fear they are casing the joint. If you save these for last and have put together a credible survey, a lot of these fears will have been stilled.

Arranging the Questions

Once you have a good opening set of questions, you can speed up questionnaire administration by remembering two things. First, keep all questions of the same format together, all multiple choice together, all rankings together, etc. This means that you only have to give directions for answering the questions at the beginning of each format group. It also means the respondent will be able to answer more easily, since he or she doesn't have to keep mentally rearranging directions.

More difficult, but important, is to try to keep the same kinds of information together. In other words, competition questions should be in one group, questions about image in another, etc. This takes a little practice, but pays off because, once again, the respondent does not have to keep doing mental shifts as you switch from topic to topic.

Another hint: Put the easiest questions to answer first. Save any ranking questions for the end. Usually, if a person has answered a substantial part of a questionnaire, he or she will stick with it. If, however, you frighten them off early in the process, they are more than willing to end the interview.

When you have asked everything you want to know about your business concerns, you need to add a demographic and psychographic section.

Getting Demographic and Psychographic Information

Depending on your business, it might be very helpful to know more about your prospective customer's lifestyle. You might ask about their favorite leisure activities. This not only tells you something about them, but will help you to choose specific media targeted to reach your audience. For instance, if a majority of people in your target says they like to go to the symphony, you could reach them cheaply and easily by buying ad space in the symphony program. If they ski, you might want to put posters up at the nearest ski lodge.

Asking what magazines they read, as I have already suggested, can provide you with a lot of insight. A reader of *Architectural Digest* and *House and Garden* has very different aspirations than the reader of *Budget Decorating*. Knowing what your customers read regularly can also help you to judge the level of expertise with which they approach your business.

Don't waste time asking about media habits. While you will eventually need to know what radio station your audience listens to and what newspaper they buy, the media themselves have research that is much more accurate and sophisticated than what you will be able to achieve.

Certain demographic information is also valuable to you. Check chapter 5, and decide which factors will affect your business. You will certainly want to note whether you are talking to a male or a female. (Hope that you can tell from the speaking voice, because asking is embarrassing.)

Age is also important. Many people will not want to admit their age, so you will have your best success by dividing your possible responses into groups: Under 18, 19–25, 25–34, 35–44, 45–54, 55–64, 65 and up.

You can make good estimates of your audience's family life cycle by asking how many children the respondent has and their ages. You will also find it handy to ask if any children are employed full time.

If income is an important factor (and it usually is) find out how many people in the household are employed. Ask their occupations. This, of course, has a major impact on total household finances.

If you want a total income figure, save this for the very last question. People do not want to tell you how much they make. They often hang up at this point, or refuse to answer. If they do, but you have asked about occupations, you can make a good estimate of household income by consulting *Statistical Abstracts of the United States*, or the census. These, available in the library reference room, will give you average incomes by occupation.

People will sometimes cooperate if you do as you did with age, allowing them to indicate a category of income. Begin with a very low category—under $3000. This artificial low helps people in lower income categories to save face. Suggested categories: Under $3000, 3–6999, 7–9999, 10–14999, 15–19999, 20–34999, 35–49,999, 50–74,999, over 75,000. Make sure you ask about total household income, or people tend to respond with their personal salary amount. In a two-income family, this could lead you to grossly underestimate the disposable income available to your target audience.

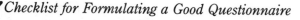

Checklist for Formulating a Good Questionnaire

- Have you opened with a screening question, that will eliminate wasting time with people who are not in your target audience?
- Have you followed this with a simple, but interesting opinion question, to get the respondent "hooked" on completing the survey?
- Have you begun with easy questions, that can be answered quickly and suggest that the survey will be quick and easy to complete?
- Are all questions of the same type grouped together so that you can give your instructions on how to answer only one time?
- Are questions grouped according to subject matter so that there is a logical thought pattern to your questions?
- Have you saved your psychographic and demographic questions for last?
- Have you asked about everything you want to know about? Your survey should include: current shopping (or service) habits; competition questions; preferences, wants and needs; psychographics and lifestyle; demographics (with the income question dead last).

Pretesting

Once you have formulated your questions and arranged them to your liking, sit down and take the questionnaire. Try to honestly answer the questions as if you were the one being interviewed. This will give you an opportunity to spot problems. You'd be surprised at how difficult it is to answer some of your own questions. Make changes, until you are satisfied. Once you have adjusted things, try the questionnaire out on someone else. This time, you are checking to see if the questions are clearly understood, and to get a rough estimate of the time required to administer the questionnaire. Keep doing this pretesting until you have a questionnaire you are satisfied with. This is a crucial step. If you rush right out with your first survey attempt, you will probably lose a lot of valuable information. Even an experienced survey-writer usually needs to make three or four drafts.

Typing the Questionnaire

When you are sure the questionnaire is ready to administer, type it up carefully. If you are going to be handing them out, make sure the form is clear, the instructions are explicit, and that it looks professional and important. (People will not voluntarily waste their time on things that they perceive to be unimportant or shoddy.) Have about 500 copies of the survey made.

If you are administering the questionnaire by telephone, you will only need one copy of the survey, but about 400 answer sheets. Record each person's answers on a separate sheet, otherwise, you will not be able to separate your results according to age, income, or any other categories into which you might wish to sort them. Now you are ready to administer the survey.

Administering the Survey

You have three major things to worry about when administering your survey: the randomness of the sample, the sample size, and the method by which you will survey.

Getting a Good Sample. *Randomness* means that, theoretically, every member of the population being surveyed has an equal chance of being asked. The population, in your case, means the members of your target audience. You need to get a list of this market, either by using zip codes, car registration and voter registration lists, or by choosing from the phone book according to neighborhoods. You can also buy lists, at a reasonable fee, from list brokers.

To assure randomness, you must choose according to some system, which numbers on your list will be called. You might take one from each column. To be totally random, you should choose a column position, for example, the eighteenth name in each column, and always use that position. If you are interested only in certain neighborhoods, you might choose every tenth name that qualifies. Stick to your chosen pattern.

If you are unsure of just who is in your target audience, you might simply call a name from each column of the phone book, and ask screening questions to eliminate anyone who obviously would not be a customer of yours.

The trick with the random sample is that you are really random. Picking and choosing names or addresses arbitrarily is not random. You must have a system. If using the phone book, which most people do, find out how many columns or pages there are. Divide that by the number of surveys you must complete. If you find that your book has 400 columns, and you need 200 completed surveys, then call one name (from some preselected position, such as first name, fifth name, etc.) from every other column.

A more refined survey method is a *random stratified survey*. Here, you are surveying your population according to some predetermined demographic method. Let's say you're interested in responses from City A, City B, and City C. Your records tell you that 45 percent of your customers come from A, 30 percent from B, and 25 percent from C. So should your survey respondents. Use your trusty phone book once again, to choose your respondents. For a survey sample of 200, 45 percent, or 90 names must come from City A, etc. Divide the columns by 90, to see if you will be calling every third column, fifth, etc. Then begin again from the beginning for City B, where you will need to reach 60 people, and C, where you need 50.

Another survey method is called the *random walk*. In this method, you knock on doors in the neighborhood you are interested in surveying. Randomness is assured by the arbitrary choice of every tenth house, or every sixteenth, or whatever figure you choose.

Alternate Methods of Sampling. Mailing out your surveys is another option. This is expensive because you not only need to pay postage on each survey you mail, but you will also need to include a return envelope. You can usually expect a low return rate. Even though many people might mean to fill out your survey and return it, they often forget. Often, people don't even open anything that they think looks like junk mail. You might need to mail out 2000 pieces to get 200 completed surveys. I recommend that, if you have enough money to do an adequate job of mailing out surveys, you save yourself a lot of trouble and simply hire a research company.

On occasion, however, you can find efficient ways to distribute your surveys. If your target population is easily accessible—downtown shoppers, or students at the only college in town—you can easily drop off your survey, or ask to have it placed in mailboxes, left at designated stores, and returned to a designated drop-off point.

It might be tempting to go out, survey form in hand, and interview people personally. Usually, this is a mistake. Students, habitually, head for the mall, where they know they can find lots of people. But mall shoppers are not necessarily typical of the general population, and they might not be the audience you want to hear from at all. Only if you define your target as "the people who shop malls" or "the students at Smith High School" does this on-site surveying pay off.

Some of my more enterprising students have succeeded in getting the competition to hand out surveys. One semester we needed information about seafood markets, the kinds of people who shopped there, their wants, etc. We random surveyed 100 people from the phone book, and placed an additional 200 surveys in seafood shops throughout the area—that of our clients, and all his primary competitors. Since the survey was designed to elicit information about seafood shoppers in general, any shop owner was willing to distribute the questionnaire in return for a copy of the results. Note: If you don't give them these results, you are guilty of highly unethical conduct. A simple percentage tally of responses will suffice, and will be helpful to those shop owners who have cooperated with you. You, however, having the questionnaires in your possession, can do a much more detailed breakdown of information.

How Many Surveys Do You Need? How many surveys must you complete? This depends greatly on the size of your market. For expediency's sake, with a self-administered questionnaire, I suggest that you complete a minimum of 200. This usually will not be enough to allow you to make accurate assessments of the market. In fact, it will give you an error factor of about 7 percent. I would not recommend, for instance, that based on 200 survey responses, you run out and build an addition to the store, or make any major business investments. You will, however, be able to get a good feel for potential problems and pluses that your business might have in the minds of your potential customers.

Introducing Yourself to the Respondent. You will need an introduction for your survey. If you are making a phone survey, make sure that you give the persons whom you are calling your name. Assure them that you are not selling anything, and that the survey will take only a few minutes of their time. Make the survey sound important and assure them that since they are part of a carefully selected sample, their responses are important. If you are distributing the questionnaire, then you will need a cover letter that conveys this same information. See Appendix for a sample cover speech.

TALLYING YOUR RESPONSES

You will need help with this. Without the aid of another person who can check off the responses as you go through the individual answer sheets, you will go mad—or at least blind.

The First Tally

When you have an assistant, sit down and go through each questionnaire. Your helper will have a blank response sheet in front of him and will simply mark off the responses as you read them. This will result in a gross tally of responses from all surveys. From this, you will begin to see certain patterns—certain qualities that emerge as being important, certain competitors that appear with great frequency, etc. You can calculate percentages for each response.

The Cross-Tabulation

You have determined, from all of your surveys, the percentage of answers to each option in the survey. You are not done. Now you want to cross-tabulate. You might have noticed, in your gross tally, that a large number of people who seem to want the qualities that you can offer fall into a certain age bracket, or tend to read certain magazines. You want to pull these out, and retabulate them to see if their responses are different from those of the total survey population. For instance, you might have been surveying the single, young adult population to see about their interests in a computer dating service. Your general tally shows that there is an interest, and during this tally, you noticed a high degree of enthusiasm in the type of service that you propose among college age students. Pull out all student surveys, and tally again. Then, separate males from females, or high incomes from low incomes, or people who worry more about looks than personality—your previous tallying and your own needs will determine which questionnaires deserve to be given this extra attention. Most often, you will end up cross-tabulating those questionnaires that fall into your two or three target audiences. Appendix B gives a sample of a research project for a small business, from focus group through cross-tabulated survey and results. Refer to it if you need an example.

Professional research firms will be able to do a lot of sophisticated analysis on these responses. They have expertise in statistical data research. You probably do not. You can, however, arrive at several conclusions about public perceptions by simply calculating the percentage of responses given for each option by the entire survey population, and then by the target markets in which you are primarily interested.

SUMMARY

Good research takes planning. A focus group, consisting of in-depth discussions with a small group of people in your target market, will help you to uncover concerns that need research. The focus group's responses to questions you have about public perception of your business will help you to formulate a questionnaire. This survey gives you a good foundation for knowing what your advertising needs to do.

7

The Mass Media and Their Characteristics

I WENT TO VISIT CHRIS SHORTLY AFTER HIS REFINISHING SHOP OPENED. BUSI-ness was slow, and he seemed confused.

"You know, right after I opened, I think every radio station and newspaper in town called me. I knew I had to advertise, so I took out ads. But they're not doing much good. I tried to read all these rate cards and statistics they gave me—but they don't make much sense. How can everybody be number one—and yet nobody is reaching the customers I want?"

Part of Chris's problem was creative. Being new to business, he let every ad salesman do his own thing. So none of Refinishing Shop's ads said what he wanted them to—or said the same things as any other ad. The main problem was that Chris didn't understand the intricacies involved in buying time and space in the mass media.

Every medium has peculiar characteristics. Newspapers seem to reach almost everyone—but not everyone in the house reads everything. So, learning to choose the right days and sections is important. Planning ahead, to take advantage of contract rates can save a new business a bundle. First, of course, you need to understand those very confusing rate cards. Which deal is best for you?

Radio can get even more confusing. The research is often poor so it's hard to tell which station will best reach your target audience. Even harder is deter-mining when your audience will be listening. Then you have to decide whether to go with a high-powered station that reaches all over town, or a smaller, less expensive one that you can afford more spots on. Plus, the rate card seems even more confusing than those for newspaper. Now the salesperson is talking about giveaways and contests. Will those work?

Finally, there's TV. You thought you couldn't afford it, but the local station seems to have one heck of a deal for you. What are the hidden costs? Will it reach the audience you want? Do the advantages outweigh the disadvantages?

These are only a few of the questions that plague the small business advertiser. Chapter 7 explains the intricacies of buying newspaper, radio, and television, the advantages and disadvantages of each, and the hidden costs to the small-budget buyer.

When we first think of advertising media, radio, television, and newspapers pop to mind. These are the mass media—the ones which reach large segments of the population almost simultaneously. From these sources, we ourselves are exposed to masses of ads at a single sitting. If you were to survey your target audience to find out where they get most of their information about the local businesses that they patronize, they are likely to name one of these three media.

Therefore, we will examine newspaper, then radio, and television in this chapter to determine how well they might fit into your advertising plan.

NEWSPAPERS

There are several types of newspapers available to the advertiser. The first one we think of is usually the local daily paper, which has a large circulation and the ability to reach your audience on the day you judge to be most effective. There are also smaller, local weeklies, which reach smaller outlying communities more directly. Then there are special newspapers, targeted to particular groups in the community, often business oriented, but sometimes cultural or consumer based. We will consider each of these separately.

The Daily Paper

The daily newspaper is the most commonly used medium for the small business. While it has several advantages, there are also a few pitfalls.

Advantages

The daily newspaper is the godsend of the retailer. In part, this is because of its circulation characteristics. A single edition of the paper reaches a large proportion of the population every day. Therefore, it is an ideal, high-reach medium. Within the paper, however, there is excellent potential for targeting. Certain sections of the paper, or special pages, appeal to very definite segments of the population. This means that you can place your ad in a section that your target market is likely to read.

Editorial Matter. The editorial matter in each newspaper is a great help to the advertiser. He or she knows that the avid cook will turn to the food section;

that those interested in style will read the women's section; businesspeople will check the stock market page, etc. Therefore, there is a logical place for your ad. The average newspaper reader also knows this, and if they are looking for something—a sale on tires, for instance—they will often grab the daily paper and leaf through the logical section to find what they want.

Stay-Around Power. This illustrates another great advantage to the paper—its stay-around power. Unlike the broadcast media, where your message comes and goes in 30 seconds, the newspaper usually lingers for at least a day. If your ad has any interest for the reader, he can spend all the time he likes studying your message. Your message might not interest readers during their first read-through, but later, when the sink starts to leak, they pull out the paper they have just laid aside to search for plumbers.

Space Flexibility. Newspaper ads are also flexible. You are not limited to a certain length of message, as you are in the broadcast media. If you need a larger ad at sale times or during seasonal highs, you can have it if you can afford it. Whereas in the broadcast media, there might not be any time available during peak advertising seasons, the newspaper can add as many additional pages as needed to accommodate the demand for advertising.

Time Flexibility. The newspaper is also flexible time-wise. You do not need to reserve your ads weeks ahead, as you do with the broadcast media. You need to plan only a day or two in advance. And your ads can change frequently.

Help with Graphic Design. Most newspapers also provide help in designing your ads. The advertising rep can show you a variety of available typefaces and clip art and give you advice on layout, ad placement, etc. If you work consistently with one representative, he or she will also give you information on special advertising rates and packages that might be helpful.

Graphic Capability. Best of all, the newspaper gives you graphic capability. As you will see when we discuss creativity in print ads, the typeface, border, and style of your ad can communicate a lot about your business in a very small space—your price range, image, even the type of business that you are. This is a blessing for those with limited budgets. Plus, if your ads must show a product—if the customer will need to see what you are offering—then newspapers can make sure we see what we need to see.

Disadvantages

There are also disadvantages to using the daily newspaper.

Limited Graphic Resolution. First, the graphic capability is somewhat limited. If the item you need to show must be very clear and detailed, then the newspaper printing process will not do it justice. You can maximize your clarity by supplying the newspaper with very large prints, but you will never get the sharp black and white resolution seen in magazine photos.

Waste Circulation. Second, the circulation is very large. If your area of trade is small, this could mean that you are buying a lot of waste circulation, where you reach people who will never be customers for your business. Many newspapers allow you to buy split runs, where your ad only appears in certain editions of the paper going to limited geographic areas. This doesn't help, however, if your target audience is limited demographically rather than geographically. If you read through the rest of this media section and still find that newspapers seem to be your best media choice, despite a lot of waste circulation, don't feel that you are necessarily being foolish. Sometimes newspaper is your best choice, and there's simply no way to avoid waste. This holds true especially if you are a new business, or one who needs to reach a lot of people in the short run, before you find your best target audiences.

Clutter. Third, we have the problem of clutter. Since so many businesses advertise in the newspaper, your ad is likely to be lost in a welter of other ads. It will take a strong graphic look and an interesting creative concept to make your ad stand out.

There is one place where clutter might seem to be a problem, but really is not. This is when the newspaper devotes a certain section exclusively to ads for a certain kind of business, or targeted to a certain theme. For instance, many newspapers run entertainment pages, consisting of hundreds of ads for restaurants and nightclubs, movies, etc. Many clients want to avoid this page, because they are afraid to be lost in the masses. The reader, however, when looking for something to do, turns right to that entertainment page. Your page two ad, for which you probably paid a premium rate, won't even be considered.

The same thinking goes if you are invited to advertise in a special section—a bridal supplement, the food page, or a financial section. The people who are in the market for your product or service will look here for your ad before they will tackle the whole paper for scattered possibilities.

Best-Customer Favoritism. Another disadvantage to newspaper is that you are not always able to get the page placement that you want. Many of the choice spots for ads in each paper are reserved for old, valued customers who buy huge amounts of ads daily or weekly. The small business advertiser can seldom compete for the pages and places on pages that are most favored.

Lack of Consistency. Finally, the very help that the newspaper provides in designing your ads can work to your detriment. Unless you have a very particular format for your ads, and specify exactly the look you want, the graphic style, and the typefaces, your ad is likely to come out looking different every week. While the content of your ad should differ, the total look and style of it should not. The ad rep, overseeing dozens of ads every day, does not have the time to worry about stylistic consistency. Therefore, while he or she can offer good advice, the responsibility for making your newspaper ads part of a consistent campaign ultimately falls on you.

Which Newspaper—If Any?

If there is more than one daily newspaper in your market, or if you have the option to buy only special editions of the paper, then you can determine which is your best buy by looking at the newspaper circulation figures. Most daily newspapers have excellent research, which will tell you approximately how much of its circulation reaches your target audience. They can also tell you about actual readership, which is different from circulation.

Circulation tallies the actual number of newspapers that are sold. However, more than one person is likely to read each copy. At home, several family members might read the evening paper. A single office copy of the morning paper might be read by several people in the lunchroom. This figure—the number of people who read each copy of the paper—is the readership figure. This is more useful to your purposes than the circulation figure, since the actual subscriber might not be part of your target audience, but the reader could be.

If your paper has good research, it might even be able to provide readership figures for the specific section of the newspaper that you want to advertise in.

Which Paper is Most Cost-Effective? If information on readership is available for the newspapers you are considering, you can use this to determine which will be your most efficient advertising vehicle. To determine the cost of reaching one thousand people in each specific newspaper (the Cost Per Thousand or CPM) divide the readership figure for your specific target audience into the cost of your ad (number of column inches times cost per inch) and multiply by 1000. This tells you how much it will cost you to reach 1000 members of your target audience in that medium.

Compare this figure with other newspapers. The best dollar figure is your best newspaper buy. If there is no demographic breakdown for a particular section, then you must use the estimated number of readers of the whole newspaper from your target audience. CPMs are your best tool for figuring out a cost-efficient media plan. You might be tempted to ignore them, while merely eyeballing the rates and making a guess. Don't. You'll end up wasting money.

Don't forget, if you have more than one target market and both might be using this medium, to include both in your calculations.

Which Edition is Best? CPM, though, is not your only consideration when buying newspaper space. You also have to decide whether you want to buy space in a morning paper or an evening paper—if you have a choice. Do you want people to read your message at work, early in the day, or at home when they are at their leisure?

If your newspaper offers you the option, you will also want to consider whether you want to buy space in every edition of the paper, or only particular ones. Editions of the newspaper are released at different times of the day. If you have a very small budget and can specifically say that your ad will be measurably more effective if read before lunch time, for instance, then you might want to buy only the early morning editions of the paper. If you are only interested in reaching people on the south side of town, see if you have the option of advertising only in that edition.

Which Section Reaches my Target? Take a careful look at each newspaper that you might advertise in. Are there special pages that seem to suit your needs? Are there special sections or supplements that seem suited to your audience? Take a good look around and see where your best placement is.

Ad Rates

Newspaper display ads (the ones appearing on the editorial page) are sold in one of two ways: by the column inch or by the agate line.

Column Inches. A column inch is one inch deep by one column wide. How much space this amounts to in real terms is determined by the specific newspaper that you are using. Some newspapers use an 8-column format, so the actual width of your column inch will be about $1^1/_2$ inches. Column width in papers using a 6-column format is about 2 inches. This information is usually included on the newspaper's rate card. To determine the number of column inches in an ad, multiply its height in inches by its width in columns. An ad that is 3 inches high and 2 columns wide equals 6 column inches. So does an ad 2 inches high and 3 columns wide.

Agate Lines. A few newspapers still sell ad space by the agate line. There are 14 agate lines to a column inch. So, an ad 2 inches high by 1 column wide would be 28 agate lines. All you are doing is multiplying the number of column inches that you want by 14.

Line or Word Charges. Classified ads, the want ads, are sold by the word or by the line. While these ads don't have the eye appeal and graphic potential of a display ad, they can be useful to a small budget, if your product or service fits into a recognized category of the classifieds—antiques, for instance, or the "Who does it" section that many newspapers offer to service businesses.

Discounts. All newspaper ads are sold at a base charge. However, as the amount of space you buy goes up, the price might go down. So, the more newspaper space you buy, the less each column inch might cost. Generally, newspapers also offer a contract rate. If you agree to buy a certain number of column inches within a specified period of time, you receive a lower rate. Often the rate decreases in increments. It is lowered once for a 200 column-inch contract, for instance, again if you buy more than 500, etc.

Special Charges. Some newspaper pages are sold at premium rates. Since page three of the newspaper is considered prime advertising space, ads on this page are often sold at a higher rate. The same might apply to the entertainment page, financial page, etc. As I stated before, this might simply be a price you have to pay if this is where your ad belongs because this is where most people will look for it.

A few newspapers will also put a higher rate on guaranteed page positions. Advertisers prefer to see their ads in the upper right hand corner of the odd numbered pages of the paper. Because of the way in which people tend to page through the paper, these are the ads that get seen first and most often. Therefore, many newspapers will charge extra to guarantee this position.

Special Sections. Newspapers also publish special sections in their Sunday papers. These sections will usually have separate rate cards, and often must be bought on a contract. These sections, however, tend to have specific target audiences that read them regularly, and so can be cost-efficient despite their premium pricing. One especially effective section is the TV guide distributed by many newspapers. This supplement has great stay-around power—an entire week. Many people will refer to the listings several times in a single evening. If your ad appears on the page they are referring to, they will see it repeatedly. In this way, a single ad achieves a large frequency just because of the way in which the TV listings are used.

Qualifying for Discount Rates. Since bulk purchase of newspaper space in either the regular section or the special section saves you money, it pays to plan your newspaper space purchases ahead of time to take advantage of lower quantity rates. The easiest way to do this is to take the total dollar figure that you have allocated to newspaper and divide that by the base cost per column inch. This will tell you how many column inches you can afford at the highest rate. If this figure is close to or higher than the minimum inches required for a quantity discount, then you can refigure at the lower rate.

Approximating a Newspaper Schedule. In order to fit this into your media plan, you must then consider the number of ads you will need in the upcoming year (or six-months—whichever time span your media calendar calls for). Divide this into your inch figure to see how large an ad you can afford. You can, of course, vary the sizes of your ads, using smaller ones during slow periods and larger ones at peak times, but this will give you a rough idea of what your newspaper schedule will look like.

Until your media schedule is finalized, this rough approximation will be sufficient. When you have roughed out your other media options, you might find that you can juggle dollar amounts from one medium to another until you get a plan that works.

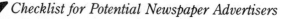

Checklist for Potential Newspaper Advertisers

Newspaper advertising will be cost-efficient for you if:

- You have a wide area of trade, not much smaller than the newspaper circulation area.
- You have a more limited area of trade but can take advantage of split runs or regional editions.
- You have a small area of trade but are a new business trying to attract customers and achieve visibility; or
- You are running a sale or special event that might attract a larger audience than normal.
- You have a product or service with which the public is unfamiliar, and you need space to explain yourself.
- You feel that the public needs to see what you are offering.

Checklist for Buying Space in the Daily Paper

- If your budget is very small, first consider whether your message will be most effective if heard in the morning or in the afternoon.
- Recheck your area of trade. Which newspapers reach this area of trade? Call each of these and request both rate cards and a copy of their circulation research report.
- Get copies of each newspaper that you are considering. See if they feature any special sections or pages that seem especially interesting to your target audience. Now check the rate card for that paper, and see if there are special charges for advertising in that section.
- Look at the circulation research. Which newspapers seem to reach your target audience most directly? Eliminate those that do not seem appropriate.
- Check to see if any newspapers offer you a split run that will allow you to reach your target audience more efficiently.
- For the remaining newspapers, figure out the cost per thousand (CPM). Take the open rate figure for purchasing one column inch (or the special rate, if that paper charges extra for the section in which you want to advertise). Divide that figure by the number of people that the newspaper reaches who are in your target audience. If you are planning on buying a split run, calculate only the target audience figure for the split run. Multiply that answer by 1000. This tells you how much it is costing you to reach 1000 members of your target audience in that particular newspaper. (Note: If the newspaper reaches more than one of your target audiences, combine those readership figures.)

- Figure the CPM for all the newspapers you are considering. Eliminate the higher priced media, and settle on the one or two newspapers with the lowest CPM.

The Weekly Newspaper

Many suburban areas, or even small geographic communities within a larger city, issue weekly newspapers devoted exclusively to local news. The rates for these papers are, of course, much lower than those of the daily newspaper because their circulation is smaller. Therefore, if you have a small budget and a small area of trade, one of these newspapers can afford you an opportunity to purchase large ads at a reasonable rate. These ads will help to avoid the problem of waste circulation.

Types of Weeklies. Most major communities have a few, limited circulation newspapers targeted at occupational or special interest groups. Many of these consist of legal or business news. Some deal with area cultural events. More and more communities are publishing weekly "shoppers," featuring classified ads and sale news. These can be of great help in allowing the small budget advertiser to target advertising demographically.

Just because you find a newspaper in your area that suits your purposes, however, does not mean that you should use it exclusively, bypassing the dailies. In the first place, many people in your target area do not receive the weekly. In the second place, many readers of weekly papers will also subscribe to a daily paper to keep up with news outside their immediate area. By concentrating your budget in the weekly paper, you achieve a limited reach and frequency. By placing occasional ads in the daily paper as well, you can maximize both.

Problems with Weekly Papers. There is only one major pitfall with some of these small-circulation newspapers. While many are sold at the newsstand and by subscription, many of them are distributed free of charge. This means that you will have no idea of how many people actually receive the publication and are exposed to your ad. Thus there is no way for you to determine whether the rates charged for advertising are reasonable. In addition, sad but true, many people still believe in the old maxim "You get what you pay for." Many free newspapers might be picked up, but often they go unread, in favor of those for which we have parted with cold cash. Therefore, there is, of yet, no solid evidence that advertising in these publications benefits the businessperson.

The Shopper—A Special Case. Depending on your product or service, the shopper publications, even if they can't give you specific circulation figures, can be beneficial. People go to the shopper in a different frame of mind than that which they take to a regular newspaper laden with ads. When they read a shopper, they are looking for products to buy, and services for which they are in the market. If your product or service readily falls into one of the shopper categories and if it seems likely that a customer would choose your new item over a used one in the classified sections, then by all means give this a try.

Checklist for Buying Space in the Weeklies

- Does the newspaper in question reach my target audience without a great deal of waste circulation? How closely does its circulation pattern match my area of trade?
- Can I get accurate circulation figures, so that I can figure out the CPM for each paper?
- Does the paper seem to be well read so that I might consider it as my primary form of print media? Do most people in the area receive it? Or will I still need to advertise in the daily paper during peak business periods?

RADIO

Radio is everywhere. Since the invention of the transistor radio, this has become the one medium that can travel with us, from room to room and street to street. Radio reaches us at home, in the office, as we wander from store to store. It goes with us down the street and travels with us in the car. In fact, 95 percent of all cars have radios. Estimates claim that, in the United States alone, there are almost 425 million radios in use each day.

This ubiquitousness makes radio an attractive proposition for the advertiser. Customers don't have to make an effort to hear your message—it practically follows them.

Advantages

Besides being everywhere, radio offers stations that appeal to almost everyone.

Formats for Every Taste. Radio stations tend to have *formats*—a plan or structure that determines the kind of music they play, the amount of talk, and the amount of news, weather, and sports they carry. Formats vary from acid rock and heavy metal stations that feature very little in the way of information, through adult contemporary stations, all talk stations, all news, jazz, classical music, etc.

Specific Targeting. Because of its diversity, each radio station attracts a specific demographic and psychographic group. Most listeners tend to find one or two stations in the market—those that most closely match their listening tastes—and stick to them. Therefore, if you have a strong picture of the demographics and psychographics of your target audience, chances are high that you can find a radio station that reaches them.

Limited Waste Circulation. Demographically, there is little waste circulation in radio advertising. There might, however, be a lot of geographic waste, depending on the strength of a station's signal. Some radio stations have weak signals, and travel only a small distance. Others can travel for hundreds of miles. Clear channel stations—those that operate at 50,000 watts—can often be heard several states away in the evening. If you need a medium that will allow you to advertise to a specific demographic segment of the market while achieving a wide reach, then radio is ideally suited to your media schedule. If you have a fairly small area of trade, however, then take care to avoid those stations with strong signal patterns reaching thousands of listeners outside your market.

Radio advertisers in mountainous states have a slightly different problem. Even a very strong radio signal can be blocked by mountains. If you are buying time on a station, you will need to find out its signal pattern. *Broadcasting/Cable Yearbook* provides maps that show the signal patterns for each station. Make sure the station you buy time on reaches the areas you want to reach.

Low Rates. Considering its capabilities, radio is relatively inexpensive. The CPM for a 30-second radio ad is very often much lower than that of a newspaper ad reaching the same target audience.

Inexpensive Production Costs. In addition to its low time rates, radio production costs can be low or even free. Most radio stations will provide production service and even write your ads for you when you buy spots on their station.

This last advantage, however, can also create problems, if you want a neat, consistent advertising campaign. If you buy spots on two or more stations, and each does their own production, then you will have two or more different radio ads. Your target audience, if they hear both, might not realize that both are for the same business. Therefore, your ad will not have the desired impact. You should supply the stations with copy, or pay for the production of a master commercial that can be distributed to each station that runs your ads. I'll discuss this more fully in the creative section.

Creativity. Producing radio ads can be a real creative thrill. Radio has often been called "theatre of the mind." On radio you can go anywhere and do anything—all at the same basic production cost. There are no sets to build, or costumes to design. This means that you can achieve wonderful advertising effects cheaply. It costs no more to be creative than to be mediocre.

Disadvantages

Radio has a lot to offer the advertiser. It has several pitfalls, too. Here are a few things to watch out for.

No Stay-Around Power. The major problem with a radio ad is that it is ephemeral. Once it has been played, it is gone. Potential customers cannot roll it back to recheck pertinent facts. While specific creative strategies have been developed to alleviate this problem, the fact remains that you will need a higher frequency with radio than with print media, simply to get your basic message across.

The Button-Switchers. There is also the dilemma of the compulsive button switcher. Especially in the car, people tend to hit the button to change stations as soon as the commercial comes on. Once again, though, good creative planning can help you here.

Background Medium. More of a problem is in the very nature of radio. Radio is a background medium. Like wallpaper for the ears, it's there, but we don't give it our undivided attention. Fortunately, listeners do tend to focus on messages that promise them something they want, so a good message that emphasizes a strong key benefit can still attract attention.

Time Scheduling Limitations. There is a great need to plan ahead in buying radio time. The radio day is finite—at longest it lasts 24 hours, and many stations broadcast for even shorter periods of time. If you haven't planned ahead, there might not be any time left for your ad when you need it most.

Over-Creativity. Finally, the very creativity unleashed by radio can spell trouble. It's easy to get carried away creating special effects—to have so much fun being clever that we forget our primary purpose—to communicate a message about our product or service. Good radio advertising requires discipline.

Buying Radio Time

Radio can be bought on a network or spot basis. Networks carry signals to many stations. If you need to reach a large national or regional audience, a network buy makes sense. One phone call will put your message on hundreds of stations.

Spot buying—the usual fate of the small business advertiser—means that you select individual stations, and negotiate with each separately.

Getting the Best Rates for Your Objectives. The first problem in spot buying is to select appropriate stations. You could try to listen in on every station in your market, until you found a few that seem to be aimed at your target audience. Or you could go to the library and look at a reference book called *Standard Rate and Data Service* (SRDS). *SRDS* has separate books for radio, television, outdoor, direct mail, etc. Many libraries only carry radio and television volumes. These books will list all the stations in your area. They will describe the general area of coverage, and the format of each station. They also give rates for advertising on that station. A look at the *SRDS* will allow you to single out a manageable number of stations that seem to suit your advertising needs, based on geographic coverage, format (which gives a clue to demographic and psychographic coverage), and advertising rates.

Once you have this information, contact each of these potential stations individually. *SRDS* will also give you the phone number and the name of the advertising representative. Do not rely on the advertising rates given in *SRDS*. For one thing, many of these are out of date. For another, the rates given on a radio rate card are often subject to negotiation. Often there are special packages available that would suit your purposes. Therefore, you will want to talk to each rep to see how much a spot on their station will really cost you.

If you cannot find an *SRDS* in your area, then get out your phone directory. Look up ''radio stations'' in the Yellow Pages. Then get your dialing finger in gear. Call up every station, and ask for rates and listenership information. You can eliminate any stations that you know are unsuitable, but collect as many rates as you can. Costs for a 30-second spot vary widely from station to station, and you might not be able to afford enough advertising on your first choice station to make it worthwhile. You need to have alternatives at hand.

Choosing a Time Slot. Next, you will need to consider the time of day during which you want to advertise. Radio advertising is usually rated according to time classes. The station usually charges its highest rates for *drive time*—usually from 6–10 a.m. and 4–7 p.m. Monday through Friday. The rates are highest then because drive time is the time when most people are available, trapped in their cars on the way to and from work.

Many small businesses automatically jump at the chance to advertise in drive time because of its greater reach. Think carefully. The car is the perfect place for all compulsive button pushers to avoid your ad. However, if the businessperson is your target, then this is a prime slot. If not, you have less expensive alternatives.

Daytime generally covers the 10 a.m.–4 p.m. time slots, and usually costs somewhat less. Some stations break the daytime slot into 10–12 noon, and noon to 4 p.m. In this case, the earlier slot has been designated as *housewife time*, because traditionally this is the time when the wife has gotten the kids off to school and the husband off to work. The breakfast dishes are done, and now she can relax over a cup of coffee, listening to the radio until her soap operas begin. While this portrait of the American woman has changed somewhat since radio time classes were developed, housewife time is still a valid idea for advertisers wishing to reach young mothers or very traditional women.

The entire daytime slot is a good time to reach workers, because radio is so often played in offices and stores. Certain stations tend to get played in offices; others suit retail establishments. The sales rep can often give you information about this; you can also wander into stores and offices patronized by the audience you are trying to reach, making careful note of the stations that they play.

This is a good buy for you if you can't comfortably buy drive time spots, or if you're afraid that drivers will hit the button at the sound of your ad.

The rates charged for daytime radio are often the same rates charged for weekend radio, 6 a.m. through 7 p.m. Since fewer people work traditional 9–5 jobs on weekends, there is no rush hour to justify drive time rates.

Still less expensive is the evening time class, usually from 7 p.m. to midnight. Most people are watching television now, if they are using media at all. Since there are fewer listeners available for radio, the rates drop. An exception to this is any station reaching the teenage audience. Teens tend to use the radio fairly heavily in the evening when they are out cruising in their cars, hanging out with their friends, or studying.

Finally, there are the lowest rates of all—the overnights from midnight to 6 a.m. The reason for these low rates should be obvious. However, if you are trying to appeal to the night owl, if you want to reach truckers, or if you operate a 24-hour a day business, then you can get some real bargains on overnight radio.

The radio *rate card* will show a simple schedule of rates broken down into time classes and discounted according to frequency. Most rate cards that you encounter will be broken down this way. If you get a rate card that cannot be deciphered, you are probably looking at a grid card.

A *grid card* is one where the rates vary according to station availability. In other words, if advertising time is selling out quickly, you will be charged a premium fee. When few people seem interested in radio time, the fee per spot will be lowered to attract advertisers. The catch: you don't know what grid the station is in unless you call and ask. You are not expected to be able to read this type of card on your own.

Program Sponsorship. On some stations, you can sponsor a specific program. Many stations have sports features, news, etc., which for a higher rate will feature both your ad and a "sponsored by . . ." tag. Often, this higher rate is worth the expense. While radio can be a background medium most of the time, people tend to stop and listen to the news, weather, and informational programs. Therefore, you have a higher rate of attention for your ad. Also, there is a psychological benefit of goodwill—subconsciously people appreciate those who sponsor programming that they value. Other high-consciousness buys include winter storm days when stations announce school and business closings or during traffic reports at rush hours.

Seasonal Rate Variations. Remember that radio rates might vary seasonally. Radio listenership is high during the summer, because unlike television (unless you have a TV walkman), it can accompany its audience to the beach, or on a family outing. Therefore, rates will reflect this higher listenership. They are also high at Christmas, when every retailer in town wants time. Those rates will drop during the remainder of winter, when people are snug inside, watching their televisions.

Frequency and Volume Discounts. Radio advertising rates are discounted in two ways: *frequency discounts* and *dollar volume discounts*. *Frequency discounting* means that the basic rate for an ad goes down as the frequency of the ad increases. This is usually figured according to the number of ads you run per week. *Dollar volume discounts* mean that your rate will drop according to the amount you spend in a specific campaign. Once again, it pays for you to plan ahead in figuring out your media schedule. Then you can contract with stations for both frequency and dollar volume discounts in order to maximize your media buying power.

Advertising rate policies vary widely from station to station. Often, if you contract for several spots during a low rate period, you can save money. You can sometimes buy a large quantity of spots and save some of them for times when other advertisers, who did not plan ahead, are forced to pay premium rates.

Special Promotion Opportunities. When you buy advertising on some stations they might give you the opportunity to take part in their special promotions. Often this involves give-aways. Listeners will call into the station and after answering a question, because they are the tenth caller, or some other gimmick, they are given a prize. The prize is supplied by one of the station's advertisers—perhaps you. So when someone calls the station and receives dinner for two at a local restaurant, you can be sure that the restaurant has first, bought paid advertising time on the station, and second, agreed to take part in the special promotion.

The advertiser will supply a free dinner for two for the listener, in return for several mentions on the radio. Often, the disc jockey will promote the promotion, telling us that in the next half hour we'll have the chance to win dinner for two at Mike's Diner. He'll repeat the name just before call-in time, and, of course, during the phone call. A bit later, he'll reannounce the winner, and the prize, thus repeating your name again. So, for the cost of dinner for two, or whatever you offer as your giveaway, you get a lot of air time. A good investment, as long as your giveaway item doesn't cost more than a regular radio spot.

What you won't get is a whole lot of selling. For the most part, these giveaway announcements do not list your benefits and promises—only your name. A few will include your slogan or tag line and address with these announcements. They are useful when your primary objective is to get your name in front of the public, especially if they are backed up by advertising in other media.

If the item you give away is less than the cost of comparable advertising time on the station, then the frequency you can get from promotional gimmicks like these can be very worthwhile. At the very least, someone will be coming into your establishment very soon to get their free gift and to see what else you have.

At best, your name will become familiar enough that the impact of your regular advertising will increase.

Warnings about "Special" Rates. Many radio stations offer special plans, called *Total Audience Plans*. This means that the station will schedule your ads so that they will run in each of the time classes, theoretically reaching their entire listening audience. Before falling for the reduced rate here, ask yourself if you want to reach the entire audience, or only a specific segment. Will your message be psychologically right if heard after midnight? If you need to reach a very wide segment of the population, a TAP plan can be helpful—if you can afford enough spots that the average listener will hear your ad at least three times. This is the minimum number of times we need to hear a radio ad before it sinks in. On a small budget, you're usually better off selecting and controlling your own times—even if it seems like you're paying a higher rate, at least you're not paying for spots that are reaching the wrong audience.

Concentrating Your Radio Buys. When buying radio spots, it is best to settle on one or two specific time slots and to concentrate all your spots here. This way, you will reach the same audience more often. If, for instance, you run spots for your "Back to School Special" twice between 10 and 11 a.m., Monday through Friday for a week, you will probably reach the same housewife and mother several times with this message. If you put some of those slots in drive time, you might reach Dad—but not with the same effect that several hearings will have on Mom. If your lunch time delivery special is heard three times a week at 10:30 a.m., you will reach many of the same office workers until it sinks in and they call for a delivery.

Choosing the Best Stations. To choose among several radio stations that seem to suit your target audience needs, use the same CPM formula that was used for newspaper. The problem here is that radio research is usually much less thorough than that done for newspaper. Estimates of radio listenership are based on ratings done by Arbitron. In small markets this is done very infrequently. Programming or even formats could change, which could drastically affect listenership, yet the available research would not reflect this. Therefore, CPMs for radio are often based a lot on hope, unless the new Arbitrons have just come out.

Small stations especially, often fail to break down their listenership into demographic segments. Try to pin the sales rep down to discover exactly what audience there is for each time slot. Run CPMs to compare time slots, if these are available. If not, well, you do the best you can. Trust the new station that has done some of its own home grown research. Assume that, in the absence of any large format changes, the old ratings and new rates are equitable. If you can't get a demographic breakdown of the audience, at least do not fail to run CPM comparisons between competing stations, in hopes that you make the best choice. No one ever said that media scheduling was either easy or foolproof.

Checklist for Potential Radio Advertisers

Radio can be a cost-efficient media buy for you if:

- You have specifically defined demographic target markets.
- Your target audience matches up with one reached by specific radio stations in the area.
- Your advertising message is brief and easy to communicate.
- You have a large enough radio budget to be able to expose your target audience to a minimum of at least three hearings of your ad within a one week period. (Ideally, you want people to hear your ad three times in a single day—nice if you're Coca Cola or Bell Telephone. The small budget advertiser has to settle for less. But never settle for less than three potential hearings—which might mean buying six ads in the same time slot.)
- There are stations in your area that reach your demographic audience without vastly over-reaching your area of trade.

Checklist for Buying Radio Time

- Either consult the *Standard Rate and Data Service* at your local library, or contact your local stations for rates.
- Eliminate all stations that do not appeal to your target audience.
- Eliminate all stations whose signal reaches too far beyond your area of trade.
- Looking at your media calendar, which of your target audiences can you reach most efficiently by radio?
- Figure out what portion of your annual budget for reaching that audience (or those audiences) should be devoted to radio. (Once again, this is just a rough guess—you'll go back and refine this after you have looked at all media choices.)
- For stations that you are considering, try to get a demographic breakdown of the listening audience from the station rep.
- Figure the CPM for any stations that you are still considering. If you can't get a demographic breakdown, give up and figure on the total listenership figure. You'll at least be in the ballpark.

The Noncommercial Alternative

I know that sounds like a contradiction. Noncommercial is supposed to mean no advertising. But I'm not talking about commercials. I'm talking sponsorship.

Major corporations like IBM and Texaco do it all the time. These corporations sponsor high-class programming—operas and concerts—over a public radio network. They don't do a lot of selling. Their name is simply associated with a production that carries a lot of prestige. These programs might not be available to the listening public without their underwriting. This creates a lot of goodwill for their companies.

You can do this on a smaller basis. Perhaps, on your local noncommercial stations, there are some programs ideally suited for your target audience. Let's say you sell sporting goods, and the noncommercial station runs a daily sports feature. You could sponsor that program. Which means that, every day through the length of your sponsorship, the announcer will tell grateful viewers that "This program was made possible through Joe's Sporting Goods, at 000 Main Street, where you can buy all your recreational equipment."

Public radio depends on listener support, or it cannot continue its programming. If your station demands that you sponsor a program for an entire season, you might find the cost too high. You have other, less expensive alternatives. Many times, during fund-raising seasons, these stations offer you the opportunity to become a *day sponsor*. What this means is that during one entire broadcast day, the station will announce that today's programs are sponsored by Joe's Sporting goods, etc. Many stations permit a small, restrained commercial along with your name. At the very least, most will give your tag line and address (Joe's—where we turn young athletes into stars).

This tactic will not work for every business. Most public radio stations tend to feature classical music, jazz, and informative programming that appeals to a well-educated, high-income section of the population. However, this might be exactly the section that you want to reach. Sponsorship on a noncommercial station can be a practical and affordable alternative to commercial advertising. Don't forget the added goodwill that you are creating.

TELEVISION

Television is the only true mass medium. Any single channel carries such a diversity of programming that everyone in the market is likely to tune in and find something it likes at one time or another during the day. It is the only medium that is capable of reaching almost the entire population of the country with a single broadcast. Except for a few thousand members of SETS (Society for the Eradication of Television), everyone has a TV set. Maybe several.

Television is the prestige medium. Advertisers gain prestige just by buying spots on television. Because television has a larger viewing audience than any single radio station in the market, its rates are higher. Because television ads require production, which can also be expensive, television advertisers tend to fall into a fairly elite group—those with big budgets. This doesn't necessarily have to be the case. With careful planning and sensible creative strategy, many businesses who would ordinarily dismiss television as being outside of their budget can find a slot within their budget.

Advantages

As I said, television is a prestige medium. Because even the most uninformed viewer has vague ideas about the expense of television programming, most automatically assume that anyone who advertises on television is doing well. People like to patronize businesses that they perceive as doing well. It establishes trust. But there are many other advantages to advertising on TV.

Reach. Television also has marvelous reach, far greater than any radio station, and more demographically diverse than newspaper. Besides, since viewers tend to have favorite programs that they view faithfully, it is easy to reach the same viewers consistently on television.

Show and Tell Capabilities. Television has the ability to both show and tell about your product. If seeing it will be more convincing than hearing about it, then television is the place—especially if you'd like us to see your product or service in action. This show/tell ability is also useful for those who wander away from the set at commercial breaks. They might not be seeing any more—but your words will still reach them. If written carefully, the ad can still communicate your benefits.

Good Targeting by Program. Television is wonderfully targeted. Not by station, as in radio, but by program. Both Neilsen and Arbitron research the television viewing audience. Your local station can usually give you a fairly accurate picture of the viewing audience throughout their program day, broken down into 15-minute segments. You can place your ad when your audience is most likely to be there.

Disadvantages

Unfortunately, technology, which made television possible in the first place, is now giving the medium trouble. The dreaded remote control has made it possible for the laziest couch potato to zap the station as soon as a commercial comes on. VCR units also allow viewers to record their favorite programs minus commercials.

Fortunately, many diehard television addicts still say that the commercials are the best things on television. And a devoted fan of a particular program will often lay aside his or her zapper for fear of missing a precious second of the show. Besides, not everyone has all this new technology or uses it consistently. So advertisers continue to use television. But there are other disadvantages.

Time Slot Expense. A major problem is expense. Advertising time on the "good" shows—the ones that have all the viewers, is prohibitively expensive. These are usually network shows, and most of the available advertising time has gone to network sponsors. Local stations can charge a premium for the few slots remaining, because these programs attract large, demographically desirable audiences.

Production Expense. Even more frustrating, those network commercials are slick, professionally produced jobs with zillion-dollar-a-minute budgets. Even if you scrimp and save to afford the time charges for a prime time slot, you probably can't afford the production charges that will let you compete with the big guys.

Alternatives to Expensive TV

Cheer up. There is more to life than prime time. Here are a few suggestions for using TV without using up your budget for the next five years.

Alternative Time Slots. Sure, the other day slots might not have the huge audiences, but those huge audiences probably had a lot of waste circulation anyway. Take a look at the alternatives—morning local shows, news shows, the time slots before and during dinner that precede prime time. How about after the late news? There are still plenty of viewers—more targeted now, which is just what you want. Ad time in many of these slots can be surprisingly affordable.

Non-Network Stations. Don't forget non-network stations. Many locally programmed stations are attracting viewers away from the networks and offer more affordable rates to the local advertiser. Cable television stations, too, often have slots for local advertisers. In some markets, advertisers can also take advantage of the new low-power television stations. These stations can be dropped into a market between the powerful network stations and operate at such low strength that they don't interfere with their bigger competitors. These stations are very local in nature and are very suitable for most small business/ small budget advertisers. Many of the non-network programming options are viewed by audiences as fully targeted as those of the typical radio station. So you'll pay less, get less waste circulation, and reach your audience in a prestigious and effective manner.

Noncommercial Stations. In addition, noncommercial television offers the advertiser the same opportunity as does noncommercial radio: sponsorship. Many programs run on the public television networks are ideally suited to the small business sponsor. To take advantage of this and to sponsor a popular program watched faithfully by a small but loyal (and ideally targeted) audience, benefits both the station, which must rely on a good deal of ingenuity to raise programming funds and the sponsor. What better advertising strategy than for a local carpenter to sponsor "This Old House?"

Ratings and Shares

In order to understand time buying on television, you will have to understand the rating system. Both Arbitron and the A. C. Neilsen Company do television audience research on a much more frequent basis than Arbitron does for radio. Program ratings, based on a sample of viewers selected because they are representative of the entire American viewing population, are therefore much more accurate and useful than those available for radio.

Definitions of Terms. Rating services take specific measurements, which we must understand before we can comprehend exactly what those mysterious and all important ratings are. The first term is *households using television (HUT)*. This measures the percentage of all homes owning television sets, which have their sets turned on. When HUT levels are low, ratings are also low; when they are high, ratings can be high.

A *rating* measures the percentage of homes that are tuned in to a specific program during a specified time period. The rating of a show measures its power to get a percentage of the population to turn on their televisions to watch a specific program. Ratings measure viewership from all households, whether the television is turned on or not.

Shares, on the other hand, only measure the percentage of people whose sets are turned on and are tuned to a particular program. This figure uses HUT as its population. Since the percentage of houses using TV is almost always lower than that of households owning TV, the share figure is based on a smaller population than the rating figure. Since, however, the number of people watching the program remains the same, the share is always higher than the rating for any given show. Shares tell us how well a program pulls against competing programs in the same time slot.

How Ratings Work. To give a simple example, we will use the town of Podunk Junction, which has six homes. One home has no television. One home has the set turned off. This gives us a population of five for ratings purposes, and a HUT level of four when we figure the share. Two homes are watching a program on ABC. One is tuned to NBC, and one to CBS.

The HUT level for Podunk Junction, then, is 80, because 80 percent of the homes in this city that own televisions are using them. The population for the rating, however, is 100 percent of the TV-owning population—all five houses, because they have TV, whether or not they are using it. The rating for ABC is 40, because 40 percent of the population of households having television are tuned to that network. CBS and NBC each have ratings of 20, because 20 percent of the population of television owners are tuned in. Since share measures the percentage of HUT, in this case only measuring a population of four households, ABC has a 50 share of the viewing audience since half the HUT households are tuned to this network.

A rating can be very low if HUT levels are low, whereas a share can be very high. If, in this same town, one lone viewer rose at 6 a.m. to watch the televised sunrise, that sunrise would have a rating of 20—20 percent of the possible television population. That same sunrise has a 100 share of the HUT audience.

Why do you need to know all this? Because when you go to buy television advertising time, you will find that the price of advertising in each of the program slots is determined by these ratings and shares. A high-rated program, such as those in prime time, might not be affordable. A lower rated program might be. Don't let a high share scare you off, though, because this simply means that the program does well against its competitors.

Using Ratings to Choose Your Best Slot. When Neilsen and Arbitron release rating information to the station, they break it down into demographic segments. If you ask to look at the ratings for shows you think would be good advertising buys, these figures will also show you what the rating and share of the audience are according to age—at least one segment of which should be compatible with your demographic target group. Every new Neilsen report also measures some other demographic aspect of the viewing audience—perhaps working women, or people with college degrees.

The moral is: Don't just look at the rate card. Rates are usually based on the total audience rating. Look at the ratings themselves, to see which shows reach your desired audience most efficiently. Once again, a CPM can tell you which shows will then be your best buy.

Using CPMs to Refine Your TV Buys. You can do a CPM based on the rating. The rating, of course, will be a percentage of the TV-owning population of the television station's viewing market. If you know that population figure, you can then figure the size of the audience. Television has achieved almost a 99 percent market saturation, which means that almost everyone in the population has a TV. So if you take the rating as a percent of the total population, your figures will be accurate enough for a usable CPM.

Keeping Production Costs Down

Before you even begin to worry about what stations to advertise on, and what programs to buy, worry about production costs. These might stop you before you even get started. If all the production staffs at stations in your market are unionized, the production costs are fixed, and often prohibitively expensive. Shop around from station to station, asking about production costs before you ask for rates. If they all seem unbelievably high, don't despair. If there is a college or university in the area that offers television production, you can often make arrangements with the department, either as part of a class project, or as an extracurricular activity. Sometimes, independent production studios can offer you rates more in keeping with your budget. Often, you are better off if you use these options. Check around first, to see if you can afford to produce your commercial. If you can't, move on to other media options.

If you can get your commercial produced through the school, or through an independent production company, then you are free to take that commercial to any area station, and they will run it. The commercial belongs to you. If, however, the local station does the production work, the ad belongs to them, and you can only run it on that station. If you plan to advertise only on that station, this is fine. If you plan to buy time on two or more stations, be careful. Your total campaign will lack consistency if a spate of different commercials, done with different people and different production styles, is launched upon the unsuspecting public. One approach to this problem is to purchase the commercial from the producing station, for use on competing stations. They are usually willing to do this, but it's one more expense for your already tightly stretched budget. Once you have the production aspect worked out, gather your rate cards.

Determining Your TV Ad Schedule

You will notice that advertising time is sold by the program. Higher rated programs have higher rates. Begin by choosing programs that you can afford. Then ask to look at the ratings breakdown to see exactly who is watching those shows. Two identically rated programs can have very different audience compositions. "The Muppets," for instance, might have the same rating as "Bowling for Dollars," but the viewers will be very different types of people. You want a show whose regular viewing audience approximates as closely as possible your target audience.

Look at the rate columns for the shows that reach your audience. Normally, there are three columns of rates here, going from most to least expensive. These columns might be headed by letters of the alphabet, roman numerals, or the letters F, P, and I. F stands for the fixed rate. This is the highest rate charged for time in that program slot. If you pay that rate, you are guaranteed that your ad will run as specified. P stands for preemptible. This means that, if someone else wants your time slot and is willing to pay the fixed rate, the station will notify you. If you are willing to pay the additional money to guarantee the fixed rate, then your spot will run; otherwise you will be bumped. Immediately preemptible (I) means that the station doesn't even have to notify you about the higher bid for the slot. You will simply have to reschedule your ad.

Discounts for TV Ad Buys. Frequency and dollar discounts are also used in television advertising. The more often you advertise, the lower the charge for each spot. Frequency discounts are usually given for purchasing a certain number of slots within a specific time period—usually a week or a month. Dollar discounts are given when you contract with the station to spend a certain number of dollars with them during the term of the contract.

Package Deals to Watch For. Television stations also offer special package deals to advertisers. Once again, take a careful look at what they offer. A rotating package that guarantees you a few prime-time slots can be good, if the ordinary cost of those prime-time slots makes up for wasted spots in the package. Even then, the prime-time shows that you get rotated into might be wasted if you have a very specific target audience. What happens if you are a lingerie boutique, and your prime time ad runs on Monday night football? You might provoke a lot of fantasies but probably not many purchases (unless it's Valentine's Day).

The moral here, as with all major media, is to be careful (but not afraid) of the package deal. Look carefully to see what you are getting. You can get some great bargains, but not if so many of your spots will be wasted that it would have been cheaper to buy them separately at the regular rate.

Nonproduction Alternatives

Advertisers who simply can't afford production costs still have options. While not as prestigious as a commercial in prime time, all of these alternatives can help to get your name and message before the public.

Cable Channels. Check with your local cable companies. Often they have a shopping channel, weather, and news channel. These channels don't run commercials, as we know them. Instead, your ad appears as a written message that is flashed on the screen for a fixed period of time. These messages are often low priced and involve no production.

Noncommercial Stations. Sponsorship on noncommercial stations is also a production-free alternative. Your message is often simply announced at the opening and close of the show. Sometimes, the station will prepare a slide, featuring your logo, tag line, address, etc.—much like your print ads, except that it will appear on the TV screen in the time slot that you sponsor.

Checklist for Potential TV Time Buyers

TV is a cost-efficient media buy if:

- You have a very wide area of trade.
- You have a small area of trade, with a large and specifically defined target audience that is reached by a particular program or cable channel.
- You have room in your budget for production costs or the potential for having your spots produced by a local college.
- Your budget will allow you to purchase enough spots that each member of your target audience is likely to view your commercial at least three times in a one-week period. (This might entail buying three spots in a single program.)
- Your product or service requires both sight and sound for effective ads.

Checklist for Buying Television Time

- Collect rates from all area stations. Don't forget the cable companies.
- Collect information on production costs from all stations, independent production companies and cable companies. Don't forget to check with local colleges and universities.
- Determine whether you can afford a produced ad, or need a nonproduction alternative.
- For produced ads:
  —Check the rate card to see in what time slots you can afford a minimum of 5 ads (to ensure at least three exposures to your ad).
  —Check with the station to see that program's rating and share for your target audience.
  —Check to make sure there is commercial time available in that time slot.
  —Compare all potential program buys by doing a CPM. Select the program or programs with the best CPM for your target audience.
- For nonproduced ads:
  —Get a program list, along with information on the audience for each program.
  —Find those programs or features that are most compatible with your business, and most viewed by your target audience.
  —Check the availability of time on those programs.
  —Check rates, and choose your best buys by calculating the CPM.

SUMMARY

Your major task, in choosing the most efficient media buy, is to see who the medium reaches and how much waste circulation it has. Calculating the CPM for your target audience can help you to make a cost-efficient media purchase, because it will allow you to make comparisons between the media, and between different options in a single medium.

While all the three major media reach large audiences, careful study of each will allow you to target your message to your audience efficiently.

Buying Magazines, Directories, Direct Mail, Outdoor and Transit Advertising

"THESE ARE VERY SPECIAL ANTIQUES," SAID MAUREEN. "PEOPLE WILL DRIVE UP from the next state to shop here. Our local radio, TV and newspapers don't reach quite far enough." We found Maureen a regional magazine for her ads, plus an insert in a regional newsletter about antiques and auctions.

"I'm a 'keep us in mind' kind of business," said Joe about his monument company. "People don't come browsing. But, when they need me, they have to be able to find my ad. I just can't afford to advertise daily." Maybe not—but a good ad in the phone book will be there when customers need him.

"I don't need to reach everybody. Newspapers and broadcasting are a waste. Only businesses and a few private individuals will call a security guard service," grumbled Wally. We advised him to work out a direct mail campaign.

"My biggest problem is location. People know I'm here, but they have trouble finding me," moaned Gordon. Mary chimed in, "The locals can find me OK, but what I want is the tourist trade." I counseled them to take a look at outdoor and transit advertising.

When we think advertising, we usually think of the big three. But many businesses have specialized needs that can only be solved by specialized ad placement. Other businesses use the mass media successfully, but find that they can profitably supplement their advertising with outdoor, magazines, directories, and direct mail.

Like any media, these have their pitfalls. They are usually not as well understood as mass media advertising, and there is not as much information available about them. Yet, for many businesses, they are indispensable.

Chapter 8 discusses the advantages and disadvantages of each of these media alternatives, tells you how to buy them, and how to use them most effectively.

MAGAZINES

Magazines are probably the most psychographically targeted of all media. If you're a cat lover or a car lover, fashion-conscious or self-conscious, money mad or just plain mad, there is a magazine especially for you. Whoever your target market might be, there are magazines aimed right at them.

Many magazines have a national circulation, many are international. These can be quite expensive but are good choices for anyone with a highly unusual product or service, or for anyone who does business through the mail or UPS. Those with more local areas of trade can often find regional magazines that circulate in a much smaller geographic area and are still targeted to specific demographic and psychographic groups. If your area does not have a city or regional magazine, check to see if the area hotels and motels have tourist publications that feature shops and services. Small, regional airlines often have publications with a limited geographic reach.

In addition, if your product or service is of interest to businesses rather than the general public, there are many trade journals and business publications that can reach your buying public.

Advantages

Specific Readerships. Magazines, as I said, tend to have very specific readerships with very specific interests. A quick check of the advertising in any periodical should tell you exactly who is likely to be reading it and what their concerns are. If your product fits, you have a ready-made, interested audience.

High Reproduction Quality. The reproduction capabilities of magazines tend to be quite high. A picture that might have disappointed you in your newspaper ad will look better here than anywhere else. For detailed photographs and close-ups, the glossy paper and sharp type of the magazine format is unequaled. If you can afford it, magazines often offer the additional possibility of color.

Good Stay-Around Power. Magazines have great stay-around power. Some people hang onto a favorite issue forever, and most leave them lying around the house for at least a week. This increases both readership, since other people will often pick them up and page through, and the frequency with which many people see the ad since many readers refer back to specific articles before they discard the issue.

Regional Targeting. Many national magazines, which would seem to have a huge proportion of waste circulation, are now offering geographic editions, with several pages of regional advertising available to the more local businesses. Therefore, many magazines can offer you the prestige of a national, high-circulation publication, without wasted expense and coverage.

Reader's Service for Mail Order Companies. If you put out a catalogue or brochure, many magazines are now offering a special reader service feature. Advertisers can buy a small listing describing their product or service and stating the price of their brochure. Readers can then order all these brochures directly from the magazine service—which takes a lot of the effort out of mail order for them. This service has dramatically increased reader interest in direct mail catalogues. This can be an effective way to increase your mailing list and your consumer list.

If you are willing to ship your products, this is a good way to increase your market. If you perform a service that can be handled through the mail, you can also use this service. For instance, a Texas company repairs antique stoves. Since this is an unusual service, which many antique stove owners need, many of those owners are willing to ship the stove or the defective part to Texas. The company owners found this market by using reader service cards in a magazine devoted to old house owners.

Disadvantages

With every silver lining, however, there are clouds. Before taking the plunge into magazine advertising, consider these drawbacks.

Waste Circulation. For the very small business, even a very local publication might offer good psychographic targeting but with a lot of waste circulation geographically. National magazines, if they do not have regional inserts, can be ideal in reaching special interest groups who would enjoy your product or service, but if your area of trade is limited to one or two surrounding states then coverage in the other 47 is wasted. Yet no other publication might be as suited to the special, miniature cheetahs you are breeding than this one national publication dedicated to specimen animals.

Need to Plan Ahead. Another major problem with magazines is their inflexibility time-wise. You must have your ad prepared and ready to go to press months ahead of time. Price, general trends, reader interest, and even your business could have changed before the magazine with your ad finally hits the stands.

High Production Costs. Production costs can also run high. Many magazines require camera-ready advertising, which means that you must have a lot of artwork and printing done before you even think about buying space.

High Space Rates. Not surprisingly, space rates for magazines also tend to run high because of their circulation, and high production costs.

Buying Magazine Space

If you have looked at the pros and cons of magazine advertising and decided to take the plunge, then you need to begin gathering information and planning your magazine schedule.

Getting Information. First, find out if there is a periodical suited to your needs. *SRDS*, once again, publishes a directory of magazines, which will give you information on over 1200 consumer magazines in 67 different classifications ranging from general to very specific interest publications. These can give you an idea on audience, geographic coverage, circulation, and the general rate structure. You can also discover whether special geographic inserts are possible. This should help you to limit your choices. *SRDS* also lists 176 different classifications of business periodicals and nearly 250 agricultural publications.

The information in *SRDS* includes circulation figures, both paid and nonpaid; these are often broken down geographically. This makes it possible for you to determine, using the CPM formula, the magazines that will maximize your media dollar. In buying magazine space, the circulation figure is your target audience figure since these periodicals are already so directly targeted to a specific audience.

If you cannot find an *SRDS*, go back to the library and check out the titles indexed in both the *Reader's Guide to Periodical Literature* and *Business Periodicals Index*. These will at least lead you to names of appropriate magazines for your purposes. Your reference librarian should be able to help you locate names, addresses, and phone numbers for these magazines, which you can contact directly.

Figuring the Costs. Periodical space is usually sold in page and fraction of page units: whole page, half page, quarter page, half column, etc. Most rate cards will also translate that into actual size for you so that you will know how big an ad you are buying.

Space buyers receive discounts both on frequency and on quantity. Frequency discounts are based on the number of times you run your ad: one issue would be the base rate, twice might be slightly lower, with the maximum discount if you advertise in every issue. Quantity discount is based on the amount of space you buy during a specified period of time. So even if you advertise in only two issues, but use fairly large ads, you may qualify for a quantity discount.

In typical magazines, premium positions such as the back cover will cost extra. Your ad rate also changes if you go from black and white to color advertising. If you want your ad to *bleed*—that is if you want the color and artwork to extend to the outer boundary of the page rather than staying within the margins, this also adds to your charges.

Many magazines also have special rate structures for different sections of the periodical. If a magazine has a special restaurant or shopping section, the charges might differ from those for a regular display ad in the front of the magazine. Mail order sections also tend to have different rates. Several magazines also feature a classified page, which has its own cost structure.

Fine-Tuning Your Magazine Buys. Do not rely on the *SRDS* alone to determine whether you will buy space in a particular magazine. Write or call the advertising manager listed in *SRDS* for a rate card and information. Although magazines do not offer special packages as often as do radio, TV, and newspaper, they can still supply you with valuable information that will help you in your media decision.

In addition, talking to the advertising manager will tell you whether or not you need to supply camera-ready advertising, or whether the magazine has a staff capable of doing this for you. You will need to be aware of advertising deadlines. Nothing can substitute for going right to the source for your information. Magazines, despite their seemingly high cost, can be the most efficient way of reaching a highly selective target market with an immediate interest in your advertising promise.

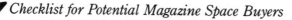

Checklist for Potential Magazine Space Buyers

A magazine can be an efficient media buy if one or more of the following conditions prevail.

- Your product or service appeals to a highly specialized interest group, especially one for which there is not a high demand in your local area.

- Your product or service is one with a very large area of trade, either because people will travel great distances, or because you can use shipping or the mail for delivery.

- Your product or service appeals to a specific interest group for which there is a magazine that offers regional issues somewhat limited to your area of trade.

- Your local market offers a regional magazine with a circulation that at least partially matches your target audience description, and your area of trade is large enough to make the CPMs (see chapter 7) reasonable.

DIRECTORIES

Most businesspeople make sure that they are at least listed in the phone book. But too many of us miss the mark here, either by buying ads that are larger than we need, smaller than our competitor's advertising, or under a misleading category heading. Many of us miss the smaller more specialized directories that could serve our advertising purposes more efficiently.

Advantages

Psychological Rightness. Directories are used by people who have already made up their mind to use a certain service, or buy a certain product. They are simply looking for a place to do this. Therefore, an effective listing in a directory can bring you business directly, because people will see your ad when they are psychologically ready to be persuaded.

Reach and Frequency in One Package. Also, the directory stays around for a long time and gets used often. This means that your ad has a high frequency for users of your product and/or service category. It also has a good reach, going out to all members of a given geographic or psychographic population.

Disadvantages

The advantages of a directory listing are great, but there are also a few drawbacks. Consider carefully whether the disadvantages outweigh the advantages.

Waste Circulation. The reach of a directory can encompass a lot of waste circulation. Your ad for hair replacement in the Yellow Pages is being directed to thousands of people who have full heads of hair. Nevertheless, it is also reaching your target audience. Smaller, more targeted directories can often eliminate a lot of waste circulation.

Display Ads Are Not for Everyone. Also, for many businesses that do not rely heavily on telephone contact anything more than the normal business listing can be a waste of money. Few people, for instance, choose their grocery store through the phone book. For those who do rely on the telephone, however, the competition is right there next to your own ad, fighting for attention. Your advertising needs to be competitive, attention-grabbing, and aimed directly at the needs and questions of the potential customer.

Choosing the Listing Category Can Be Hazardous. Perhaps the major disadvantage, or at least difficulty, of directory advertising lies in choosing the category under which you wish to be listed. If, for instance, you remodel bathrooms and kitchens, you could equally well be listed under kitchen remodeling, bathroom remodeling, and contractors. You will, in this instance, need to buy a display ad rather than a single line listing if you want to hold your own against your competitors. But with a small budget, you can't afford displays on all three pages. It will take some research and good hard thought to decide which listing is your best bet for a display ad, and it will take a bit of budget stretching to make sure that you are at least listed under every logical category where a customer might look for you. Check with your phone company, because often you can get a cross reference rather than paying for three separate ads.

Special Considerations

Too often I have had clients refuse to consider anything but a basic directory listing, because "I've never had any luck with it." Often, this turns out to be because the listing was not placed under the most effective category. Often it was because the client, aghast at the yearly cost of a display ad, settled for a small listing while his bigger competitors used larger, more informative ads. The undecided customer looks to the directory for information and generally calls those businesses that supply information in their directory listings. The trick here is to make sure that your display ad answers the questions that the directory reader is most likely to have. Often, you can get by with a smaller ad, if it gives exactly the right information to the potential customer.

Display, or Line Listing? Some businesses need display advertising. Generally, the higher the cost of your product or service, the more likely the consumer is to want information before they give you a call. Other businesses, however, tend to be spur of-the-moment types of places—places where we go on impulse, or where we give little thought to quality, price, reputation, or atmosphere. Small lunch counters, convenience stores, retailers dealing in low-priced merchandise—few of these will need more than a basic listing, just in case people call with a particular question.

If, however, your product or service depends on reputation, if it is a service that people know very little about, or if your product represents an investment, then you need a larger ad. If yours is a phone-order business, as with florists, if people need to call for appointments or reservations, then your competition will be buying display ads, and so should you.

Types of Listings. Some businesses fall between the extremes. They don't need a big display ad, but a small line listing doesn't seem to be enough, either. If you fall into this category, you might want to consider a **bold listing**, where your company name is printed in darker, heavier type than that of the regular listing.

You can also get extra lines within your regular listing—just enough to describe specifically what you do. A *space listing* will get you a small border around the ad to make it stand out in a column of competitors. This often includes your tag line, and other extra lines, as well as some variations in type size.

Some businesses can take advantage of special categories within a set of listings. All Chevy dealers in a market have the option, for instance, of not only their listing under their business name, but also an additional listing under ''Chevrolet Dealers,'' for potential customers who have a particular car in mind. If you carry a particular name brand of merchandise, check into the possibility for a *trade name* listing.

For some businesses, directories offer a special listing within your category according to geographic location. Restaurant listings are sometimes done according to types of food as well as alphabetically. Check to see if there is some special category for your business that can help you to stand out. Figure 8-1 gives samples of available directory listings.

THE RESTORATION SHOP

FOR A FINE
FURNITURE FACELIFT
Stripping, Refinishing
Reupholstery
Free pickup and delivery

Rte 6, Tnkhanck. 587-5064

1 1/2 " SPACE

THE RESTORATION SHOP

FOR A FINE
FURNITURE FACELIFT
Refinishing, Reupholstery

Rte 6. Tnkhanck. . . . 587-5064

1 INCH SPACE

Trade cross reference listing

FURNITURE , REPAIR
See "Restoration Shop"
under this clasification

Regular listing

Restoration Shop, Rte. 6, Tnknk 587-5064

Semi-Bold listings

RESTORATION SHOP
Rte 6, Tnknck. 587-5064

Bold Listing

RESTORATION SHOP
Rte 6, Tnknck. 587-5064

Extra Line Listing

RESTORATION SHOP
Refinishing, Reupholstery
Rte 6, Tnknck. 597-5064

Fig. 8-1. There are many different types of directory ads. Here are a few of the most affordable offered by the Yellow Pages. Make your choice of ad style based on your budget, the degree to which your business depends on the telephone, and the advertising of your competitors.

Buying Space

If your business is very local, then you need only to buy space in your city directory. However, if your area of trade encompasses several outlying areas, you will want to be listed in several directories. NYPSA (National Yellow Pages Service Association) puts out a Rate and Data publication that covers more than 5,800 telephone directories in the country. Concentrate on those directories that reach areas heavily populated with potential customers. Check to make sure that directories for small towns are not duplicated by a larger, metropolitan directory.

Getting Preliminary Information. You can call the National Yellow Pages office and talk to a representative there if you are dealing with directories in more than one state. Otherwise, your own phone book should lead you to your area's regional sales office.

The Donnelley Directory, which is very much like the Yellow Pages, is gaining great toeholds in many areas as an alternative directory. While its coverage of the population doesn't equal Yellow Pages, in some areas it is the preferred directory.

Rate Structures. Rates will vary heavily from area to area, depending on the population, and on the number of different phone companies that service the area. A basic ad is the least expensive form of listing, usually coming free with your business phone. Rates increase as you add options. Discuss these with the advertising representative.

Checklist for Directory Users

You need only a basic line listing if:

- Yours is a product or service that is usually purchased on impulse, or is low priced, and if your competitors have no more than a line listing.
- If yours is the only business in a certain category, and your product or service is one for which potential consumers do not require additional information and explanations.

You need a larger listing if:

- There is a lot of competition between yours and similar businesses.
- Your competitors use special listings, or display listings.
- Your potential customer demands a reputable business, or looks for information about specific services.
- Your price is high enough that people might want to call for information before they come in.
- You depend on the phone for orders. In this case, you need an ad that is as large as those of your closest competitors.

Specialized Directories

Many professions, associations, and special interest groups publish directories for their members. Directories are getting more popular every year. Now you can buy a special Women's directory, one for businesses specializing in products for old houses, one for businesses with 800 numbers, etc. Many of these directories are listed in two special editions of *SRDS*: *Business Publications* and *Consumer Magazines*. The advertising policy of these might differ greatly from that of the telephone company. Many will accept only standard listings. Some are arranged by business category, while others are strictly alphabetical. Many accept display advertising. Most of these go to highly targeted audiences. The major question for you, as advertiser, is whether the target audience to whom the directory is being sold is also your target audience.

DIRECT MAIL

So far we've looked at advertising media that involved the purchase of either time or space. That cost was controlled by the media. Direct mail, on the other hand, is an advertising expense that remains largely within your own control. You decide what kind of advertising material you want to reach your customer, how much of it to send, and to how many people. The only thing that you cannot change is the cost of postage, although you even have some flexibility here if you opt for second class or bulk mailings. The mailer you choose to send, its quality and complexity, is strictly up to you.

Advantages

Great Targeting. Direct mail is probably the most directly targeted of all advertising media. Some advertising books claim that, with direct mail, there is no waste circulation. This is not strictly true—every mailing list reaches people who are not interested, and even people who won't open your mailer. Nevertheless, there is less waste circulation with direct mail than anywhere else.

Control over Reach. You have total control over who is to receive your advertising message. You can select specific target groups and send each a message suitable for their psychographic characteristics. You can send one message to regular customers and a separate one to those people you hope to lure into your business.

Direct Feedback Opportunities. Direct mail also provides you with a chance to get direct feedback to your advertising message. You can include a coupon or a request form for those who desire further information. This will allow you to gauge the effectiveness of your advertising appeals and the benefits you are featuring. You can even pretest advertising appeals that you hope to use in major media campaigns. Try out one or two benefits that you are thinking of using as your major campaign theme in direct mail campaigns. The one that draws the best response is probably your best bet.

Protection from Competitors. Direct mail is also a very private medium. As long as no one from your competition is on your mailing list, your campaign ideas and promises remain safe from their prying eyes. This will make it more difficult for the competition to position itself against you.

No Limitations on Length. One of the major advantages of direct mail is the possibility for complicated messages. The length of the mailer is up to you. While newspaper, radio, and TV space and time characteristics necessarily limit the amount of information you can cram into a single advertising message, with direct mail the amount of information you include is only limited by post office weight specifications. If you have a complicated product, or need to get a lot of information across to an uninformed public about yourself, this is the place.

Disadvantages

High CPM. If you try to figure out the CPM for direct mail, you might go into shock. Whereas you can get a good reach and frequency on radio for about $4 per thousand people, the equivalent direct mail CPM might be $100 or more. This is not as extravagant as it seems, however. As long as you have a good mailing list, the control you exercise over circulation and creativity makes direct mail a more efficient way to communicate.

Unreliable Mailing Lists. Mailing lists can be a problem. Many lists are compiled by using the names of people who have ordered specific products through the mail. I am on a list of direct mail targeted to senior citizens, even though I have just turned 40. I was placed on that list because of a gift I ordered for my father-in-law. The list-compiler has no way of knowing this. Some waste circulation cannot be avoided.

"Junk Mail" Prejudices. Perhaps the most difficult problem with this advertising method is that of getting people to open their mailers in the first place. Unfortunately, the affectionate name for direct mail is "junk mail." Many people simply toss this away without a second glance, especially if there is nothing on the envelope to indicate that the contents might be of special interest to them.

Nevertheless, direct mail has been enjoying unprecedented success in the past few years. Despite the "junk mail" nickname, people have begun to seek out direct mail packages that will give them information on products and services which interest them. Check the back of many current magazines, and you will see a reader service card bound into the pages. This card allows the reader to use the magazine as a clearing house where they can request mail information from hundreds of different companies. And they do.

The main thing is—if your direct mail piece offers information to people who are interested in your product or service, they will read it and perhaps respond to it. Since this is the one advertising medium that you can tailor precisely to your budget restrictions, for many small businesspeople, direct mail cannot be overlooked.

The Mailing Piece

Direct mail pieces range from the postcard to the elaborate, four-color, glossy-paged catalogue and a dozen in-between options. The choice is up to you. You can choose to simply write a letter to interested target customers, informing them of your service, hours, reputation, and anything else you deem essential. You can enclose samples, coupons, reply cards, photographs—whatever seems useful in provoking a response.

Multipiece Packages. Direct mail research has shown that for most product advertising literature, the response rate goes up with the number of separate pieces included in the envelope. That's why, if you get a piece trying to get you to subscribe to a new magazine, you will find inside a letter, a fold-out brochure showing pages and features from past issues, a reply postcard, and usually, a sealed packet that says, "Don't open this unless you intend to say no." Each piece is designed to interest you in subscribing to that magazine. Every one takes a slightly different approach. If one piece doesn't grab you, the next one might. According to all the current research, this works.

Multipiece packaging, however, is expensive. Printing costs alone can run high, especially if you use the four-color attention-grabbing printing that these professional packages use. This doesn't even take into account the time spent stuffing the envelopes.

Self-Mailers. Many advertisers have had success with a *self-mailer*—a brochure that is folded so that one portion of the back is used for the address of the intended recipient. These brochures can be multicolored, or simply one color; they can use pictures, illustrations, or simple, attractively laid out type. They can include inserts, reply cards, and coupons. Because the printing is simple and the folding can be done by machine, the expense for these self-mailers can be low. Plus, you save the cost of envelopes, and the time needed to stuff them. In addition, because there is no envelope to open, the self-mailer often exposes the recipient to at least part of your advertising message, even if they never unfold your entire brochure.

Postcards. The extremely low cost variation of this is the postcard. Postage is low, there is no envelope to stuff, and printing costs are minimal. Your recipient will have to read your advertising message if only to discover whether to throw it away. This method, of course, doesn't allow you to include a lot of complicated information or selling tactics. But to announce a sale, grand opening, or any special event you might be running, this is by far the most cost-efficient way to go.

Coupon Cards. Postcards are also useful as coupons. The customer can be asked to bring the card into the store for a discount, a free gift, or a free demonstration. The advantage to the coupon offer is that it allows you to collect the actual responses in order to compile a more targeted mailing list. Anyone who comes in with a card is a potentially regular customer, who will take notice of any of your future mailings. Coupons also might be just the impetus needed to push a potentially interested customer into one who makes the effort to come in to your business before the coupon expires.

Catalogue and Price Lists. A final way to use the mails for advertising is with a catalogue or price list. A new restaurant, for instance, could send out sample menus. This lets people know what you have to offer and what your price range is. A stereo shop could make up a black and white brochure including many of the more popular pieces of equipment and parts that they stock. Small plant nurseries often have great luck with simple typed lists of their annual and perennial plants, along with prices. The interested browser, if they can see for themselves that you have something that they want, just might give you a call.

Getting People to Open the Envelope

If you choose to go with a mailer in an envelope, you have to do something to make sure that people will open it. The direct mail industry has resorted to hundreds of ploys in the past, a few of which have worked well over time. A few seemingly clever tricks have bombed dramatically.

In the past two years, mailers have attempted to scare you into opening the envelope by disguising themselves as telegrams or Federal Express mailing. This backfired because people felt cheated by the time they ripped open the envelope and found themselves faced with a mere ad. If you want to avoid making your target audience angry, you need to be honest with your envelope strategy.

Plain Envelopes. Many mailers have great success with the plain envelope. A typed return address and a handwritten or typed address often makes people suspect that this might be something personal. We have learned that this type of envelope often encloses advertising messages, but curiosity often makes us open it anyway, just to make sure.

Odd-Shaped Enclosures. Another good way to get that envelope opened is to include some object inside. Maybe it's only a small pencil or a penny, but we can't resist opening packages to see what's there.

Envelope Ads. A final, worthy way to attract attention is to use the envelope itself as an ad. If your mailer is reaching a carefully selected target audience, then it is reaching people who will want the information you have to offer. If your dress shop is offering a giant, end of the year sale, then an announcement on the envelope will ensure that fashion-conscious consumers will look inside to see what you have to offer. Maybe they won't, but often the advertising on the outside of the envelope will be enough to get your point across.

The Mailing List

The whole success of your direct mail campaign depends on your mailing list. You cannot afford to send pieces out at random, hoping that some of them will hit an interested customer.

List Brokers. The most common way to acquire a mailing list is through a list broker. A check through your phone book should show several companies that rent out mailing lists. These are usually segmented in many ways: geographic, demographic, and psychographic. Often, business magazines like *Entrepreneur* can lead you to catalogues of lists available through national brokers.

The brokers do not own these lists. Instead, they act as agents for many large companies who will rent out their personal lists for a fee. You will be charged a certain dollar amount per thousand names on the list. For instance, if you have a camping goods store, you might want to rent the list for an outdoor magazine, because its subscribers are clearly interested in the kind of goods you sell. You would not, however, want the national list, because this involves waste circulation. Instead, you might buy the portion of the list, in units of 1000, drawn from your area of trade.

As a Rolls Royce dealer, you might choose the mailing list of a company like Tiffany's, which caters to a high-income clientele. You might ask them to break down the list to only those people within a certain income bracket in your area. As an appliance repairman, you might want to get a list of people who have bought appliances in the past five years. And so on.

The thing to remember with a list broker is that you are only renting the list. You can rent for one-time use or multiple uses, but you cannot photocopy the list and go on using it beyond the terms of the contract. Every rented list contains one or two "dummy" names. Anything mailed to these dummy names goes to an address maintained by the list broker. So if you try to cheat with your rented list, you will probably be caught and charged—or even prosecuted.

One good source for mailing lists is SRDS. They put out a *Direct Mail List Rates and Data* catalogue twice a year, which includes sources for lists, CPM, categories and breakdowns of lists, etc.—about 21,000 lists in all.

Direct Buy from Compatible Business. Instead of going to a list broker, you might be able to do business directly. If you know of a company whose list is likely to be compatible with your target audience needs, you can often arrange to rent or buy the list from that company. Larger companies, especially magazines, usually rent their lists broken down into very specialized classifications such as occupation, hobbies, income, style of furnishings, etc. Small, local companies probably do not have these resources, but they do offer localized lists that might be precisely suited to your needs.

Sometimes you can form a co-op with other businesses in your area. If you have a merchants association, for instance, you might propose that businesses with similar audiences and clientele share their lists.

Compile-Your-Own Lists. On a less expensive but more time-consuming scale, you can compile your own lists. A bridal consultant, for instance, might check the newspaper daily for the names of those who apply for a marriage license. Furniture stores might use the list of people who are moving in the area. Cemetery and monument companies often use the death notices for their mailing list source. The telephone book, real estate transaction records, and the Department of Motor Vehicles can all be good sources for your personal lists.

Another good source is your own sales records. You will usually have the names and addresses of all charge customers. You can get names from the upper left-hand corner of all checks that you accept. Many businesses make it a practice to ask for the name and address of all customers, even if they pay in cash. Some businesses leave out a guest book for customers to sign or leave postcards at the cash register for those who wish to be on the regular mailing list.

This list, since it consists of people who have already patronized your business, is not useful for extending your target market. It can, however, be helpful in creating repeat customers and ensuring their loyalty.

Special Word about Mailing Cost

If you are planning to do a lot of mailings, then you would do well to check with your post office about either a second class or bulk mailing permit. These are purchased on an annual basis for a small fee. If, however, you are only doing a small mailing to a select group of customers, it may be more cost efficient to go ahead and use first class mail. For one thing, research has shown that envelopes with first class postage get opened more often than those with metered or second class postage. For another, the additional cost of the first class stamps for a small mailing may be less than the cost of the permit. Check your costs, and make sure that you really need a permit. Your local post office will be glad to provide you with information.

Checklist for Direct Mail Users

- If you are trying to maintain the loyalty of current customers, or to encourage them to use your business more often, you can get a list by:
  —Marking down return addresses on all checks.
  —Noting addresses on all charge orders.
  —Having customers sign a guest book.
  —Leaving postcards or slips of paper by the register that customers can use to request inclusion on your list.
- If you are trying to attract new customers you can:
  —Rent a list from a list broker.
  —Rent or purchase a list from a noncompeting business with a similar target audience.
  —Compile your own list from public records: newspaper listings of realty transactions, birth, wedding, and death notices, lists from the Department of Motor Vehicles, etc.
- Check to see if your list is the best possible for your money.
  —Do people on the list live mostly within your area of trade?
  —Do they come from the right income level?
  —Does the type of list you are considering indicate that these people have interests similar to those in your current market?
  —Can you determine from the list description whether these names are for people with a lifestyle similar to those of your desired target audience?
  —Can the list be broken down into segments small enough to match your requirements? If not (if you require fewer than the 1000 names that are the usual minimum), is the list so targeted that the cost of the names is worthwhile?
- Does the message that I need to communicate require a lot of explanation? Pictures? Color? Have I checked area printers to see what this type of package might cost to produce?
- Can my message be communicated on a single folded page, or will I need inserts, and therefore envelopes? Have I checked with the printer for costs on these?
- Am I making an offer that can be communicated on a postcard? Would this be the most efficient way to reach my customers? Have I checked printing costs?
- Is my mailing large enough to justify getting a bulk or second class mailing permit? Will I be sending out more than one mailing this year? Have I checked with the post office, explaining the type of piece that I am mailing, to see which would be my most cost-efficient way to mail?

OUTDOOR ADVERTISING

There is a wicked rumor that people don't read billboards. This is demonstrably untrue. Several years ago, an outdoor advertising company tried an experiment. They first did a survey to determine how many people could name the current Miss America. Few could. They then mounted billboards across the country with Miss America's name and picture. Nothing more. While many people later surveyed still claimed that they never read billboards, the number of people who now knew Miss America's real name had risen dramatically.

Advantages

Outdoor advertising is an effective tool for getting your name out in front of the public. It stimulates awareness and has many advantages for a small business advertiser.

Very Low CPM. Outdoor advertising has the lowest CPM of all the major media. You can reach a large percentage of the population with a single ad, and you can reach them several times. Most people drive the same routes repeatedly, and therefore see the same billboards day after day.

Flexibility. Outdoor advertising is also extremely flexible. Depending on your contract with the outdoor advertising company, your ad can be moved to reach differing segments of the population; it can be changed seasonally to meet new advertising needs.

If you have a location problem, especially if you are hard to find, outdoor advertising is especially valuable. It can be placed in locations that will help to direct people to your place of business. The ad itself can incorporate directional arrows or directions.

Mandatory Exposure. One great advantage to outdoor advertising is that it requires no special effort by the consumer. They do not have to turn on the TV or radio, or buy a periodical in order to be exposed to your message. As long as they are out in public, on their way to work or the store, they cannot help being exposed to your message.

Visual Impact. Outdoor advertising is extremely visual. It can help to create a graphic image of your company, and to establish your logo and colors in the minds of the public.

Disadvantages

Outdoor advertising almost sounds too good to be true, when you look at its advantages. Maybe it is. Look at its disadvantages and consider how severe these are when applied to your own particular advertising objectives.

Not a Selling Medium. As visual as it is, outdoor advertising cannot be used to really sell a product or service. Because the audience is usually traveling by your ad at 25 miles an hour or more, they do not have time to read complicated messages. Therefore, outdoor advertising is better for reminder ads or for creating awareness than it is for persuading people to buy.

Imprecise Demographic Targeting. In addition, outdoor advertising is not very targeted, at least demographically. Your ad will reach not only your specific target, but anyone else who happens to drive along the road where your sign is. Therefore, you are likely to pay for a lot of waste circulation.

An Environmental Issue. Finally, for some people, outdoor advertising creates a psychological problem. Many people are opposed to outdoor advertising as an unsightly scar upon the landscape. This feeling leads some to boycott any advertisers who resort to outdoor ads, simply on principle.

Forms of Outdoor Advertising

While many signs are posted outdoors, they are not necessarily outdoor advertising. Your store sign, directional signs posted on utility poles, etc., will be considered in the next chapter. Outdoor advertising is limited to a few, very traditional forms: the poster, the bulletin, and the spectacular.

Posters. Posters come in two basic sizes. The first, the familiar large billboard along the highway, is called a 30-sheet poster. This is the largest available, and gives you an area for advertising copy that measures 259 inches long and 115 inches high.

A 24-sheet poster has a copy area of 104 inches high by 234 inches long. These are measured in sheets, because outdoor billboards actually consist of several printed sheets of paper that, when pasted together, make up the complete ad. New printing technology has reduced the actual number of sheets that make up these boards, so that a 30-sheet poster actually has 14 sheets, and a 24-sheet poster is made up of only 10; the industry, however, continues to use the old terminology.

A junior panel, also known as an eight-sheet panel, measures 8 feet 7 inches high by 4 feet 10 inches wide, and is made up of three sheets. The junior poster is most likely to be found around suburban malls and in urban areas with limited space, especially near neighborhood stores and parking lots. Many companies, however, also make these available for urban highways, and they provide a less expensive alternative for the small business.

Bulletins. A bulletin is a permanent billboard. In other words, it is a board that is painted, rather than one made up of pasted sheets. The ad is painted onto movable sections and assembled on site. Because each board has been painted rather than printed, this is a much more expensive alternative for the advertiser.

However, these boards do have advantages. While the sheets on a poster can be damaged by weather or vandals, painted bulletins rarely are affected. The piece-by-piece assembly means that the bulletin can be taken apart and moved to different locations during the contract period, thus letting you reach more people with a single ad. Painted bulletins can often be embellished with cut-outs or special effects.

Spectaculars. The final form of outdoor advertising is the spectacular. These are usually found only in heavily populated urban areas, because they are too expensive to be cost-effective unless you are reaching a tremendous number of people. Spectaculars have no standardized size or shape; they could resemble giant tires or hot air balloons; they make use of very elaborate lighting and special effects.

Outdoor Advertising Research

Outdoor advertising is sold by *showings*. A showing of 25 means that 25 percent of the population will be exposed to your ad. A newer term, replacing showings in many companies, is *Gross Rating Point* (GRP). Since a rating point is equal to one percent of the population, a gross rating point measures the percentage of the total population reached by your outdoor advertising schedule.

If you wanted to reach 50 percent of the total population with your message, you would contract with an outdoor advertising company for 50 GRPs. How many posters this would require depends on where you are advertising. In a small, rural area, this might require only one poster; in New York City, it might require several hundred.

Many companies, especially the large, national firms like Patrick and Gannett, can provide specialized research that can give a more demographically oriented breakdown of the population. This will allow you to target your message to the high-income section of the population, to a certain ethnic group, and so forth.

Research that determines how many posters you need is based on data from the Traffic Audit Bureau. They issue a publication, *The Audited Circulation Value of Outdoor Advertising*, which gives the average traffic count for every area of the country. These are then converted into figures that show how many potential viewers will see a particular billboard. These figures determine the cost of a billboard in a particular location.

Choosing a Site

Consider where the most effective placement for your message will be. Which side of the street you place your ad on can make a difference in its success. If you are located in the downtown area of a city, for instance, you will want your advertising located on the side of the highway facing motorists going toward downtown. For these drivers to see your poster on the way home is almost self-defeating.

You will also want to check the distance at which your chosen board can be seen and read. If your ad is placed right around a bend in the road, the driver will have little time to see and absorb your message before it is gone.

Although, especially with tourism-based businesses, placement on a major highway is ideal, you might want to consider a site on a busy major road with traffic lights. The slower the traffic, the more time it has to see the message. A poster located by a traffic light at a major intersection can provide lots of reading and absorbing time.

Will you need lighting? If you are advertising in the summer, you might not need this added expense, because of the long daylight hours. In the winter, however, short days plunge many billboards into darkness before they have achieved their full reach potential. If your location is well lit, this might not be a problem. On a stretch of road without streetlights, however, you might need to get illuminated billboards.

Buying Outdoor Advertising

To contract for outdoor advertising, you will have to go through your local outdoor advertising plant. These plants might be very local in nature, servicing only your community. They might also be branches of major outdoor advertising firms. If your message is one that needs to be located in many areas of the state, or country, then you will want to contact a national firm; otherwise a local company might be more cost effective.

Gathering Information. Plant operators either own or lease property in each community that has legal clearance for the erection of outdoor advertising media. Every firm owns different locations; if you have a particular location in mind, then contact the firm that handles that space. The name of the advertising company can usually be found underneath the poster or bulletin. If you are uncertain, contact all outdoor advertising firms in your area. Rates from company to company can vary vastly.

Contact the firm, and find out what areas they have available. They will provide you with a map showing the various locations, and the GRPs for each location. Before settling on a particular site, go out and look at it for yourself. Make sure that your ad will not be hidden behind trees, buildings, or other billboards.

Signing a Contract. You will be asked to contract for your outdoor advertising. These contracts can take many forms. Your shortest available term is usually one month. Many contracts are taken for three months, with an agreement that the poster will be relocated each month. Painted bulletins, which usually have a one-year contract, sometimes provide for seasonal repainting—at this time you often can change the message on the bulletin.

Costs. How much should you pay? Well, the cost of your billboard is affected by many factors: the traffic count in the location you select, the size of the poster, the lighting, and the amount of rental that the advertising company pays to lease the property on which your ad is to be located. In addition, you will be paying a production fee for the manufacture of your printed sheets and their paste-up. The cost-effectiveness of the advertising site can be determined by using a CPM calculation. As for production costs, you will just have to shop around to see if the rates you are quoted are in line with what other companies charge.

Comparison Shopping. Sometimes, it pays to shop around. If you find several suitable locations for your advertising message, leased by several companies, contact all of them to get your best price. The cost of a poster or bulletin can vary widely, depending on the size of the firm, their skill in negotiating land rental fees, and their own operating costs.

Checklist for Users of Outdoor Advertising

- Is my advertising objective to create awareness, reach a new target audience, or to overcome a location problem?
- Can my message be communicated quickly enough to be readable in a fast-moving car?
- Can much of my target audience be reached by placing outdoor advertising in one or two specific locations?
- Are most of my customers environmentalists who might be offended by billboards on their landscape? If so, I might want to consider some other way of reaching them.
- Are there outdoor advertising sites available in the area in which I want to advertise?
- Would it be best to reach my customers with my message on the way to work? On their way downtown? On their morning, or afternoon drive?
- Will people need to see my message after dark in order for it to work for me? Are there available sites with street lights, or must I pay for a lighted sign?
- Do I need more locations than I can afford in a single month? Would a painted sign, movable by the month, suit my needs?
- Do I need a full-sized board, or can I be effective with a smaller one?
- Would my best location for advertising be in a crowded area where small movable boards would be most effective?
- Having looked at the locations and size of board that suit my needs, have I contacted several companies to see whose rates are most advantageous to me?

TRANSIT ADVERTISING

Transit advertising is another very visual form of media. The signs on the backs and sides of buses, the posters we read when traveling in a bus or train, and the displays we see in airports, train stations, and bus terminals are all forms of transit advertising. The traditional categories for this form of advertising are: exterior transit, interior transit, and station posters.

Exterior Transit

This refers most often to signs that are found on the sides and fronts of buses. In some areas, taxi cabs also carry some form of exterior transit advertising.

Advantages and Disadvantages. The main advantage to this type of ad is that, unlike outdoor advertising, where the viewer must drive to the ad, exterior transit travels past the viewer. These types of displays generally have a very high reach and frequency for a very low CPM. Unfortunately, the research for exterior transit advertising is not very precise; we know where a bus is likely to travel, which will allow an advertiser to somewhat limit the area of coverage and eliminate waste circulation. We don't have any method, however, of breaking down the reach of exterior transit advertising demographically.

Placement. You have three choices in placing a bus ad: back, sides, and front. Logically, front and side positions carry a greater reach. Front posters will be seen by all traffic headed in the opposite direction. Posters on the side of the bus are seen by street traffic and all traffic on the cross streets intersecting the bus route. The poster on the back of the bus, while it is seen very well and for long periods of time by its audience, is limited to those cars that are stuck behind the bus. While this might amount to a large number of drivers, the actual reach is generally lower than for the other positions.

Buying Exterior Space. Exterior space is sold by the showing or GRP. Therefore, buses traveling through heavily populated areas will be more costly than those in rural areas.

An advertiser can often buy only certain routes. This can help to eliminate waste circulation. For instance, if your business appeals to a high-income audience, then buying only the bus routes that run through the areas of town most densely populated with these people will help you to target your message. If yours is a downtown business, you might want to buy only those routes that end up in the center city. If your business is located along a bus route, you might want to purchase only that route.

Production Considerations. Like the outdoor companies, exterior transit companies can provide you with help for your artwork. Remember to keep your ads consistent with anything you are doing in other media. Your bus cards must have the same format and theme as any other print advertising you are using; use the same type styles, the same style of artwork, and the same colors.

Interior Transit

Interior transit advertising gives you a captive audience. Your ad, posted inside a bus or train, is often the only thing that the passengers have to look at for the duration of their ride. This is an excellent opportunity to sell. Because the viewer has the opportunity to study your ad, you can use a fairly complicated message. You can also attach coupons, fliers, or reply cards for interested travelers.

Targeting. Interior transit is an excellent way to reach the businessperson. Many people commute to work rather than fight city traffic. In metropolitan areas, the commuter trains are heavily populated with upscale workers—especially the new, executive woman.

Frequency. The frequency for this medium is excellent, as is the CPM. In addition, interior transit advertising is a good way to reach audiences who are not heavy users of other media. If you are also using newspaper as part of your media plan, you have a possibility of reaching the same commuter twice—once in the newspaper they read on board, then immediately afterward with your interior poster. If your car card includes a *take one*—a tear-off reply card or coupon—you can greatly maximize the impact of your advertising message.

Disadvantages. Of course, with this form of media, you are missing all people who do not ride mass transit. In small towns with no real traffic problems, this means that you are mainly reaching senior citizens, young teens, and people who don't drive—which can be great, if these are part of your target audience. If not, despite the low cost, this form of advertising can be inefficient. In large cities, where many people prefer mass transit to being stuck for hours in traffic, this can be a beneficial way to increase reach and frequency with a low budget.

Buying Interior Transit Space. As with exterior transit, you might buy a whole run (all the buses and trains in service), a half run, or a quarter run. If you are buying less than a full run, ask to see which lines will be included in your contract. Try to choose those routes that best match your area of trade.

Station Posters and Displays

Station posters are those cheerful ads that greet us as soon as we step into the airport or off the bus or train. These are especially useful media for the restaurant or hotel owner, or for businesses that cater to tourists.

How it Works. While the average traveler might not pay much attention to your poster while in the station, there is a later, psychological impact. When that same traveler gets to his or her hotel, and opens the phone book or the local tourism magazine to find a place to eat or shop, they might run across your listing. For some reason, your name seems familiar to that person. Almost inevitably, this rings a little bell in people. "I've heard of that," they say to themselves, although they're not sure where. Inevitably, the next line comes. "It must be good." The universal tendency, if we cannot trace our knowledge of a place to a specific advertising message, is to assume that some friend or colleague has recommended the place.

Target Audiences. Remember, though, that not everyone who gets off a plane or bus is a tourist. Many are residents returning home. Many people might be coming into town on business or to visit family. Many might be taking advantage of medical facilities or educational institutions. Before considering a station poster, determine who uses your station, and for what purpose. If the most common type of traveler is also someone who might be a good customer for you, then station posters are an economical advertising investment, especially when supplemented with newspaper and directory advertising.

Production Specifications. Station posters come in many sizes, from a single panel 46 inches by 30 inches, through an 84 by 42 inch, three-sheet poster. They are much like outdoor advertising, in that people are likely to be passing them in a great hurry. Therefore, they must be graphically simple. They are primarily recognition-creating media, rather than persuasive messages.

Placement. Location is a factor here. A poster located near the ticket desk, or around the baggage collection area will get more attention than those on corridors full of bustling travelers running to catch a plane.

Station posters must be contracted for with the transit company. You are generally responsible for supplying the posters; you merely lease space from the company.

If you are interested in any of these forms of transit advertising, you can usually find the companies with which you need to deal in your phone directory under "advertising." Call each company and get rate information. When you get to the chapter on media scheduling (chapter 10) you will save a lot of time and trouble by having rate cards in hand, and CPMs all figured.

SUMMARY

There are many options for the small business advertiser, aside from the prominent mass media. Magazines and direct mail provide excellent opportunities to reach a very specific target audience. Directories allow head-on targeting against the competition, while providing good reach and frequency and magnificent stay-around power. Outdoor and transit advertising provide excellent reach and frequency for a very low cost per thousand.

The challenge, in using these various media, is to maintain advertising consistency while meeting your advertising objectives. All your advertising needs to be thematically and graphically consistent. Having achieved this, your choice is then determined by your objectives. Outdoor and transit advertising are excellent for advertisers who need to achieve a high reach; it familiarizes us with your name and purpose. Magazines also achieve a good reach within a very specifically defined target audience.

Directory advertising rarely reaches consumers until they are actively seeking out a particular product or service; this form of advertising is crucial if your business is one where people are making a large investment in either time or money, or if your product or service is one about which the public is likely to have a lot of questions.

Direct mail is perhaps the most targeted of all media. Despite its high CPM, this form of advertising can stimulate a direct response from the consumer, and can be used as a research tool to gauge the success of different advertising approaches you might be considering for the mass media. Since there is no real restriction on the length of message in direct mail, this media can be used to explain complicated techniques, products, or services to the consumer.

9

Using Nontraditional
Forms of Media

"SURE. WE CAN SEND SOMEONE OVER TOMORROW. DON'T WORRY, MR. Marquand—we'll have your place in shape in time for the party. And can I ask you how you heard about us?"

"Funny thing," replied Marquand. "It was at the Little League field. My wife kept nagging me about this party when the centerfielder caught a long fly— and right behind him was your ad, right on the fence."

Vi was delighted. She had only bought that sign because she believed in Little League and wanted to support it. This was the fourth customer it had brought her.

Sometimes ads come in strange sizes and shapes. They show up on bulletin boards or get handed to us as we walk down the street. They walk before us on the backs of T-shirts or pop up on a potholder. They amble down the street on shopping bags or descend from the heavens on balloons.

Miniature media are some of the most misunderstood forms of advertising. Many merchants invest large sums of money on specialty items—pens, calendars, and notepads—without knowing how to best distribute them. Too often, the minuscule budget means that a business owner resorts to handing out flyers on the street, and then can't understand why no one will take them. How many of us ignore the earnest high school student who wants us to buy an ad in the school paper, or the volunteer worker who thinks we need space in the symphony program? It's easy to fail with these media, if we don't understand how they work. It's just as easy to succeed, with a little background strategy.

Chapter 9 examines the many forms of miniature media, their advantages and disadvantages, and the best ways to select and distribute them. Often overlooked forms of advertising—your own sign, shopping bags, and stationery—are examined, as well as some very nontraditional ways to advertise that will not only attract public notice, but maybe garner you some free publicity.

Big time advertising books rarely talk about these small forms of media. Some of them are so basic to your business that most of the books don't even think of them as advertising. These include media like your store sign, any trucks or cars you have on the road, and your stationery, business cards, shopping bags, and boxes. (These, incidentally, are not things that come out of your advertising budget. They do, however, help to bolster your advertising appeal.) Others are simply forms of media that have low circulation, and generally low cost—too low for the average ad agency to be bothered with.

Most businesses would love to be able to launch a full-scale mass media campaign, using the media discussed in the last two chapters. Some businesses, however, are simply under-capitalized in the beginning. As much as you know that you have to advertise to get customers in the door, sometimes the money for radio or newspaper just isn't there.

Other times, we can afford to schedule a traditional media campaign, but want something more—some neat form of continuous advertising that will continue to work for us even during those periods when our schedule is light. If you fit into any of these categories, this chapter is for you.

MEDIA YOU ALREADY HAVE

Every business has certain equipment that simply goes along with the business. Most of us either send bills or give sales receipts. Most of us have business cards. If we sell a product, we either bag it or box it. Several types of businesses either travel by truck, or use a delivery car. And most of us, of course, work out of some kind of building, which has a sign to show that we are there, doing business. Any or all these necessities can do double duty for us, not only performing their basic function, but also acting as advertising.

Your Sign

Your sign, for instance, is by far your most important investment. It's a one-time cost, and it might be expensive, but it works hard. The look of your sign gives the public clues about your personality, and the type of business you do. It helps people to locate you, or simply creates awareness in those who walk or drive by. In other words, it functions as advertising; it projects an image, creates awareness, and hopefully gives your target audience an impetus to come in and see what you have to offer.

Your sign is important. It is a part of your campaign. The lettering you choose should be the lettering you use in your logo. The colors you choose should be the ones that appear in any color advertising you do and in your decor. Those same colors should provide strong hints about the paper and ink you use for business cards, trucks, bags, boxes, and anything else you do. Your sign sets the tone and image for all your other advertising.

Changeable Signs

If you can, and if zoning laws permit it, take advantage of a second sign—one that changes. People pass your sign daily, which makes it a great high-frequency medium. Like all things that we see every day, we soon forget to notice it. Signs that change—those that have a space for daily specials, for witty sayings, for community service announcements, for a time and temperature reading—continue to get noticed. We make the effort to look at them and see what's new.

Maybe you can't afford the digital clock and temperature read-out that the banks use. You might be able to use one of those new changeable signs that look like neon. Or even one of those tacky yellow-lighted signs. Sure, they're ugly, but they work. That's why we keep seeing them. Use your sign to notify the public about different features of your business, of special events, or key benefits. Think of it as a three-dimensional print ad. Once you have paid for the sign, your only investment is in the time it takes to post the information. One of these days, the information you post is going to be that last lure that finally entices the customer in.

Your Building

Your building, too, functions as advertising. Its style, the way that you arrange your windows, the degree of cleanliness, and state of repair—all these give people ideas about who you are and what kind of place you are likely to be. Is your door clearly marked with your logo? If you have awnings, can they also become little ads? Is your window clean, and does it show us something persuasively inviting? Can passers-by see your sign?

Your building, in itself, can be a sign. If you have a clear side, facing a parking lot or corner, you can paint that side as though it were a permanent billboard. This not only identifies your building to pedestrians who are looking for you, but becomes such a prominent feature as we drive down the street that it has the same impact on people as the billboard—but at a one-time cost to yourself.

If there is a college or university in your area, check with their art departments. Often you can find talented students who will paint these signs for you very reasonably. Sometimes trade schools and technological institutes also have students who can help you, at far below the cost of hiring a professional.

Company Vehicles

Another way to get your name around town is to make sure that your company logo and tag line are prominently painted on any cars or trucks that you use for business. These vehicles should all have one color scheme—your company colors. Treat them like transit advertising. You eliminate waste circulation, since you're using the vehicles within your area of trade. Once again, once your ad is painted onto the door, it belongs to you. No more space rental fees.

Business Stationery

Stationery, too, should work for you. (See Fig. 9-1.) It's tempting to go for generic bags, boxes, receipt pads, etc. But why not go to the printer, and have him put your logo, name, and address on all of them? The additional expense is not high, considering that customers will carry those bags and boxes down the street, showing your name to all who walk by. Portable advertising like this helps to make your name familiar. In the end, it pays for itself.

With Compliments

finishing touches for your wardrobe

1151 Grove Street , Clarks Summit   18410   587-1414

Fig. 9-1. Your letterhead should wear your logo as well as tag line.

Figure 9-2 shows a shopping bag that simply uses the logo for its design. Because the logo is so visible, it is also an effective ad.

One inexpensive way to customize your bags, boxes, and stationery is to have a print shop make stick-on labels for you, using your logotype and colors. These can then be gummed onto any blank paper materials that you would like to have personalized. If you sometimes use very large bags and boxes and other times very small ones, have the labels made in two sizes.

If there is any place to have your name embossed, painted or printed, do it. The more we see it, the more familiar it becomes. The more familiar you become, the more likely we are to think of you when we are in the market for your product or service.

Checklist for Maximizing the Impact of Media You Already Have

- Is my business name printed on anything—signs, bags, etc., in something other than my logotype and colors? Check prices to see about having these changed.
- Are there places where I could use my logo, but am not? Check prices to see about having these personalized. Check into labels that can cover old, inaccurate printing and personalize new blank items.

- Is my sign working for me? Can it easily be seen from the street? Is it using my company logo and colors?
- Can I take advantage of a changeable sign to inform passers-by about specials, changes, or just to give them friendly messages?

VERY SMALL BUDGET MEDIA

Sometimes, there's no money in the till for mass media advertising. Or sometimes, we need just a little more impact than our mass media ads are giving us. That's when we turn to leaflets, flyers, and bulletin board cards.

Leaflets and Flyers

Many a small business has relied on the leaflet or handout to call attention to itself. You've been there—walking down the street minding your own business, until some guy on the corner thrusts a paper into your hands, or panicking at

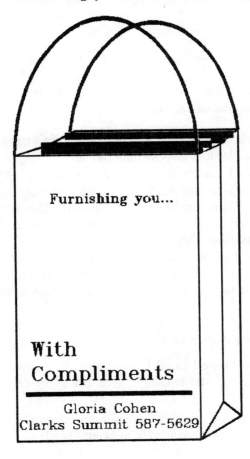

Furnishing you...

With Compliments

Gloria Cohen
Clarks Summit 587-5629

Fig. 9-2. Your shopping bag will work as a traveling ad, if it wears your logo.

what you think is a traffic ticket stuck under your windshield, only to find out that it's a flyer for some local business.

Most of us, annoyed or busy, thrust these away—usually unread. Yet businesses continue to use flyers, and have since ancient times. They must work—at least sometimes. Think back to those few flyers that you did read. What made them different?

Factors that Help Acceptance. There are a few small principles that tend to work. One is locale. If you are in a tourism center and many of the passers-by are tourists, unfamiliar with the area, then they can and will accept handouts, if only to make sure that they don't miss something interesting.

Your chances of success are better if your distributors look wholesome and all-American. Too many of us are wary of the handout these days, after spending the '60s besieged by tracts from Hari Krishna and other cults. There is, too, a reluctance in us, based on our mother's admonition never to take candy from strangers. So, if you hire someone to pass out flyers on the street, make sure they look like someone we wouldn't hesitate to nod and say hello to.

Postcard-sized flyers, on heavy stock, tend to rate more of a glance than regular-weight, $8^1/2 \times 11$ papers. Perhaps this is because it takes more effort to crumble the heavy paper. But also, heavier stock seems to denote quality to us. The very feel of your handout will help to dispel the notion that you are some cheap, fly-by-night operation. Coupons, if they are immediately apparent, also stop the impulse to discard. Americans seem to have gone coupon mad.

Illustrations with large, eye-catching type and a brief and easy-to-absorb message will help your flyer to get at least minimal attention. Figure 9-3 shows a flyer that is eye-catching and informative enough to rate a second glance.

Alternative Ways to Distribute. Face it, though—the handout in the street is probably the worst way to go. You would be much better off to find some other method to distribute your flyer. First, who do you want to receive it? If your ad is aimed at downtown shoppers, why not see if some noncompetitive business will put your flyers by their cash register? Maybe you can get the cashiers in the grocery store to stuff it into bags along with the groceries. If you want the workers, hire someone to use up a little shoe leather delivering them to the businesses in the area. If these seem to be more effort than the street-corner handout, think again. The chances of having your ad read increase when you focus on your target audience.

If you must use the under-the-windshield-wiper method, by all means avoid any leaflet that even remotely resembles a traffic citation. Use bright colors. Make sure that the flyer is folded so that any coupons or specials show at first glance.

Some enterprising entrepreneurs get great distribution by bribing paper boys. The youngster who has the business route, or who goes to the residents

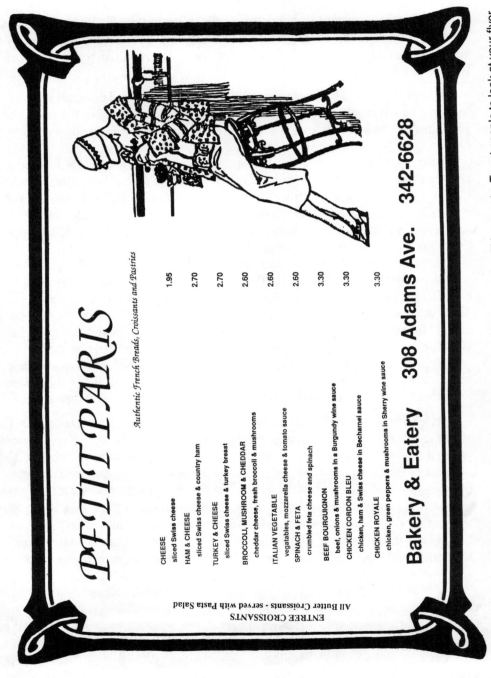

PETIT PARIS

Authentic French Breads, Croissants and Pastries

CHEESE	1.95
sliced Swiss cheese	
HAM & CHEESE	2.70
sliced Swiss cheese & country ham	
TURKEY & CHEESE	2.70
sliced Swiss cheese & turkey breast	
BROCCOLI, MUSHROOM & CHEDDAR	2.60
cheddar cheese, fresh broccoli & mushrooms	
ITALIAN VEGETABLE	2.60
vegetables, mozzarella cheese & tomato sauce	
SPINACH & FETA	2.60
crumbled feta cheese and spinach	
BEEF BOURGUIGNON	3.30
beef, onions & mushrooms in a Burgundy wine sauce	
CHICKEN CORDON BLEU	3.30
chicken, ham & Swiss cheese in Bechamel sauce	
CHICKEN ROYALE	3.30
chicken, green peppers & mushrooms in Sherry wine sauce	

ENTREE CROISSANTS
All Butter Croissants - served with Pasta Salad

Bakery & Eatery   308 Adams Ave.   342-6628

Fig. 9-3. An eye-catching menu with prices is a handy flyer that many people will hang onto. To get people to look at your flyer, you must make it attractive. A strong graphic, such as the picture here, might arouse enough curiosity to get people to read your ad before they toss it away. (Clip art from Carol Belanger Grafton, *1001 Spot Illustrations of the Lively Twenties*, courtesy of Dover Books) Ad by Matthew Brown.

in your area of trade is often glad to earn a few extra dollars dropping your flyer off along with his newspapers. In fact, a few enterprising newspapers feature a bulk-mail package, where for a small fee, they will bundle your flyer in with the newspaper, and make sure that it gets delivered along certain routes. Check with your newspaper to see if this service is available in your area.

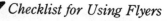

Checklist for Using Flyers

- Will the flyers be distributed in a tourism area, or one where people are likely to be open to such solicitation?
- Is the person doing the distributing one who looks open and trustworthy?
- Is my flyer eye-catching, communicating quickly what my business is and what type of offer I am making?
- Is there some way that I can have my flyers distributed to my specific target audience, other than mailing them?
- Do I have a noncompetitive business that might be willing to distribute my flyers in an area that caters to our shared target audience?
- Do the local newspapers offer a bundle-and-deliver service? Must I use their entire circulation, or can I limit my distribution to my area of trade?
- Remember to get costs for both printing and distribution if you plan to use flyers in your media plan.

Posters

Posters always seem like such a good idea. They are inexpensive, nice looking, and informative. The problem with these is distribution. Who will want to hang your poster? Very few people will oblige even the worthiest nonprofit organization when they want to hang posters in the front window. Your chances, as a bona-fide business, are remote.

Small cards, however, larger than a business card but similar in design, can be placed on those bulletin boards that are often prominent in grocery and drug stores. People read these. If you attach "take-ones" to your poster—slips with your name and number, or a small box that holds several of your business cards—then you might see some response from this ad.

OTHER SMALL CIRCULATION PRINT MEDIA

They come to your business almost weekly: high school kids wanting you to take an ad in their yearbook, the university students who think you should advertise in their newspaper, the charitable organization who wants you to buy space in their program. Should you be a good guy and pay up, or an ogre who says no to good causes?

Who Is the Target Audience?

Sometimes, it pays to say yes. Once again, take a good look at the audience to whom these small-circulation pieces will go. Are the people who will attend that charity auction part of your target audience? Do you get a lot of business from those students? Or the faculty? If you do, then this is an excellent, affordable way to reach a target audience.

School newspapers are excellent places for small businesses to advertise, if your product or service appeals to a young audience. The cost per thousand is apt to be high, but the waste circulation is apt to be very low. College radio stations can also be good buys, if they are over-the-air stations that can be heard over more than a three block radius. (In addition, if you buy time on college radio, you can often arrange to have some good commercials produced that could be used on other stations.)

You might want to think twice about the yearbook. A high school yearbook will reach young people (and parents) who are probably local and will remain in your area of trade. College yearbooks tend to be distributed at the end of the school year, however, when half of your target audience is going home for the summer.

Evaluating Programs

Symphony programs, sports programs, and souvenir booklets for cultural events—what can they do for you? Each of these will undoubtedly go to an audience that is very psychographically targeted. If the audience fits your target audience profile, then you might want to consider buying space. However, think too of the circumstances in which these booklets will be looked at. If you are a late-night eatery, then your ad in a theatre or sports program can be just the suggestion needed to bring these people through the door after the event. If you are a daytime only business, then all these programs achieve for you is some additional frequency to help in name-recognition. There is, however, an added good-will factor, which could be especially valuable if you are trying to overcome an image problem.

With programs for athletic events, you are reaching sports-minded people. The program for an antiques show will reach people who enjoy rare items, unusual, or traditional objects, etc. Take a good look at the audience, and see if it is one that you would like to have knowing your name. Then decide if you want to buy.

Church Papers

One small circulation print media that is often overlooked is the church paper. Many people seem to think that to advertise in this paper is like taking advantage of God. Not so. These weekly bulletins depend on advertisers to pay their costs. Without you, there might not be any church paper. People tend to go out of the way to patronize businesses that support their church paper. Of course, not every ad will be appropriate—but many service businesses, especially, can profit from the weekly parish bulletin. The area of trade tends to be small, although the demographic spread can be wide. The cost is always reasonable. The goodwill generated is invaluable.

Checklist for Buying Small Circulation Print Media

- If the medium is a charity special event program, is the cause one that I want to support? Which my target audience is likely to support?
- Is the medium likely to circulate primarily among people who are in my target audience?
- Will my ad reach that audience at a time when they will be in the market for my product or service?
- If your answer to the above questions is yes, you are looking at a cost-efficient media buy.
- If you are planning your yearly media purchases, you are probably not yet aware of the programs, yearbooks, etc., that you might be approached with in the coming year. If you think this type of advertising will benefit you, you might want to set aside 5 – 10 percent of your budget so that you can afford to take advantage of these opportunities as they arise.

SPECIALTY ADVERTISING

Let me say one thing right off the bat: Specialty advertising is not cheap. Your cost per thousand can be astronomical. But specialty advertising is a medium with an extremely controlled circulation—you probably won't even need a thousand of anything to achieve your objectives.

What Is It?

Specialty advertising includes all those small items that we receive from the businesses we regularly patronize, complete with advertising name and message. They are not selling media. No one decides to buy insurance from you because they saw your pen. Rather, they are reminder media, which keep your name in front of your regular customers, and help to create good feelings about you and your business. If your advertising objectives include maintaining customer loyalty or increasing business among the current audience, then consider specialty advertising.

Choosing the Right Specialty

Choosing the right item to give to your intended audience requires careful thought. The most common, least expensive forms of specialty advertising are tempting, because they're easy. They might also be a waste of money.

Pens are probably the most common form of specialty advertising. They are small, and often inexpensive, so they are popular. Too popular. I've surveyed audiences time and time again, and almost no one can tell me what is advertised on the pen they are using. Most people have to check to see if the pen has advertising at all. Writing instruments are just one of those things that we take for granted. Half of all Americans probably come home each night with a different pen than the one they had when they left the house, but they will have no idea of when and where the switch was made. So, inexpensive or not, the pen might not be the best form of specialty advertising for you. Unless you get a very good pen that people make a point of keeping or an unusual one (such as the crooked pen favored by chiropractors), it will fade into oblivion.

The reason the chiropractor's crooked pen works when others don't is twofold. First, it is different. People notice it. Second, that pen visually tells us what a chiropractor does—he straightens out kinks in people.

The key to a good specialty advertising medium is suitability. When we look at the item that you have given us, is there anything that will associate it with your type of business? A store that sells water skis, for instance, makes an impact with their floating key-chain, suitably printed with their name, address, and logo. A beauty shop can give small purse mirrors to their customers. Smirnoffs vodka one year gave out tiny screwdrivers emblazoned with their logo.

Making a Selection

A call to a specialty advertising company will get you a catalogue listing thousands of items like these. One or more will suit your business. Generally, the items available fall into a few basic categories: wall items, desk items, pocket and purse items, household items, and apparel. Wall items include calendars, clocks, thermometers, and even posters. Desk items include note pads, appointment books, telephone dialers, ashtrays, and memo pad holders. Pocket and purse items include matchbooks, mirrors, rain hats, small sewing kits, lighters, pens, pencils, and pocket secretaries, among the most obvious. Under household items, we find everything from rubber jar openers and potscrapers to potholders, coasters, and little stickers for your phone that list local emergency numbers.

Avoiding Problems

A few of these items are prone to pitfalls. Calendars, for instance, face heavy competition. Every year, dozens of companies hand them out. There are only so many places where we can use a calendar. The trick is to get yours chosen. A beautiful design helps. Monthly coupons, recipes, first aid hints, or any information that makes your calendar a reference guide as well is likely to give your calendar a position in the home or office. (This gives you a possible frequency of 365 for a single ad.)

Matchbooks, of course, are useful only to smokers. Keychains are almost too popular. So are note pads. The trick is to choose an item that is useful, and is unusual enough to not be taken for granted. Choose anything, as long as you can afford it, and your customers will see how the item you give them relates to your business.

Distributing your Specialty

The idea is to distribute these to your regular customers. You decide who you want to give these items to and under what condition. They can be given out after a certain dollar amount of sales, or along with a specific type of purchase or service. You can give them out at holidays or special events. You can give them only to those people that you like. It's up to you.

Apparel is a special case. T-shirts and caps, especially, are very popular items. Bars, entertainment facilities, car dealers, etc., often find that the shirt they bought for their employees has a hot market value. People actually want to pay you to get that shirt, and, in effect, to walk around advertising your business. To sell or to give out, to award as prizes, to raffle off at special events—it's up to you. Wearing apparel functions like a walking billboard for your business. And you might be able to get your advertising dollars back.

Checklist for Using Specialty Advertising

- Is my advertising objective either to strengthen the loyalty of my present customer, or to encourage more business from my present customer?
- Do the specialty advertising companies in my area (listed in the phone directory either under advertising, or specialty advertising) offer a useful item that customers will associate with my business?
- Does the item I am considering have room for my name, logo, and address?
- Is the item unusual enough that it will not get lost among a welter of similar items?
- Is the item inexpensive enough for my budget?
- Do I have a plan for distributing these to the appropriate customers?

SPONSORSHIPS

One way to get people to wear your name and logo is to sponsor a team. While this might mean that only the 14 men on the baseball team or 5 bowlers are wearing your ad, there are also a lot of spectators. Teams and leagues usually make an effort to be grateful for your sponsorship; they try to send business your way.

In addition, if the team you sponsor gets media coverage, then your name (the team name), gets printed or mentioned on the air every time they play, absolutely free. If it's a really hot game, the newspaper might print a game picture—and there are your shirts and caps right on the sports page.

If team sponsorship is a bit over your remaining budget, consider stadium posters. Little League fields, especially, have signs around the outfield rented by local companies. Once again, all the spectators see your sign for an hour or two, several times a week, all season. So do newspaper readers, every time an outfielder makes a photogenic catch.

NONTRADITIONAL WAYS TO ADVERTISE

Some experts have claimed that the average American is exposed to something like 16,000 advertising messages a day. If you are inclined to doubt this, just sit back and think for a minute. Not even counting all the media I have covered in the past few chapters, there are countless places where a company name or logo could appear. Some of these are emblazoned on designer clothing, luggage, etc. Many times we see the brand name on a product, just as part of the general design. Watch a TV show, and you'll see the characters using products with the brand names prominently displayed. These companies often pay the producers to feature their products with their target audience.

Maybe you can't compete with these ideas, but the idea is to get all kinds of ideas about places where your company name can appear. Here are a few ideas.

Utility Pole Signs

Depending on the restrictions in your community, you might be able to put small signs on the light posts or telephone poles in your area. This is especially useful if you have an out-of-the-way location. A small sign with directional arrows can inspire leisure drivers to seek you out on impulse, and it will alleviate frustration for people who have never been able to find you.

Any reputable sign company can make you small, attractive and weatherproof signs bearing your logo, an arrow if you need it, and even your address, slogan, etc. The trick is in getting them up. Check with the city, or with the utility company who services the poles you are interested in. In our city, no one seemed to know who was in charge of granting permission for this. The advice from the city, the electric company, and the phone company was to go ahead and put them up; the worst they can do is tell you to take them down. So far, dozens of small merchants with out-of-the-way locations have done this, and many signs have been up for five or more years.

Sandwich Boards

We don't see too many of these any more—the poor soul who wanders the streets with an advertising board strapped fore and aft. For that very reason, the sandwich board man attracts attention. If you can get an attractive board painted up, this can be a creative way to make people aware of your new business or of your special event. It is also one way to make people accept any flyers that you want distributed. Since they already know what the flyer will be about, they will take one. If interested, they might read and use it.

Once again, a good sign company can make a sandwich board for you that includes your logo, address, phone, etc. You can ask them to leave a space for you to fill in changeable information as the need arises.

A Shower of Balloons

Kids love balloons. So do adults, although they won't admit it. If you can launch a whole shower of balloons out of an upper story of a building, you'll have people chasing them down the streets and carrying them all through the city. Make sure your name, logo, and any pertinent information about you is clearly printed on the balloon. This is an interesting way to get people talking about you, and the balloons are little, portable ads.

Hot Air Balloons

On a slightly larger scale, maybe you could rent a hot air balloon, and tether it outside your place of business. People are fascinated with these and will walk or drive out of their way to see one up close. If you can advertise free rides (or even paid ones), this is an additional crowd drawer. This idea can be especially effective at a grand opening when you need to have people know where you are and what you do. Often, it rates a newspaper picture, thus garnering free publicity. (Hint: Call the local papers and clue them in. Newspapers and even TV stations love stories with visual interest.) You will want to get all the publicity you can out of this stunt, because, while it is effective, it is not cheap.

Sky Writing

Nothing stops people in their tracks faster than a sky writer. We rarely see these nowadays, and, as an advertising medium, they might be even more ephemeral than radio and TV. One good breeze, and your message is literally gone with the wind. However, on a clear sunny day when people are out and about, you can write your message for the whole city. People are bound to start talking. For getting word of mouth started, you can't beat it.

There are many more ideas you might try. Let your imagination run wild. Keep your eyes open. See what attracts your attention; see what others pay attention to. There are interesting, and often inexpensive advertising ideas everywhere, if you know where to look.

SUMMARY

A very small budget advertiser might be able to create an effective advertising campaign without ever resorting to the major media. Especially with a limited target audience or a small area of trade, alternatives such as church papers and school yearbooks, flyers, and utility pole signs can get your name and message to the public at a low cost.

Most important of all, however, is to make sure that your business tools—signs, cars, bags, etc., work for you. Don't pass up any possible opportunity to keep your name and logo in the public eye.

10

Planning a Media Schedule

"I'D REALLY LIKE TO REACH THE YOUNG, NEWLYWED CROWD," SIGHED HERB TO his assistant. "I think I'll try advertising on radio."

"Great," enthused Tim. "How about that new rock station?"

Herb shuddered. "No—I can't stand that kind of music. But I had a media rep in here the other day with a great deal—fifteen spots for only $9 a piece, and he says they're number one among 25–34 year olds."

"When do the spots run?"

"Oh, that's up to them—whenever they have time. That's why I save so much money. It's that superstation—goes all the way into the next county—you know, the easy listening one?"

Tim tried his best to explain three things to Herb. First, most young newlyweds think easy listening is something that belongs in a dentist's office. Second, that's probably where most of them hear it, which is why the station can claim such a large audience of young people. And third—if Herb leaves his radio schedule to the station, his spots are likely to run at 3 a.m. when no one else wants radio time. It's unlikely that his desired audience will be listening.

Herb has fallen victim to a problem common to many small businesses—he doesn't understand media scheduling. Nor are the time and space salesmen who inundate his office likely to be of much help. They all have one purpose: to sell ads. They're not interested in Herb's over-all media schedule.

A smart businessperson plans their media purchases ahead of time. Taking advantage of contract rates can save you money, and ensure you time and space when you need it. Planning ahead also allows you to coordinate media so that you can reach more of your target audiences more often. Planning also helps you to resist the sensational ploys of those salespeople. Because you will have already done your homework, you will know what media are best for you and your advertising objectives.

Chapter 10 will tell you how to create a six-month or yearly media calendar that will maximize the reach and frequency of your advertising while avoiding waste circulation. Waste circulation means that you waste money reaching people who are not in your target audience. This chapter contains valuable warnings about the many traps that await the small business advertiser—bargain rates that are no bargain.

The best way to have an effective advertising campaign is to reach your audience with a meaningful message on the media that best suit your advertising needs, objectives, and target audience. This means that you have to consider several factors before you jump in and start buying time and space for your media message. First, you must look at your budget to determine what media you can afford. Second, you must look at your area of trade to see how large a market you need to reach. Third, you must look at the demographic and psychographic profile of your target audience to see which media they are most likely to use. Finally, you must go to the media to see which ones among those that suit your purpose will use your advertising dollar in the most cost-efficient manner. You have already collected rates from the various media that appear to suit your business needs. Now we will learn how to select the best media at the most appropriate times in your annual plan.

THE MEDIA SCHEDULE

Your advertising budget has a great deal to do with where and how you will advertise. To look merely at the dollar amount you have set aside for ads, then calculate how many inches of newspaper you can afford or how many spots on a local station, does not tell you much. To form an effective advertising campaign, your media must be incorporated into an effective schedule.

When we examined budgeting in chapter 2, we laid the basis for developing a media schedule. In the exercises, you developed a calendar that marked out the amount of money you had to spend each month on advertising and the times of year when you most needed to advertise.

As a quick review, several things determine the amount you will spend on advertising each month. The most important follow. First, determine when your fast and slow months of business are. You will need to spend on advertising during your busy months. This makes the audience aware that your business can provide the products or services when they are most likely to want it. You do not want to spend a great deal during the slow months since people can rarely be induced to buy when they are not in the mood or in the market. Second, you need to spend when your competition does so that they do not achieve prominence in the customer's mind. (As a rule, your competitors will be spending during busy months, too.) Third, you need to earmark dollars for those times when you have any special sales, events, or celebrations that you will want people to know about. Your budget should be apportioned on the calendar in a way that will allow you to advertise heavily and lightly, as needed.

SCHEDULING STRATEGIES

Once you have decided what you have to spend and when you need to spend it, you must devise an overall spending and scheduling strategy. Your budget determines the strategy you choose.

The Continuous Advertising Strategy

Major companies use a tactic called *continuous advertising*. Their media schedules are always full; you will see ads in every night's newspapers, and probably hear them on carefully targeted radio and TV stations. The names of these companies are rarely out of the public eye. Department stores, chain stores, and national products with multifigured budgets use this tactic explosively. You can barely avoid seeing an ad for K-Mart, for instance, if you read the papers at all. Smaller businesses can also use continuous advertising, but on a smaller scale.

If, for instance, your budget analysis tells you that you have no slow seasons—that yours is a business that has a steady market year round—then you will want to advertise continuously. As a small businessperson, however, you will be unlikely to afford to do this on the scale of Bloomingdale's. Instead, you must choose one or two affordable media, and run carefully scheduled, small ads daily, three times a week, or whatever you can afford.

Pulsing Strategy

A second media planning strategy is called *pulsing*. This means that the advertiser runs a small base of continuous advertising, but accelerates the media schedule during peak periods. For instance, a florist might run a newspaper ad twice weekly year round. Around Mother's Day, Valentine's Day, etc., when floral gifts are traditional, she might increase her media buys substantially. She might run ads in the newspaper daily and also advertise on radio and smaller weekly newspapers. When the season for giving is over, she cuts back to the lighter schedule.

The very small business version of pulsing is to run ads only at the busy times. You might choose to eliminate advertising in the very slow months and to concentrate all your budget into those times when customers are readily available, and competitors are spending heavily. While this is risky during your off months, it does attract people to your business when they are in the market for your product and service. These people might then continue to be your customers during slow times. You would be better advised, however, to run at least one ad during those slow months as a reminder that you are still around. Or, better still, take advantage of some of the lesser forms of advertising that I will discuss under "Media you might not have considered." These will at least keep your name visible, if not exactly prominent.

Flighting Strategy

A third strategy, somewhat similar to very small business pulsing, is one called *flighting*. With this plan, the advertiser strives to maximize the impact of his or her schedule with a minimal investment. The theory in flighting is that no one except you, the advertiser, waits with bated breath for your advertising message. Therefore, if you are on for a short period, then off, then on again, the average consumer will assume that you have been advertising all along, but that they somehow missed the message.

Practically, flighting works something like this. Assume that you have analyzed all the media in your area and know that in order to reach most of your target audience, you need to be in both the morning and evening paper, and on a certain AM and FM radio station. Your budget, however, will only stretch to include one newspaper, and one radio station. With flighting, you buy time and space on all four—but you alternate times. One week you use the morning paper and the AM station. The next, you use the evening paper and the AM station. Next, the morning paper and the FM station, etc. Psychologically, people will perceive that you are advertising more than you are.

This perception has a certain, limited advantage in your plan. People tend to believe that businesses that advertise a lot are successful, and therefore must be good, or at least trustworthy. However, the fact that people think your message is on a lot, but are not seeing or hearing it, is a minus. For an ad to be effective, it must be heard often enough for it to sink in. This is where the important concepts of reach and frequency come in.

REACH AND FREQUENCY

All good media plans are based on these two concepts. *Reach* is the average number of people who are exposed to your media message at least once. *Frequency* means the average number of times that one person in your target audience is exposed to your message. We have looked at media in terms of how many people they reach, and which will enable you to reach people most often. Now you must decide which concept best suits your objectives.

Reach vs. Frequency

Reach determines the rate structure of a medium. The more people reached by a given medium, the higher its rates will be. Therefore, if you plan your media schedule to reach a large number of people, you will necessarily be able to buy fewer ads. This means that you might reach all your target audience at least once, and the avid media user might hear your message several times. If your budget is limited, and you devote a great portion of it to achieving a large reach, then your frequency might be adversely affected. As reach goes up, frequency goes down. As frequency increases, reach decreases. And every ad needs a minimum frequency before it has an impact. So which should you aim for?

Frequency. At a bare minimum, a person needs to hear or see an ad at least three times before it begins to sink in. So you must have a frequency of at least three, or you are wasting your ad dollar.

Assume that you follow this advice quite literally and buy three radio ads on a station targeted to your market. Can you ensure that the same listener will be present for all three ads? Probably not. To achieve a frequency of three, you need to buy five, or maybe six radio ads all on the same station, and all scheduled in the same approximate time slot—when your customer is likely to be tuned in.

Only the most exceptional ads can afford to ignore this rule. If you are offering free diamonds, then a single exposure to your ad might lure enough people into your store to justify the advertising expenditure. Usually, however, people are not really paying attention to advertising and will not grasp your message until it has appeared several times.

Frequency, as a more general concept, helps convince a well-defined target audience to patronize you, helps keep already attracted customers loyal, and helps communicate difficult or complicated messages. Advertisers usually opt to use their budgets to achieve frequency once they have developed a well-defined target audience, and once they have achieved a basic level of awareness with that audience.

Reach. Reach, on the other hand, helps to develop awareness and to begin the word-of-mouth process. The new advertiser usually opts for reach, at the beginning, in order to familiarize the greatest number of potential customers with his business. Once a recognizable segment of the market emerges, he then should concentrate on reaching that smaller group more often.

Using Reach and Frequency

Reach and frequency are important concepts in helping you to achieve your advertising objectives. The owner of a small, downtown lunch counter, for instance, would first want to reach all the workers in the area who go out for lunch. She might do this simply by sending fliers out to all the stores and offices, including a sample menu. She might also place ads in a business journal to reach executives, and buy pre-lunchtime spots on one or two radio stations commonly played in downtown office buildings and stores. By doing this, the owner has done her best to achieve a wide reach for all potential customers.

Eventually, however, she might notice that she is doing a thriving business at lunch time, but that the bulk of this business comes from the lawyers and clerks from the courthouse across the street. If these people give her enough patronage to satisfy her, the owner can then concentrate on ads in the legal news, and more fliers and specials aimed at this group. The business journal can be dropped, as can the radio ads on popular stations that are played in the downtown boutiques. The advertising budget can now be used to reach the likely audience more often and more effectively.

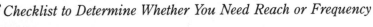

Checklist to Determine Whether You Need Reach or Frequency

You need reach if:

- You are a new business.
- You are not sure who your best target markets are.
- You find that your business has a very small recognition factor.
- You have made major changes in the business that might attract new target audiences.
- Your advertising objectives include reaching new target audiences or increasing your volume of business.

You need frequency if:

- You have a well-defined target audience.
- You have a good recognition factor in your area of trade.
- Your advertising objectives specify that you want your current customers to come in more often.
- You are satisfied with the volume of business you are doing now.

MAXIMIZING REACH AND FREQUENCY: The Media Mix

Few people would deliberately choose to concentrate on a small segment of the population at the expense of other potential markets that might provide regular customers if they only were aware of your business. A good media plan strives to achieve a good balance between reach and frequency. The best way to achieve this is through a media mix.

A media mix is simply a combination of media, rather than exclusive dependence on a single medium. For example, you might choose to advertise on the 6 o'clock TV news, and in the morning paper. Some of your target audience do not get the morning paper, but they will see you on the news. Some watch a rival TV channel but will see the newspaper ad. Some will see both. So you have achieved a greater reach by using two media instead of one. You have also achieved a greater frequency among some of your target population.

Increasing Reach

Too many small business advertisers tend to rely on a single medium to do their advertising work. This is almost always a mistake, unless your budget is so small that there is no other way to achieve a minimum frequency. By relying solely on billboards, for instance, you are passing up huge segments of your target market that do not drive on those particular roads. Not everyone watches much TV or reads the paper. Your message is much more effective if used in a media mix.

Increasing Frequency

Similarly, you maximize your impact if you use more than one vehicle within a medium. Radio, for instance, is highly targeted to specific audiences. In most markets, there are at least two stations that reach your potential customer. People tend to be loyal to their preferred station. To ignore one station, concentrating on the other, means you miss a segment of your market.

If you have an extremely small advertising budget, then make your choices in at least two media. As your budget increases, expand your time and space purchases within a media category—more radio stations, more billboards on different routes, both newspapers, etc. Do not, however, forget the basic frequency rule. To achieve a media mix at the sacrifice of minimum exposure to your message will considerably lessen the impact of your campaign.

COORDINATING YOUR MEDIA

To further maximize your media plan, you want to make sure that the media you choose work well together. When, in the next few chapters, we consider the characteristics of each medium, we will discover how some media perform certain functions better than others. For instance, print media allow you to present complicated messages because the reader, if interested, has the time to study your ad. Print media also allow you to use coupons and reply cards. Radio, while reaching a more targeted audience in a creative and interesting way, does not give the audience time to think about your message. Once the message is heard, it is already gone. Few people, listening to their favorite station in their cars, will be able to jot down your address or phone number. So, if your campaign calls for heavy advertising in a certain month, and you are using a combination of print and broadcast media, make sure that you coordinate them.

Coordinating your media means paying attention to both your scheduling strategy and creative message. If you are running a series of radio spots featuring your grand opening, and you will also have ads in the newspaper, mention these. Telling the listener to ''Watch for our ad in tonight's *Free Press*'' will alert interested listeners. Then the newspaper ad you run can fill them in on any details that couldn't be included on broadcast media. This helps to maximize your reach because you are using a media mix; it also improves your frequency because you might motivate people to seek out your print ads.

HOW MUCH ADVERTISING IS ENOUGH?

A major question that many advertisers ask at this point is, "How much advertising reach and frequency is enough—and how much is too much?" Enough, as I have stated, is a minimum frequency of three exposures to your ad, reaching everyone in your most likely target audience. More is, of course, better.

The Value of Frequency

The more times people hear a statement, the less likely they are to question it and the more likely they are to accept it on face value. In the early days of radio, advertisers used repetition within an ad very heavily, assuming that when something is heard often enough, we tend to believe it. If, for instance, someone told you right now that the ice age will be here next July, you would doubt it. The second time you hear the statement, you will still be somewhat scornful. By the tenth time, however, you might begin to wonder if there isn't some truth to the statement. The same goes for advertising. The more we hear or see it, the less inclined we are to question it. Therefore, the greater the frequency you can achieve while still getting a good reach, the better.

The Saturation Point

There is, however, a saturation point, when the ad has appeared too many times to have any more impact. No one knows what that point is since it is an individualistic reaction. If you've ever pasted a picture of a fat person on the refrigerator door to remind yourself not to snack, you'll know what I mean. We see that picture for the first week or two, then we simply quit noticing it. It might as well not be there, for all the effect it has on our snacking habits.

Advertising can suffer the same fate if the same ad is repeated too often. Few small businesses have the budget to achieve this saturation point. However, a smart business will make sure that, in every ad campaign, the individual messages include some variations on your basic campaign theme—enough to keep the audience paying attention. For this same reason, it is not enough for you to prepare a single ad, and then use it forever. Your creative strategy must be consistent, but you will need more than one ad per medium to achieve impact. While this idea will be discussed in depth under creative strategy, I want to note here that when you can only afford a small newspaper ad, then you can maximize your message by changing the ad often to include a changing array of information that can keep potential customers informed about all your products and services.

THE TARGET AUDIENCE MIX

If you were paying attention in chapter 2, you will remember that, undoubtedly, you have more than one target audience. Your advertising budget was divided among these audiences, with the largest amount devoted to reaching your primary target, and lesser percentages devoted to lesser targets.

The same rules of media scheduling apply to any target groups you wish to reach. All must receive the messages you intend for them at least three times. All must receive those messages at the times when they are most likely to be in the market for your product and service. What will vary, in your media calendar, is the media with which you reach those audiences.

Demographic and Psychographic Needs

The demographics and psychographics of your audience will help you to determine which media and which vehicles within those media will best reach your audience. Some media are better at reaching a particular audience than others.

Newspapers. Few teenagers read the newspaper, except for the entertainment page, and maybe the comics. The most brilliant ad campaign in the world, aimed at teens and placed in the newspaper, will probably fail. So, in this instance, an entire medium is demographically inadequate for the needs of advertisers seeking the teen market.

Radio. Radio, on the other hand, is used by everyone. However, the individual stations have widely varying demographic and psychographic targets. Stations that feature heavy metal music have a teen audience, those which play the classics have a generally upper-income, highly educated older audience. Talk stations have large percentages of elderly people in their audiences. So the medium can theoretically reach almost everyone, but the choice of station is what determines the success or failure of the media schedule.

Television. Television is much like radio, only it is the individual program, rather than the station, which determines the audience. Especially since cable television and the remote control, few viewers are consistently loyal to a single network or station. People are, however, loyal to certain shows, and can be reached consistently by advertising on those shows that appeal to the demographic segment you are trying to reach.

Magazines. Magazines are media that also appeal to an infinite number of highly targeted audiences. There is a magazine for every possible interest, from old house rehabilitation to fly fishing. Magazines also lean heavily on psychographic appeals. Some go to those people who see themselves as traditionalists, some appeal to the nouveau riche, others to the nonconformists. You can usually tell who a magazine is trying to reach by flipping through the ads.

Buying Ads by Demographics and Psychographics

The same principle holds true for any mass medium. For the most part, the ads will provide a good clue to the audience. Of course there are mistakes—

advertisers who don't properly understand targeting, and simply did what the business down the street did, or who bought space from the first media salesperson who walked through the door. But if you study each station, program, newspaper, or magazine carefully, you will notice that most ads seem to aim at a particular audience.

If you are considering a media purchase, study that medium first, to see what other ads they are carrying and who those ads are trying to appeal to. Sometimes the program itself can be misleading. For instance, the show *Charley's Angels*, featuring three unbelievably gorgeous women, seemed to be a male fantasy. Many people assumed that this would be the ideal place to reach men with their ads, but not so. Women turned out to be the primary audience for this program—something that should have been obvious from the preponderance of perfume and cosmetic ads run in this time slot.

In order to achieve a target audience mix, you must take the percentage of your budget that you assigned to each target group and spend that amount on media that are most likely to reach that group; the remainder is allocated to media that reach the secondary audience, etc.

Targeted Media Buys: A Case History

A small shop devoted to selling pottery and handcrafted items might look at its customer pattern and realize that there are two main types of customers patronizing the shop. The first consists of older women, who have developed their own, highly individualistic tastes, and who have enough disposable income to afford one-of-a-kind handcrafted mixing bowls and spice jars. The owner might estimate that this audience makes up about 70 percent of her clientele so she devotes 70 percent of her ad budget to buying media that will reach these women. She takes space on the fashion page in the evening newspaper, buys time on a soft rock/oldies station, and advertises in a monthly city magazine devoted to arts and cultural activities.

There is, however, a smaller audience of young women, mostly in their early twenties, mostly just about to be married and seeking to set up their homes in a highly individual manner. The shop owner will therefore spend the remaining thirty percent of her budget trying to reach these brides-to-be, advertising her bridal registry. Here, she would buy rock stations on radio, and perhaps space in the bridal supplement of the newspaper. She might also comb the newspaper for lists of those who apply for marriage licenses, and send a direct mail piece to each of these couples describing her wares.

WHEN DO I BUY?

Scheduling your ads can be a tricky business. The crafts shop owner described earlier might reasonably expect that June is the best time to reach brides. She would be wrong. Her ads need to reach the engaged woman long before that, when she first starts registering for gifts. Travel agents want to advertise when people begin to plan for their vacations—not during the peak season, when people have already made their plans.

When Is the Market There?

The first thing to do is to consider when people begin to look for information about the product or service that you offer. Is your business one that people make long-range plans before using? If so, you need to be buying ads well before peak season time. If, on the other hand, yours is a spur-of-the-moment type of purchase, then your media schedule should be concentrated during those times when business is naturally heavy.

When Do I Need Advertising?

Scheduling your media buys depends not only on the customer's tendency to buy by the season, but also on your own special needs and plans. Look at sales, special events, time of day when the audience is available and paying attention, and a number of other factors before finalizing your schedule of advertising.

Sales and Special Events. First, consider the business events that you have planned. Plan to start advertising at least one week before any special event or sale. People like to be able to plan ahead in budgeting both their time and money.

Scheduling by Time of Day. Time of day can make a difference in the impact of an ad. Plan to schedule your ads so that they reach people during those times when they are most susceptible to your message. Ads aimed at businesspeople should be scheduled to reach them during the day when they have the ability to act on your suggestion. Lunch businesses, for instance, will want to reach the worker in the morning, about the time when thoughts begin to wander towards food and lunchtime.

Ads for major purchases, such as cars or furniture, might be better if received in the evening, when the family can discuss the expenditure and make decisions.

The Best Days. Time of week or month can also affect ad responses. Many housewives, for instance, save their food shopping for the days when newspapers run coupons and food supplements. This seems to occur midweek in most cities. Shoppers might notice your ad on Monday but by the time they have pored through the Wednesday food section, your message has been replaced by several others.

Furthermore, pay dates greatly affect shopping habits. If there is a major industry in your area, then there are also predictable paydays. When people have more disposable income, they are more likely to shop or to take advantage of nonessential services. The same goes for predictable dates for welfare checks and social security. Spending always goes up when the checks arrive. This might be the best time for your advertising to appear.

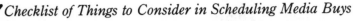

Checklist of Things to Consider in Scheduling Media Buys

- Who is your primary target audience? What media are they most likely to expose themselves to?
- Is your product or service one that people buy on impulse? If so, consider media that will reach people when they are likely to be available to your business.
- Is your product or service one that requires discussion? If so, schedule your ads to reach your target audience when they are likely to be able to discuss it with their family.
- Is your business seasonal? When do people begin to plan for the season? (Ex: Many people begin Christmas shopping in October. They plan summer vacations in February. And so on.) Make a note of the planning season in your media calendar. You will need to begin your ads for that season when people begin to plan.
- Are you planning sales or special events? How far in advance do you need to make the public aware of these? Note this in your media calendar.
- When are paydays in your area? What are the prime shopping days in your area of trade and for your target audience? Make a note of these, because they will affect the days on which you schedule your ads.

SPECIAL CONSIDERATIONS THAT MAY NARROW YOUR MEDIA CHOICES

The best way to achieve maximum efficiency with your advertising dollar is to avoid waste circulation. Waste circulation is any advertising that reaches people who are not in your target audience. To a great extent, your area of trade determines what is waste circulation.

Area of Trade Limitations

If your primary customers are drawn from an area within six blocks of your place of business, then you have a very small area of trade—a six square block area. To advertise in the daily newspaper, which reaches a 37 square mile area, means you are paying a large price to reach thousands of people who are simply outside your area. Your ad is wasted on them—and so is your money. Similarly, the most popular radio station in town might reach the age group you want but also thousands of other people in that age group but outside city limits. Yet you're paying a premium rate just because of this too-wide circulation. Therefore, businesses with a small area of trade will want to go with low reach media, to avoid waste circulation. The general reach potential of each medium is discussed in chapters 7, 8, and 9.

Demographic Limitations

Another way to waste circulation is to buy into a medium that reaches an appreciable number of people outside of your demographic audience profile. A radio station sales rep might come into your place of business proclaiming that his station is number one in reaching adults, 25 – 34. This is the audience you want, so the purchase of time seems to make good sense. Look again. Who else is that station reaching? If it is a high power station, chances are that your target audience is not even the primary listening audience for that station. Chances are that most listeners are 18 – 25—but because there are so many listeners for that station, spread over a wide geographic area, that station happens to reach more of your target audience than a rival station more specifically targeted to that group. So why not go ahead and buy it? Go ahead—if your secondary audience also happens to be the one listening to that station. Otherwise, your dollars would be more efficiently spent on the station that does not have all that waste circulation, and so is undoubtedly charging a lower rate.

Avoiding Waste Circulation

The best way to avoid waste circulation is to get accurate audience figures from the media with whom you are dealing. This is easy with major media in major markets, and sometimes impossible with small media and in small markets where little accurate research can be done. However, find out to the best of your ability exactly how many people in your target audience will be reached by your ad on that medium. Divide that figure into the cost of the ad, and multiply the result by 1000.

What you have now is a figure which tells you exactly how much it is costing you to reach 1000 people in your target audience by using that medium. This formula is known as determining the cost per thousand (CPM). Compare that with the cost per thousand viewers of the smaller station. The one which allows you to reach 1000 people in your target the least expensively is your most efficient media buy. This formula:

$$\frac{\text{cost of ad}}{\text{number of people in target audience} \times 1000}$$

can be used to determine your most cost-efficient buy for any medium of advertising. You can compare newspaper with radio, or compare the relative efficiency of two competing stations. Do this before you make any commitments to purchase space or time, or you might be wasting your advertising dollar.

There is one special case where you can avoid figuring CPMs—direct mail. The CPM for this is shockingly high, but there are many instances when this is your most effective approach to advertising. This is discussed in the "Direct Mail" section of this book.

Maximizing Your Schedule with Trade-Outs

One last consideration when deciding between two media vehicles that seem equally desirable is whether one of these will allow you to trade out your products or services in return for advertising. When you are making your calls for rates, inquire about their trade-out policy. You might be able to get substantially more ad space or time in one medium than another simply because you offer a product or service that they can use. All other things (target audience, CPM, availability, circulation, etc.) being equal—go with the medium that gives you the most.

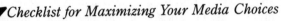

Checklist for Maximizing Your Media Choices

- Gather together all the media information that you have collected so far. Exclude any media that you have eliminated from consideration.
- From the media that remain, choose the medium in which you want to spend the largest percentage of your advertising dollar. Don't worry about specific stations or newspapers, etc., yet—just media categories.
- Now look at the remaining media. Look through the categories carefully, and choose the other categories that best fit your media objectives. If your budget is small, you might have to limit yourself to only one other choice so be very selective.
- How important are each of the media categories that you have selected to your plan? Assign a percentage of your budget to each according to the weight of importance you attach to them.
  NOTE: In selecting your primary and secondary media, consider not only total reach and frequency, but also the effectiveness of each media type in reaching all your target audiences. You will want at least one medium that reaches each group effectively, and a secondary medium to increase your reach and frequency with those audiences.
- Look at your budget figures. How much of your budget does the percentage you have assigned to each medium represent? Give it a dollar figure.
- What strategy do you need to use to maximize your budget: continuous, pulsing, or flighting? Do the media you've chosen have rate structures that will allow you to do this?
- Now that you have narrowed down your media choices, what percentage of the total dollar amount per medium will you spend in reaching each of your target audiences? Translate this into a rough dollar figure.

- Now take a look at the individual media vehicles: individual newspapers, radio stations, etc. Which reach your primary audience most effectively? (Look at your CPMs.)

- Look at the rates for the first media vehicle that seems to be your best primary audience vehicle. How much can you afford to buy on this station, given the dollar amount you derived previously? Is this enough for you to get at least the minimum frequency during the months you will need it? If not, select another vehicle, and figure the same way.

- Do this for all the media that you are considering, using the amounts you have budgeted per target audience per medium, until you have made your final media selections. Don't forget to check the possibility for trade-outs.

- Appendix C gives you a sample media plan. Check with this to see if yours is on the right track.

COMMON PITFALLS FOR THE SMALL BUSINESS ADVERTISER

The small business owner, faced with a media plan, faces three major pitfalls that few advertising books ever talk about. Most books are aimed at major advertisers, who have a high enough budget to withstand some waste circulation, and mistakes. You, however, do not have any margin for error.

The Over-Zealous Sales Rep

We discussed your first pitfall. This is the media sales rep who comes in with impressive statistics about the station and its relative strength in the market. He or she usually comes complete with a set of handouts that show how they lead the area in just about everything. Ask for copies of these handouts. Collect them from every rep who seeks you out. Then take them all out and study them carefully. Notice anything? They all seem to be number one.

The problem is that these handouts were written by advertising people, who have lots of experience in making their product seem like the most desirable alternative for your business. They are trying to do the same thing you are, and most do it very well. The thing you need to do is to become an informed consumer. Stick to basic facts—how many people do you reach in my specific target audience? Then, a few comparisons of CPMs, and you can avoid being bamboozled.

The Not-So-Special Special

Another pitfall for the small business is the advertising special. The sales rep usually offers you a special schedule of advertising at reduced rates. These always look great at first glance because suddenly you can afford twice as many ads as you could before. Once again, study these specials carefully. When or where will your ads run? Is this what you want? How many ads will be run in places or at times when your audience is not likely to be tuned in? How many do you think will reach your audience? Add up the cost of the ads that appear in time slots that your target audience uses, and see how much each ad is costing you. It might not be such a bargain any more.

A typical standard feature for radio and television advertising is a plan called the *ROS* (*run of schedule*). This allows you to buy ads at a reduced rate, but often allows you no control over their placement. The station uses ads bought on the ROS plan to fill in any program time when they could not sell ads at the regular rate. During slow months, this could mean that one or two of your ads will run in premium times. If you buy ROS when advertising time is tight, your ads will probably be running at 3 a.m. or whatever other time slots were rejected by the knowledgeable advertiser. Unless your potential audience is available and likely to be listening heavily around the clock, these so-called bargains could wind up costing you more than the full price rates.

Not all these bargains are bad for you. Look at each offer individually, and see how much control over placement you get. Also, consider the time of year, and the general demand for advertising. Television stations often offer some very good bargains during the summer season when TV viewership is low. Radio station rates tend to go very low after Christmas, because the demand for time drops so drastically with the new year. You might run into some very good deals at these times. But never buy a bargain rate at Christmas when every retailer in town is clamoring for time.

Personal Prejudice

The final, and most difficult pitfall that most small business advertisers have to overcome is their own personal prejudice. All too often, when I have worked with a client, I find that they refuse to advertise on a particular medium, because they tried it and it didn't work. It is difficult to explain tactfully that it might have failed because the ad itself was bad, or because they advertised on the wrong station or time slot.

One furniture shop owner with whom I worked—a man in his mid-sixties—wanted to reach the younger newly affluent portion of the city's population. I suggested a mellow rock station. The client adamantly refused; he hated their music. Another client refused to give up her spots on an oldies station that had the lowest ratings in town and was totally wrong for her target audience, because she loved the music. It might be difficult to imagine purchasing time or space in media that you yourself despise, but if that is where the customer is, that's where you need to be. It might be tempting to imagine that your best customer has the same tastes as you in music, and TV shows, but don't count on it.

Another ugly prejudice that often rears its head at media buying time is a personality problem. The media rep and you might not hit it off. This can make for difficult working conditions. But if that salesperson represents a medium on which you need to be advertising, don't let your personal tastes get in the way of a good business decision, as I have seen happen all too often. If necessary, call the station or the newspaper, and see if there isn't someone else you can work with. Don't let your prejudices keep you away from the media that reach your target audience.

HOW TO CREATE YOUR FINAL MEDIA SCHEDULE

Now that you have made your close-to-final choices of media, you are ready to create your media calendar. This will take a lot of scrap paper, and a lot of patience, but remember, planning a media calendar will not only help you to reach your target audience efficiently, but also save you money. So go to it!

The Media Calendar

The first thing you need to do is get your media calendar. By now, each page should have several notations on it: the amount you have to spend that month, the percent of that amount that is devoted to reaching each target audience, and the dollar amount that this percent represents. You should also, if you did the previous exercise, know approximately what percent of the budget for the month is earmarked for each medium.

In addition, your calendar should already be marked with the dates when you need to advertise, because of special sales and events or because these are the best days for business with the target audience you are trying to reach. Once again, check Appendix C for a sample plan and calendar.

Calculating Yearly Spending by Medium. Before you begin to allocate dollars by the month, you need to make one more calculation. Total up the amount that you are spending on each newspaper, radio station, etc. This will help to see whether you qualify for any bulk. The amount of space or time that you need to buy to qualify for a bulk discount will vary with the individual medium, but your rate cards will give you this information.

Allocating by Medium and by Month. First, take the total figure you have for spending on a specific newspaper vehicle. Let's say you have $4000 to spend in the morning newspaper. Divide that figure by the base cost per column inch. How many inches does this allow you to buy over the year? If the number is close to or more than the amount listed for a contract rate (which is lower), divide your $4000 (or whatever amount you have to spend) by this new, lower figure. This tells you how many inches or minutes you have to spend over the year.

Now look at your monthly figures. What percentage were you planning to spend in the morning paper for January? How many inches does that give you of your yearly total?

Next, look at your calendar. How many ads will you need to run in the morning paper for January? Does this inch figure allow you to accomplish your objectives? Do the ads seem too small? If so, perhaps you can borrow budget (and inches) from months in which you do not need to advertise very heavily. Or perhaps, taking a look at your target audiences for this season, you can use money allocated to media that reach audiences that are not important to your January business. Or, you can simply run smaller ads. (Whether you want to shrink your ads depends a lot on the page where you are advertising. If everyone else on that page tends to run large ads, you might get overlooked.) Either reconsider your page position, or borrow money from less important months.

If your budget seems to give you too much space, don't be afraid to run nice, big ads that will get noticed. Or, if you think that your morning newspaper budget is giving you more ads than you need, take a look at your secondary medium. Can you use more money here?

Continue to allocate ads until you have distributed the budget through all your planned media for the month. Then move on to the next.

Refining the Calendar

Remember, when you move through the months, to indicate not only the size of the ad (2 columns by 3 inches) but also the desired page placement. This might vary within a single medium when you are appealing to different target audiences. For instance, your January ad might be in the women's section, because your primary target audience is women. But some of your February ads should be placed on the business page or in the sports section, if you want to reach the men who will purchase your products Valentine's Day.

Remember when buying broadcast ads to indicate not only the number of spots that you have purchased each day, but also the time slots in which you want them to run. Check to make sure that you have clustered broadcast ads so that your target audience will be likely to hear at least three of them during the week. Since you must purchase a minimum of five ads per week to be effective, check to see if this qualifies you for a frequency discount.

If you are using flyers, schedule not only their distribution day, but also the day when you need to order them from the printer. For direct mail, note printer deadlines, mail days, etc. In this way, you will create a calendar that not only shows you how to allocate your media in a cost-efficient way, but which will also serve as a reminder to you to check with media reps, write new copy as needed, or do whatever you need to do to keep your advertising on schedule.

Checklist for an Efficient Media Calendar

- Have you figured out whether you qualify for any bulk discounts in the media you plan to use?
- Have you checked to see for which frequency discounts you might qualify?

- Have you spent your budget monthly in accordance with sales?
- Have you allocated extra funds for months that have special needs, sales, etc.?
- Have you saved 5 – 10 percent for emergency expenditures and opportunities?
- If you are using media that involves production costs, have you figured these into the monthly budgets?
- Do your monthly plans use media that reach the target audiences that are most important that month?
- Do your monthly plans give you enough reach and frequency to be effective? Does this hold true for all media and all target audiences?
- Have you scheduled your media buys for the times that are psychologically best for your target audiences (example: reminding them at home so they can discuss the purchase with family members, advertising near paydays when they are financially prepared to buy)?
- Call the media with which you plan to advertise and arrange for all your contracts. If media reps offer you any special rates, check to see if they are real bargains. If so, accept them and refigure your budget to take advantage of the new rates.

SUMMARY

Scheduling your media effectively means advertising at the times when customers are most likely to be in the market for your business. With a small advertising budget, advertisers often take advantage of pulsing or flighting strategies to achieve a maximum impact without maximum expenditure. Ads, however, must be purchased in such a way that they reach enough of the target audience to draw in the amount of the business you need. These ads must be scheduled so that your potential customers are exposed to them a minimum of three times each.

In order to create an effective media schedule, you must look at each medium that you might use, and the demographic and psychographic characteristics of the audience. You must then look at the geographic area that the medium reaches to see how closely this coincides with your area of trade. When you find something that seems to fit your needs, figure out how much it costs you to reach 1000 people on that medium. By comparing this figure with the CPM of other potential media buys, you can achieve the most efficient use of your media dollar.

11

Finding the Right Advertising Message

"SOME OF MY ADS WORK BETTER THAN OTHERS," MUSED GINNY. "BUT I'M damned if I can understand why."

She showed me one ad she'd been especially proud of. Nicely laid out and easy to read, it gave all the pertinent information about her insurance agency. "Look—it shows all the types of insurance we offer, and tells people how much training and experience I've got. Plus, it says we have low rates. So how come it flopped, and this crummy little ad for motorcycle insurance was a smash?"

I looked at the new ad—only one column inch. "Motorcyclists!" its headline proclaimed. "You can get affordable insurance at Walker's."

"Don't you see the difference? The first one looks good, but all it tells us is what you've got. This little guy tells the customer what you can do for them. That's the whole key to a successful ad—making a meaningful promise."

Sad to say, but your potential customers don't care what you've got to offer. They're too busy to take time to read your list of boasts. They do care what you can do for them.

Your entire advertising campaign should be customer-based, offering benefits rather than listing selling points. A successful ad makes a meaningful promise to the consumer, assuring them that you can make their life happier, more profitable, easier, or more secure.

The success of the promises you make depends entirely on the wants and needs of your customer. This chapter tells you how to take the research material you gathered in chapters 4, 5, and 6 and use it to determine what your ads need to communicate in order to motivate your customers. Do you need a factual promise—saving money, time, or trouble? Or would you be better off with an emotional benefit—fun, prestige, or maybe security? Which promises will best set you apart from your competition while being attractive to your target audiences? Which promise can you make that will form an effective theme for your entire campaign?

CREATING AN IDENTITY

In the old days, before mass production and mass media, creating an identity for a business was easy. There wasn't much competition. All a businessperson needed to do was proclaim "Here I am." As business boomed and competition increased, each small shop and service realized a need to set itself apart from everyone else. On Madison Avenue, advertising executives created a method for achieving this known as the *Unique Selling Proposition (USP)*.

The Unique Selling Proposition

The USP simply pointed out, through advertising, the ways in which you were unique. Not necessarily better than the competition—but different from them. At first, this worked well. With fewer businesses, there were plenty of meaningful differences to go around. Business A had a strong reputation for service, its Competitor B had good prices, and C had the best quality of merchandise. D had a bigger selection than anyone else. And so forth.

Eventually, though, as business E, F, and G started up, the meaningful differences were all taken. G had to resort to saying "The store with the red awning." This was not a great selling point, even if it did make G easy to recognize. A new advertising tactic was called for.

Positioning

When uniqueness became too difficult an advertising concept, Madison Avenue invented *positioning*. Positioning refers to the way in which your product or service is positioned in the mind of consumers—the way in which they think of you and the prominence you assume in their mind when they are in the market for your type of product or service. What positioning did was to allow advertisers to depart from advertising mere physical attributes and instead use image advertising. Or, advertisers could make other types of benefit claims, depending on their understanding of the target audience.

Ways to Position Your Business

There are many ways to position a business. Your best method depends on your advertising objectives and the wants and needs of your target audience. Keep a careful eye toward what the competition is doing.

Positioning by Unique Attribute. The first positioning technique, if you can do it, is to use a meaningful USP. If there is something truly better about your business than what the competition can offer, then you can still set yourself apart this way. Few of us are lucky enough to get off this easily. So we try other tactics.

Positioning by Attribute. You could position yourself by attribute. This simply means choosing some feature that the competition is not claiming, and using that as your identifying characteristic. In other words, if the competition and you are identical, but she has chosen to emphasize price in her ads, you might choose to emphasize selection. If she seizes upon both price and selection, you advertise price and quality. Toothpastes do this all the time. One is a cavity fighter, one promises whiter teeth, one has a good taste. All three have the same qualities, but each chose to emphasize a different one. In our minds, however, we think of each as having a separate and most important identifying characteristic. So, if we are buying toothpaste for kids, we grab the cavity fighter. The insecure adolescent gravitates toward the whiter teeth promise. Reluctant brushers choose good taste. All the toothpastes are basically alike, but they are positioned in our minds as ''the toothpaste for cavities, etc.''

Positioning by Use. You can position your business by use. This means that your ads concentrate on telling people when they need to come to you. A downtown restaurant, hoping to take business away from the bar with the fabulous happy hour might advertise that they are famous for their British afternoon tea. A preventative health clinic advertises ''See us before illness strikes.'' A small winery tells us that ''Valley Wines make lunchtime luxurious.'' Since many people think of company wines as being foreign, relatively medium-priced, and for consumption with and after dinner, Valley is hoping to inspire you to treat yourself, even when there's no company and have Valley's wine with lunch.

Positioning by User. You can also position by user. This suggests to people that they want to do business with you because that's where other people in their reference group go. Thus, you become ''George's Diner—Where the Beautiful People Eat,'' or ''Maxine—Plumber to the Stars.'' This does not mean that only bona fide stars will call Maxine. Everyone who wants to associate themselves with the stars or to claim that they can do business in the same lofty category as these people will be attracted to her, in preference to ''Bob—Plumber to the Working Class.''

Virginia Slims positioned itself by user. It has such a strong identity as a cigarette for women that men are embarrassed to bum one. Hallmark Cards is also positioning itself by user when it says that its cards are ''For those who care to send the very best.''

Positioning by Image. Another alternative is to position by image. Image advertising often avoids making any factual claims at all. Image advertising depends largely on the look or sound of the ad to convey a certain corporate personality. This form of positioning works a lot like positioning by user; the customer tends to choose the business with an image that matches his or her self-image. Trendy, old-fashioned, friendly, exclusive, expensive, efficient, luxurious, down-to-earth, a bit zany—all these are images that can attract.

The important thing to remember, in attempting to position your business in the public mind, is to offer your potential consumer a benefit. That benefit can be psychological, or it can be a real, dollars and cents bonus. Consumers of advertising, as a rule, will not act on the advertising message unless they perceive in that message some advantage to themselves.

Checklist for Finding Your Best Position

- Find your competitors' ads. Check the Yellow Pages, the newspaper, and if possible, the broadcast media. What promises are they making?
- Is there any promise that you can make that the competitors are not making?
- If you do find a promise that sets you apart, check your research. Is this promise one that is meaningful to your target audience? If not, try a different positioning approach.
- If you don't find a different promise, try one of the remaining positioning tactics.
- By use: Is there some way to use your product or service that the target market might not have thought of? Are there any emotional uses for your product or service, such as feeling secure, satisfying curiosity, looking and feeling up to date, appearing to be trendy etc.?
- By user: Who are your customers? How do they like to think of themselves when they see themselves as users of your business? Can you find a meaningful way to describe yourself to this audience? Is it different from what the competition is saying?
- By image: Do you project a different image from your competitors? Is this an image that your target audience will find appealing? Is it meaningful enough to make some of them prefer you to the competition?

The following discussion of selling points and benefits might help you to discover a position that will create a successful advertising identity for your business.

BENEFITS AND SELLING POINTS

Benefits are meaningful promises about what you can do to make your potential customer's life happier, more fun, more secure, or easier. You derive benefits from your selling points, which are the positive features that your business can offer.

Selling Points

As a business, you have many, many features that you designed to serve the public. You might have a great degree of expertise in your field, or excellent credentials. You might have a good location, attractive decor, knowledgeable help, a great selection, soothing background music, or an impressive clientele. If you deliver, have free parking, take charges, or do special orders, these are all selling points. So is the fact that you've been in business fifty years, or that you're new. Selling points are all the things that you have and do that will make your business attractive to your customer.

List Your Selling Points. Simply making as complete a list of your selling points as possible will be a great help in showing you what kinds of promises you can make to your target audience. But taking the time and trouble to list all your selling points has another, hidden benefit—it can help to show you what you have to offer that is different from your competition.

Compare Selling Points with the Competition. Since one of the goals of advertising is to set you apart from the competition, one of your first goals should be to discover in what ways you are already different from your competitors. Many of the differences might not seem meaningful at first. You might have a contemporary decor, and your competitor looks more traditional. You might deliver in a red truck while she uses a blue one. Nevertheless, these differences provide the public with a means of distinguishing between you. Surprisingly, for many of your potential customers, your decor, color scheme, or the neighborhood in which you are located will give you a psychological edge over your competitor. If I feel more at ease in a chrome and glass atmosphere, I might tend to prefer your modern store to the competitor's wood and chintz environment. One group of people might enjoy telling friends that they bought that tablecloth in a little shop in the Village, while another enjoys the snob appeal of saying she bought it on Park Avenue.

In determining your selling points, then, it is a good idea to list all the tangible and intangible aspects of your business. Look at location, decor, services, merchandise, clientele, your degree of expertise, store layout, years in business, color, texture—even the music you play. Any one of these things might make a difference in how customers perceive you. Therefore, a list of selling points includes a complete list of everything that answers the question: ''What have you got that makes it pleasant (or efficient, or sensible) to do business with you?''

Make as complete a list as possible of everything you have that might be perceived as a good selling point for your business. Then try to check out your competitors. How are you the same? What is different?

Relate Your Selling Points to the Customer. If you have carefully researched your target audiences, an inventory of selling points should be able to take you far. Look at your lists—what you have, what your competition has, and what your similarities and differences are. Now take a good look at your audience, their desires, likes, dislikes, and general style. Which items on your lists seem to be most meaningful to your audience? If you have written a target audience profile, as I suggested in chapter 4, you should be able to decide which features are most likely to be meaningful to that hypothetical typical customer of yours. Which of these meaningful items that you have chosen are either not available from the competition, or are not featured in your competitor's ads? This is the list with which you will work to formulate your advertising campaign.

Using Your Selling Points: A Case History

As an example, let's say that you offer a typing service to the local university. You will do term papers, theses and dissertations for $1.50 a page. Your selling points? You type 120 words a minute. You won the state typing championship in 1983. You have an IBM PC, with a letter quality printer and automatic footnoting and bibliographies. You are familiar with all the recommended styles for academic papers. You can pick up and deliver your work. You also have an IBM Selectric typewriter with five available typestyles for special work. Your computer can draw charts and graphs. You work at home, and clients can easily reach you there by phone. You tend to do mostly doctoral dissertations and masters theses. You can read even the worst handwritten drafts. Plus, you take Mastercard.

Your competitor offers the same service. She can type 120 words a minute on her IBM PC. You don't know whether she ever won any typing awards, but if she did, she's not advertising it. Her IBM Selectric has seven type styles. She works 9–5 in a rented office, but you can always reach her answering service after hours. She doesn't take any charges. The bulk of her work is undergraduate term papers, and she promises overnight service.

Your audiences, as you have analyzed them, are not 9–5 people. Many of them do not have cars. They don't care how fast you type, as long as you can get the work done when they need it. Getting things done according to the right style manual, however, for your thesis and dissertation customers, is crucial. There is very little demand for any but the standard type available on your letter quality computer printer. Many of your customers are short of cash most of the time, but can always manage to put a bit more money on the old charge card. Therefore, your flexible hours, delivery capability, knowledge of style manuals, and charge card service are meaningful selling points that set you apart from your competitor. These are the basic selling points that your ad campaign will need to feature.

Let us imagine a bit further that you and your competitor are identical in services, hours, and expertise, and are in neck and neck competition for the same target audience. The only difference between you is that you deliver your work in a beat up VW Bug, and she drives a regular Buick. While your Bug might not seem like a very good selling point in comparison to your competitor's nice, but more conservative car, it does make you stick out a bit and gives you a certain personality. This, too, is a selling point.

Checklist for Determining Your Selling Points

- List every service that you offer, including those that you don't seem to have any demand for. (The lack of demand could be due to lack of awareness.) Which of these do the competition offer? Are there any that you offer that the competition does not? Are any of these meaningful to your target audience?

- List all types of merchandise that you deal with, including all popular brands and styles. What do you offer that your competition does not? If you offer the same line, do you in any way improve on their offering—price, guarantees, etc.?

- List your price range, and the ways in which this differs from your competition.

- Look at selection. How is yours better than and different from the competition?

- Look at your place of business. Describe everything in it that might appeal to the customer: wide aisles, decor, carpet, music, cleanliness, signs to help people locate items, etc. In what ways is this different from your competitors? How is it better?

- Look at your staff. What do they have to offer to your customer? Does this in any way differ from what your competitors offer?

- Look at your customers. Who are they? Do they fall into any group classification that gives you an identity—are they all smart shoppers, the very elite, those with great taste, or people who appreciate good work? Would knowing this influence your target audience?

- Look at your image. Is it different from your competitors image? How attractive is your present image to your target audience, according to your research?

- Make a record of all the meaningful differences that set you apart from your competitors. Make a second list of those points that you share with your competitors, but the customer will need to know about in order to be attracted to your business.

Benefits

Selecting your main selling points is important to a good advertising campaign—but the next step, turning them into benefits—is crucial. A benefit doesn't talk about what you have, it tells your potential customers what that selling point will do for them.

Why a Benefit? Turning your selling points into benefits is crucial because people, even the kindest, don't care what you have. They only care about how you can improve the quality of their own lives. If you're completely honest with yourself, you'll admit that your basic response, when listening to a radio ad that says "We have 12 stores under one roof, and the largest selection anywhere. Our specially trained sales staff and newly remodeled floor plan offer the ultimate in up-to-the-minute design," is a kind of disinterested "That's nice." Face it, there are simply too many advertising messages out there, competing for our attention. We don't have time to translate all those "we haves" into "you'll gets." A good advertiser does this for you. Instead of 12 stores under one roof, tell them "Our twelve shops mean you can take care of all your shopping needs in one easy stop. Our specially trained staff will help you to choose the equipment best suited to your needs—and in an atmosphere designed to make shopping easy for you."

Converting Your Selling Points. That's the trick with a benefit. Take your selling point one step further, and translate it into a promise to the consumer. Don't talk about what you have. Talk about what we'll get.

Try to look at your business from the customer's viewpoint. What do they hope to get from you? Good service, certainly. And merchandise that offers quality at a good price. A pleasant atmosphere. All this. But think a bit more. Why do they come to you? What are their emotional hopes? Does your electrical service offer them peace of mind? Does your clothing selection help them to create and/or maintain the self-image that they would like to hold of themselves? You're not just selling a product or a service, you are selling emotional overtones. Security. Trendiness. Sex appeal. Maybe even patriotism. A chance to fit in with the crowd—or to stand out from it. A feeling of self-worth, or knowledgeability.

Emotional Benefits. You cannot necessarily see, hear, and touch the benefits that your customer might receive from doing business with you. These intangible, emotional benefits, however, might be more important than your list of such easy to spot things as parking, wide selection, and lots of help. These emotional benefits should supplement your list of selling-points. These are the personality of your advertising, the real motivators that create good ads. Plus, these less apparent benefits are exactly the tool you need to set yourself apart from the competitor. Let him sell mouthwash. You can sell security. Let her sell pottery, while you sell individual self-expression. Let them sell air conditioners, while you sell comfort, or freedom from the heat.

DETERMINING YOUR KEY BENEFIT

A key benefit is the central point of your entire advertising campaign. This is the single, most meaningful promise that you can make to your potential customer. Your key benefit is a promise that you will make over and over again in all your advertising. It becomes the theme of your campaign, and a powerful means of creating a special identity for your business in the consumer mind.

Key Benefits in Action: A Case History

A good key benefit makes a promise to the consumer that is meaningful to him or her, and that is different from what the competition is promising. For instance, you have a jewelry store, and so does Josephine. Both of you specialize in costume jewelry of a good quality, but at reasonable prices. That's what Josephine advertises—good quality at a reasonable price.

Josephine is telling people what she has. While this is an attractive selling point, it is not as powerful as a benefit. If you advertise that "With Jewelry by Jennifer, you'll only look expensive." You're saying the same thing as Josephine, but you're also making a promise. You're telling all those costume jewelry buyers out there what you can do for them.

Now, imagine that Josephine is a fierce competitor. She sees your ad and realizes the error of her ways. She writes a target audience profile and sees that her most frequent customers don't care about wearing real diamonds and gold. They like to have lots of "fun" jewelry to accessorize and complement their outfits. They enjoy blatant fakes. Josephine realizes that, to her typical customer, looking expensive would not be the key that would draw them into her shop. The key benefit to her customers is that her jewelry is inexpensive enough that they can buy enough to go with everything. She advertises "Josephine's Jewelry—fun for all your fads and fancies."

Does this approach mean that people will shop with you when they want elegance without expense and shop with Josephine when they want something frivolous? Maybe. What your key benefit does is create a certain image of you in the consumer mind. It fosters a certain way of thinking about who you are and what you offer. But if a customer in search of inexpensive elegance notices your display of plastic bangles and likes them, she is just as likely to buy from you when the frivolous mood strikes.

Key Benefits and the Audience

In formulating your key benefit, you should first look at your target audience profile. Then look at your list of selling points and decide which of these is most likely to influence the person described in that profile. Check your research to discover exactly what points are most likely to influence your market. Finally, take a look at what your competition is promising in their advertising.

Key Benefits and the Competition

You can feature the same selling point that your competitor does, as long as you turn your selling point into a benefit that is meaningful to your potential audience. If your competitor is already featuring the same benefit that you wanted to highlight, you have a couple of options.

Differing Benefits. One is to choose another key benefit. No one makes a decision to act based on a single motivation. Therefore, your target customer for a beauty shop might be motivated by an ad promising glamour. He or she could also be mightily moved by an ad promising Parisian chic, or individuality, or sex appeal. The same wallpaper buyer who is attracted by easy care and washability also hungers for style and self-expression. The woman who calls your plumbing service wants assurance that you won't charge her an arm and a leg, but she also chose you because your ad conveyed great professionalism. There is no single promise that will work for all your customers all the time. Therefore, if your competitor is already making your favorite benefit promise, there might be several others that will work equally effectively.

Double Benefits. If you can, however, you might consider promising a double benefit. If your competition offers low, low prices —"We're passing on our savings to you,"—then you might offer low prices and a big selection—"Any look you want at the price you want." The only thing you need to be careful of with this strategy is that you don't make too many promises. More than two benefits, and you begin to seem dubious, even if everything you claim is true. More than two benefits, and you also begin to muddy your public identity. People might remember you as the glamour place, or the fun place—or they might remember you as the place that offers glamorous fun. When you start promising glamorous fun at a savings, we start getting confused.

Keep it Simple. The sad fact is, few people out there pay 100 percent attention to advertising. They have some vague notion of your identity, if you happen to be in a business that they might have a want or need for. They do not, however, check the paper each night, eagerly searching for your promises. So you have to keep those promises simple, meaningful, and memorable.

RATIONAL VS. EMOTIONAL BENEFITS

There are two main types of benefits, the rational and the emotional. Rational benefits are those that talk about real promises you can make to the consumer, such as saving money or finding everything you need under one roof. Emotional benefits address the less tangible wants and needs of your audience. Emotional benefits promise security, popularity, freedom from guilt or fear, or just plain fun. The type of promise that you make depends on both the type of business you are advertising and the audience to whom you are speaking.

Rational Benefits

Several bits of information that you have gathered about your target audience will help you to determine whether you would do best with a rational benefit. Educational level, sex, the perceived expense of the item, and several other factors will determine whether you must give your customers logical reasons to buy, or if an emotional appeal would be more effective.

Education. As we mentioned in the chapter on demographics, the more educated your audience is, the more they demand rational proof that they are making a wise decision. Men, too, prefer to find some rational justification for making a buying decision, and this preference strengthens as the educational level rises. This does not mean that these people will not respond instinctively to emotional appeals—they do. But they need to be able to justify this response in rational terms.

Expense of Service or Goods. As the expense of a purchase rises, so does the need for rational benefits. If you are considering a new refrigerator, no matter how emotional you might be, you tend to look for appliance stores with good reputations. People might respond emotionally to color, shape, and all the neat little gadgets that come with some of the floor models, but when the purchase represents a substantial cash outlay, they need rational justification.

Cost Perception of the Audience. Expense, of course, is in the mind of the purchaser. The Astors and the Vanderbilts could afford to lay out enormous sums for fancy cars and gadgets, without ever having to consider practicality. Today, advertisers of Mercedes and Lincoln know that they can sell pure image and emotionality, because they are talking to people who can afford the asking price without wincing. But if your target audience is likely to consider your products to be an investment, then you must offer them rational reasons to choose you.

On the other hand, not even the most hidebound, rational male Ph.D needs logical reasons to justify indulging in a candy bar. If it tastes good, and the chocolate seems soothing on the roof of his mouth, and he can reach into his loose change to buy it, then you can give him a purely emotional appeal and he just might respond.

Type of Product or Service. Besides cost, your choice of a rational versus an emotional appeal might be affected by the type of product or service that you offer. For instance, there seems to be almost no way that you can use a logical appeal for selling perfume. Perfume is purely emotional. Cost is the only practical factor that affects our choice of scent. Other than that, you are selling hope, or femininity, or sexuality. It would be difficult to use this same approach in selling stocks and bonds. While the investor might have high hopes for what his money can earn, he also wants good, solid reasons for making a particular investment, even if it's only in penny stocks.

The Competition. The decision to use one type of key benefit over another, then, rests heavily on the needs of your customer, and the perceived cost of your product or service. Your decision should also take the competition's offerings into account. If emotions sell well for them, they might very well work for you also. If they are having great success with facts and figures, you might want to compete on the same basis. Just remember not to set yourself up as a clone for your competitor. Promise as much or better than they promise—but promise your customers something that they want or need.

Combining Rational and Emotional Benefits

I don't mean to suggest that your ads must be either wholly rational or totally emotional. A successful ad, especially for a small retail or service business, is usually both. You might offer a potential customer a car that will make them feel young, sporty and affluent, then back up your promise with EPA ratings, cost figures, etc. Offer them clothing that will totally express their individuality, then point out that they can achieve this at less than it would cost to shop with the masses.

This double-barreled approach to advertising is generally the wisest way to go. Our motivations for buying are not always clear, even to ourselves. We might have a strong emotional attraction for an item, but need logical reasons before we will convince ourselves to spend. Or, we might know logically that we should use a certain service, but lack the motivation to actually call for an appointment until something pulls at our heartstrings. The ad that reaches its customer with both rational reasons and emotional appeal will have a better chance of success than one that ignores the head/heart nature of humankind.

Making the Most of Your Benefits

When choosing a benefit to feature in your advertising, make sure that you distinguish between the benefits that come from doing business with you, and the benefits that come from using your type of product or service. Too many ads give the customer great reasons to use a travel agency—but no particular reason to use yours. Or they feature a dozen great reasons for painting the house—but never tell us why we should use your brand. Your key benefit—the promise that becomes the tag line to all your advertising—must make promises about the advantages, either emotional or logical, of doing business with you.

Individual ads within your campaign, however, will want to feature a particular product or service. As an insurance agent, your campaign theme, your slogan, might stress that "you can feel secure with us." The headline for your ad for motorcycle insurance might stress "lowest rates in town"—at "GRE— where you can feel secure." Thus, in a single ad, you combine both rational and emotional—the best of both worlds.

Checklist for Determining Your Key Benefit

- Look at your list of selling points. Which are most important to your target audience? Which emerge as the ones that best set you apart from your competitor? Make a separate list of these.
- Of these, which seem to be the most important to your target audience, as discovered in your research?
- Look at your price category. Do you need to make rational promises to justify your cost? If so, which selling points on your list most logically convince the customer that they should do business with you?
- Looking at your target audience, do they seem to want more of an emotional, or a rational reason to do business with you? If emotional, look at your selling points to see what you can most convincingly promise. Do the same for rational promises. If you think they require both, choose two promises that seem to go together. Do they make convincing points that set you apart from your competition?
- When you have narrowed down your list to one or two most important points, turn these into promises. Don't worry about wording. Simply list what the selling points that you have singled out will do for the customer. This idea will form the basis of your campaign theme.

WHICH BENEFIT WHEN?

I mentioned above that the headline in your ad can feature a benefit that differs from your key benefit. Not only can these benefits differ, they should. Every good advertising campaign has two aspects: permanence and change. Part of your campaign never changes—the total theme, the look and sound of your ads, your name, hours, logo, and tag line. Parts of your ad must keep changing.

The Perils of Permanence

As a business owner, you are probably the only person in town who actively seeks out your advertising message. The rest of us must be enticed, in some way, to notice what you are saying. We tend, as a rule, to notice mainly those ads that have some relevance to us. If I, as a newspaper reader, am in the process of redecorating my home, I will tend to read ads for paint, wallpaper, furniture, etc. Once I am done with my project, I will quit noticing your ads until it's time to redo another room. During the redecorating phase when I am paging through, and notice your ad for the first time, I will read it to see if you sound like you fit with my plans. I might continue to do this for a week or so. If after a period of time, your ad hasn't changed and told me more, I will stop reading. You have nothing new to tell me. Soon, I won't even see your ad as I flip the pages. And, I still haven't bought my wallpaper.

What happened? After all, I was in your target audience. The answer is simple. The ad I saw didn't quite hit a responsive chord in my mind. Whatever you chose to feature wasn't exactly what I was looking for. I kept reading, however, because I knew that you weren't telling your whole story in a single ad. I hoped that tomorrow or next week, you would feature something that I was in the market for. Instead, your ad remained static. So I tuned out.

The Benefits of Change

If, as discussed earlier, you had constantly changed the subbenefits in your ad, I would have continued to discover new things about you. I would continue to read your ads. If someday you were to feature exactly what I was looking for, I'd grab my coat and head to your store.

This is the reason for making a totally thorough list of all the benefits that you can offer a potential customer. While your key benefit becomes the tag line or slogan of all your ads, the additional benefits that you offer can form an ever-changing array of information designed to interest the consumer. You can feature different benefits at different times of the year as the headlines and body copy of your print ads, and as the message of your broadcast ads. Be consistent with your main theme and benefit.

This plan to change the featured benefits of your ads also is budget wise. When you sit down and try to figure out what you would like to tell members of the public about your business, you have a long, long list of messages. Sometimes, at first, it looks like you'll need at least a full-page ad. Your budget, however, might tell you that you can only afford a four-column inch ad—not nearly enough to say what you want to say.

In that case, choose your permanent element, the key benefit that you want people to identify with you. This becomes your tag line, and appears in every single ad. Then, choose one or two pertinent things from the list of other benefits. The next week, choose two or three different items. In this manner, you can tell the public a lot about yourself in a small space. Plus, you're giving them a reason to keep reading your ads as they appear. You're forcing them to pay more attention to your ad than they might have if it didn't change. This repetition makes more impact on a potential customer than a single exposure would. Every new benefit that you feature is one more chance to hit upon exactly the promise that will motivate someone to act on your ad, rather than just think about it (Fig. 11-1 illustrates a series of ads that rotate benefits).

Shall I Chintz It?

We can recover your upholstered
furniture in chintz--or tiger printed
velvet, quilted homespun--whatever
you fancy. If you can dream it,
we can do it.

Give your furniture a Facelift

the **Restoration Shop**

Route 6, Tunckhannock 587-0574

Fig. 11-1. Each of these three ads highlights a different service that this new business provides. This not only gives the reader a reason to keep on reading your ads every time they
appear, but also gives you, as advertiser, a chance to keep giving out new information that
doesn't comfortably fit in a single ad. (Clip art from Carol Belanger Grafton, *Love and
Romance.* Courtesy of Dover Books)

Want to Strip???

Poor stripping of fine wood furniture can loosen joints and weaken your treasured pieces. Let us do it right--so that you get what you want, and keep it for a lifetime. Plus--we can refinish it to give you a fine, renewed look at reasonable prices.

Give your furniture a Facelift

the Restoration Shop
Route 6, Tunckhannock 587-0574

Fig. 11-1 (continued).

Bored with your Boudoir?

We can give that room a whole new look with our custom wood finishes. From faux marble and tortoiseshelling to Chinese lacquer and clear wood finishes. In any color your heart desires.

Give your furniture a Facelift

the **Restoration Shop**
Route 6, Tunckhannock 587-0574

Fig. 11-1 (continued).

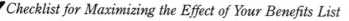

Checklist for Maximizing the Effect of Your Benefits List

- Look at the points that remain now that you have selected your key benefit. Do any of them appeal more to one target audience than another? Make separate lists, for each of your target audiences, of all the selling points that appeal specifically to that audience. Any that are common to all lists have key benefit potential.

- Do some of your selling points have only seasonal appeal? Separate these from the rest, according to target audience.

- During the year, will you feature special products or services at specific times? Are there certain selling points that make these appealing? List these in their own category.

- Make a set of lists that can be used to create ads targeted to specific audiences and occasions. Your next step is to turn those selling points into benefits. Looking at the audience and occasion, what does each selling point do to make your audience's life happier, easier, etc.? (Appendix D gives examples of selling points turned into benefits.) Turn these into benefits now, and putting your specific ads together during the year will be a simple matter of choosing the points you wish to feature.

SUMMARY

The key to successful advertising is to develop an identity for your business that customers will associate with a benefit that you offer to them. This benefit, called your key benefit, is the most meaningful promise you can make to the type of customer you wish to attract based on both their motivations and your need to set yourself apart from the competition. The key benefit becomes the theme for your advertising, and is usually expressed as a slogan or tag line that people associate with your business name. That slogan can be either a tangible promise, an emotional one, or a combination of both logic and emotion.

All the other benefits you can offer potential customers, whether they be temporary or permanent services and features, become the changing elements of your advertising campaign. This keeps ads from becoming static, and therefore, less noticeable. It also allows the small-budget advertiser to convey a lot of information to the public at a low cost, while encouraging that public to read your ads more often.

12

Keeping Your
Ads Consistent:
The Campaign Concept

BUTCH'S ADS WERE VERY CREATIVE. ONE WAS DONE LIKE A COMIC STRIP WITH every panel featuring a new benefit. Another was serious, but striking. A third used a house-shaped border, with the theme "Everything for the whole house." Most customers who responded to an ad for the first time commented on it favorably. Good as each ad was, however, as a package they didn't bring in the amount of business that Butch felt they should.

His biggest problem? Butch had great ads, but he didn't have a campaign. Since none of the ads resembled any of the others, readers had trouble recognizing them as coming from the same business. Butch had no theme—no key promise that gave his business a particular identity and a meaningful difference from his competitors.

A successful ad is one thing; a successful advertising campaign is another. Campaigns have a common theme, and a common look and sound. They are based on a key benefit, which helps to establish your business identity. They aim at accomplishing the specific long- and short-range objectives that you have established.

Chapter 12 explains how to create a unified campaign that will accomplish all these things. You will learn creative techniques for developing campaign themes and the formulae used on Madison Avenue and by persuasive theorists for creating an effective ad. You will also learn how to keep your campaigns consistent in all media.

There are two types of consistency in a good campaign. The first is *campaign consistency*—a thread of thematic unity that runs throughout all the ads, in every medium of your campaign. The second is *within-media consistency*—a basic similarity of format and execution in each ad developed for a single medium. The first will be dealt with in this chapter, the latter in chapters devoted to the separate media.

THE ADVERTISING CAMPAIGN

Probably the most frequent problem encountered by the advertiser is that they don't understand the idea of "campaign." As various media salesmen carry off our time and space orders, it becomes all too easy to write one kind of ad for one radio station, another for a second, and something altogether different for the newspaper. The penalty we pay for this scattered approach is an immense loss in the frequency with which our target audience perceives our ads. They might see every piece of advertising that we put out, but, because the ads are so different in concept and execution, they might fail to realize that all these ads come from a single business.

A study of advertising formulated by the major agencies for million-dollar clients should give you a clue about what I mean when I say you must have a campaign theme. Take a look, for instance, at the ads that have been running for over a decade for Palmolive dishwashing liquid. They each have a central character—Madge the Manicurist. They each have another changing character—a woman who has dishpan hands. They have a central theme—dishwashing liquid so mild you can soak in it to soften your hands before a manicure. This theme is the real key to the campaign consistency. Every ad, whether in print, on radio, TV, or billboards, shows us the phenomenon of dishwashing liquid so mild that it seems to benefit our hands.

The TV ad provides us with the entire array of characters. There is a format to this ad, although much of the content changes. We always open with a woman sitting down for a manicure with Madge. Madge always makes some sarcastic remark about the state of the woman's hands while the customer complains about the ravages of dishwashing. Madge then delivers a small lecture on the benefits of Palmolive. The woman acts incredulous. Madge then tells her that she's soaking in that very Palmolive. The TV camera focuses on the clear bowl of recognizable green dish soap, with a manicured hand soaking. The commercial always ends with a visualization of benefits—the woman returns with beautiful, soft hands while Madge cracks a joke about the woman's former ignorance.

On radio, the dialogue from the TV commercial can run minus pictures. On billboards, we usually focus on the hand soaking in Palmolive—a device that has become instantly recognizable to us through the TV ads. It communicates the benefit instantly and graphically.

If you page through the women's magazines, you will see Madge and her client seated at the manicure table with the client's hand still soaking in Palmolive.

Consistency by Situation

Every ad in the Palmolive campaign revolves around a single idea—the product benefit. Every ad does this consistently, by using the same tag line or slogan, the same graphic devices, the same characters and types of situations. While Madge's clients change, as do her jokes, the rest of the ad and the situation in which the product is used remains amazingly the same, and has for years. This is the essence of the advertising campaign.

Some companies are a bit freer in their interpretation of consistency, and yet still achieve recognizability over the years and across the media. The telephone company's suggestion that we ''Reach Out and Touch Someone'' has been running for years. No matter what the medium, we see the same situation—someone calling long distance to keep in touch with a loved one that they separated from. The people and their reasons for separation are different in every ad, but the idea—that we can get a lot of warmth and love across by calling long distance—never varies.

Consistency by Audio or Visual Symbols

Some ads use a visual or audio signal in every ad that ties the campaign together. The fizz of Alka-Seltzer, for instance, could be heard in every broadcast commercial and portrayed visually in every print ad. Old Spice used to use sounds of the sea and creaking boats—another audio symbol that was easy to show in print. As long as the elements can be both heard in broadcast advertising and be visualized in print, they can help to tie your ads together into a cohesive campaign.

Consistency of Theme and Attitude

One last way to create unity in your advertising is to use an emotional theme or attitude consistently. For instance, your ads could all lean heavily toward the idea of romance. Print ads will be full of lace, ribbons, and flowers, while broadcast ads use music and sound effects to portray romantic words. Your new personal shopping service ads could feature a variety of people, all being ecstatic about the wonderful choices that you have made. Their consistency of attitude will help to tie your campaign together across media.

At any rate, make sure that all your ads in every medium contain some common elements. The best way to achieve this for your own campaign is to choose a theme for your advertising that can be expressed in a tag line or slogan, and a key visual.

The Key Visual

A *key visual* is some graphic device that appears in every print ad, and relates to the campaign theme in some meaningful way. In the Palmolive ad, the bowl of dishwashing liquid with the fingertips soaking is the key visual; with Bell Telephone, we have not only the visual and recognizable logo, but the inevitable sight of the situation hero or heroine using the telephone.

Your logo is a key visual, and must be in every ad. If your campaign also calls for illustrated print advertising, then find some way to give all pictures some common theme.

The Advertising Format

The secondary ploy in campaign creation is to develop a recognizable format that never varies for each medium, even though the additional benefits and information might change with each new ad. In print, this means that you have a specific layout that remains consistent, a particular selection of typefaces, and an identifiable border style. You also have a never-changing logo. In radio, this means that you have a recognizable style to your ad—either a straight announcement always done in the same voice, or a consistent form of dialogue, or a recognizable character who speaks for your business. This same character and situation should be employed in your TV ads, and on any billboards or other visual media you employ. The main point of every ad, no matter what the media, should be to communicate your most important benefit to your target audience and supplement it with additional benefits.

TURNING YOUR KEY BENEFIT INTO A CAMPAIGN THEME

You should already have your key benefit—the most meaningful promise that you can make about your business to your target audience. Now it's time to play with words. Turn your benefit into a catchy phrase that you can use in your ads. This phrase must be memorable, because it is the central point to your campaign. If your campaign is successful, this is the phrase that will automatically pop to mind when people hear the name of your business. Your campaign theme will also become your business identity.

Some people are lucky enough to be able to come up with catchy tag lines immediately. Most of us are not. A brainstorming session can be helpful. Gather together a few friends or associates, and explain the simple ground rules. They are to try to come up with a snappy (or simple and memorable) way to communicate your key benefit to the public. They can say anything that pops into their mind, no matter how stupid it might seem. Often the silliest remarks are the ones that provide someone else in the group with inspiration. In a brainstorming session, no idea is dumb. Any phrase that seems possible should be written down. At the end of the session, all these phrases should be compared with your campaign objectives and the key benefit to see if any one of them do an adequate job of expressing your benefit to your target audience in a successful manner.

Checklist for Creating a Successful Tag Line

- The tag line should be short. You want people to be able to remember it easily. You also want it to be brief enough to fit into even the tiniest of ads, to be short enough for motorists to easily read on billboards when flashing by at 60 m.p.h., and to be small enough to fit on any matchbooks, pens, etc., that you might distribute. It must be included in all your broadcast ads, no matter how much other information you might have to cram into them.

- The tag line should tell your target audience what you can do to make their lives better. A slogan that only communicates what you have will be less effective than one that tells us what we will get out of doing business with you. Most people don't care about you; they care about themselves.

- Linguistic devices such as rhyme or alliteration often help. Don't overdo it, though, and have every single word in a ten word slogan start with the same letter. This only gets silly. Consider the rhythm and memorability of ''Everything's Better with Blue Bonnet On It.'' A hint of alliteration, an internal rhyme, and you've got a very catchy tag line.

- Don't forget that the benefit you offer can be psychological, rather than logical. If people will feel more important, sophisticated, or secure, then let them know.

- Avoid overused claims. Unique, for one, is a word that should be abolished from advertising. Everybody tries to claim that they are unique, but few people are. If you want to make this claim, tell us how you are unique, and why we should care. Another claim, the one that most businesses want to make as their key benefit, is that you offer quality goods at a good price. Two problems here. First, most of your competitors are probably also making the same claim so this will not help you stand out in the public mind as a distinct and meaningful place to do business. Second, you are talking about yourself, your prices, and your selections, and not your audience.

- Avoid imprecise words. Don't tell us something is good, or different. Tell us how and why. Specific information not only makes more interesting copy, but it seems to contain an element of proof that makes it more believable and acceptable to the audience. Certs didn't tell us that it was a better breath mint—it told us why. That sparkling drop of retsin (which, if you check the list of ingredients turns out to be a sparkling drop of vegetable oil) gave them a definite edge over the competition.

- Make sure that the slogan or theme you choose sets you apart from your competition. If the only meaningful key benefit that you have is one that your closest competitor is already claiming, make sure you say it differently. If your discount record shop and your competition have similar price structures, then you could both claim to have the lowest prices in town. If he claims ''Top Rock Records at Rock Bottom Prices,'' then you claim ''More Hits for Less Cash—Ralph's Records.''

- If your creativity fails when trying to better the competition at their own claim, try making two claims. In the earlier example, ''More Hits for Less Cash'' makes your shop sound like it has both low prices and a larger selection than the competitor.

- Always try to connect your slogan to your name so that the two will be associated in the mind of your audience. For instance, a downtown lunch counter, whose key benefit was that none of the food was frozen, used a visual and audio symbol of a cow as part of the logo. The tag: ''Branded Billy B's for freshness.''

- Make sure that you can back up your claim. Honesty is crucial in advertising. To lie, or even slightly to deceive only backfires when the new customer walks into the store feeling hopeful, and right back out feeling cheated.

- Make sure that the tag line that you create makes a promise that will benefit all your target audiences. The tag line shapes the general theme of your campaign. Any specific targeting that you do centers on creating individual advertising for each target group, designed to fit the media that best reaches that group.

- Make sure that your tag line is one that you can live with over a long period of time. This is your business identity—and you don't want to have to keep changing it so often that you look schizophrenic.

THE CREATIVE PROCESS: An Illustration

To develop a tag line that fits all the criteria in the checklist is a challenge. Even the people who consider themselves creative can find that this is one of the hardest parts of campaign planning. If you don't consider yourself creative, then you might be tempted to give up before you even start. Don't!

In order to help you to understand the way a tag line is developed, I am going to lead you through the process of creating one, just as I experienced it. Not every tag line is created this way, of course, but the thinking that goes into creativity and the devices used to get you started, are usually similar to the ones that I will present here.

The Objectives

My objective was to create a tag line for a young woman just getting started in the catering business. Her first advertising objective, at start-up time, was to make the public aware that she was in business. This meant that she needed to reach her target audience with ads that told them who she was and what she did. She was starting very small, cooking on the side while she worked a 9–5 full-time job. She began by simply using business cards with her business name and phone number.

Now, if this were you, what else would you put on that card? After all, until you get established in business, this is your sole form of advertising.

You would include the fact that you are a caterer. But why pass up the chance to be more informative? Ask yourself what your public is likely to want to know about you. What type of meal are they likely to demand? What image do you think they will want to present to their guests?

The Target Audience

Whether you use the brainstorming method, or simply rack your own mind for ideas, you must begin by looking at your target audience and their desires and motivations. The process will work something like this:

> My typical customer is a very affluent businessman, about 48 years old, married to a working spouse. They both have college degrees. She reads *Gourmet* magazine, and experiments on him when she cooks dinner. He has been complaining for a while that all catered parties have a boring similarity. He is tired of chafing dish manicotti, and wants something that will show his clients and friends some ingenuity and sophistication. Because this man and his wife are both so heavily involved in both business and community affairs, they are likely to hire a caterer even for their smaller dinner parties.

Assuming that you decided to go into business to fill this need, you now know what information, if communicated to the public, could make them call you instead of their regular caterer. The theme of your campaign, beginning with the tag line that you place under your name on the business card, must make people aware that you are a caterer with flair who can handle everything from the intimate dinner for four to the huge charity ball. The image that your theme projects must be sophisticated and original. Both your objectives and your target audience description tells you this.

The Brainstorming Process

Once you have your objectives and audience firmly in mind, it's time to begin brainstorming. There are several approaches you can take, to get those creative juices flowing.

Try Alliteration. You could go wildly alliterative, and tell your audience that you do "Food from the foreign to the familiar, for four to four hundred." This, however, is not only labored, but unwieldy. So try again, remembering that your tag should tell your prospects how they will benefit from using your service. You come up with "We cater to your every need." Not bad—it's short, kind of cute, and communicates a benefit, but it's likely to be trite and doesn't set you apart from your competitors.

Associate with an Image. Step back a second. What will communicate sophisticated and elegant dining to your audience? Just throw a few ideas out. You might come up with a list like the following: cordon bleu, Julia Child, the Four Season's restaurant, Epicurus, caviar, champagne, and so on. If nothing turns you on here, ask what is currently "in" in dining. You might come up with Cajun-Creole, Tex-Mex, arugula, and gourmet pizza. Do you see the germ of an idea here? Try associating one of the classic symbols of fine dining—cordon bleu—with one of the current fads—Cajun. Pairing the two in your tag line might suggest that you are both well trained and trendy. Plus, since the two terms begin with the same letter, you gain a bit of alliteration to make your tag line more memorable. So your card might read "Marjorie Allen: Fine catering from Cajun to Cordon Bleu." Yes?

This tag identifies you, tells the public what you do, and sets up your limits: trends or classic cooking. It is not particularly dazzling in its creativity, however. Worse still, it's talking about what you have to offer. You need to change it in some way to suggest that your customers will benefit from your service.

Get Out the Thesaurus. Okay. Let's try out synonyms. The thesaurus might tell you that synonyms for food include such words as victuals, fare, provisions, and cuisine. Cuisine is a sophisticated word so maybe we can work with it. From Cajun cuisine to cordon bleu? No—there's still no benefit. Let's take a look at the customer again. What kinds of adjectives might be used to describe them?

You might come up with a list, based on your target audience profile, that includes words like finicky, picky, gourmet, sophisticated, suave, social, and so on. And what do these finicky gourmets want? Well, based on that same profile, they want food that's out of the ordinary. Creative cuisine!

That works. We can promise them creative cuisine for—who? Gourmets? Maybe, but that particular word is overused and misunderstood, and is probably part of the ads of all your competitors. How about sophisticated? Creative cuisine for sophisticated socials? Not bad—but if you plan to use radio eventually, you may regret all those "s" words—they come across as though a snake is hissing through the microphone. How about "Creative cuisine for finicky food fanatics?" Nope—too insulting. How about a synonym for finicky—particular.

Refine Your Ideas. Now we have creative cuisine for particular people.

Can we refine it a little? Limiting the audience to particular people almost sounds like a restaurant ad. You're catering parties, aren't you?

You settle on "Creative cuisine for your most particular parties." The alliterations make this tag line easy to remember. Creative cuisine suggests that you will offer your client something different. To target your services to the client's most particular parties suggests that you are a caterer for the sophisticate, when he or she wants to make an especially good impression. Parties is ambiguous, but at least suggests that you are equipped to cater to both large affairs and small groups.

That's how the creative process works. You ask questions, try to associate what you do with ideas people might have about you, try out a lot of synonyms and rhymes—and eventually, you come up with something usable.

REVIEWING YOUR OBJECTIVES

Before you decide on any single tag line, you need to step back and look at all the background work that has led you to this point. Review your advertising objectives. You should have two sets: one objective that you want your entire campaign to accomplish, and a second, specific objective for each particular ad.

Accomplishing Overall Objectives

The theme for your campaign should be developed with an eye toward accomplishing your overall first objective. Therefore, if your objective is to create awareness of your new business, your theme should be aimed at telling us exactly who you are. If your aim is to attract a new target audience, then your theme should try to tell us who you're for. If the overall object of this year's campaign is to change an image, then your campaign theme must establish the new image that you want. If you want to stimulate your current customers to do business with you more often, then your campaign must give them logical reasons to do so.

A good tag line will be associated with your name in the mind of your target audience. If you decide to take out newspaper ads, this tag will run right alongside your logo. On radio, it will be heard following your name. Of course, in every ad you write, your overall objective is to make sure that you stick to the theme and identity set up by this tag.

Accomplishing Specific Objectives

Once you have your general theme, you can begin to develop variations. While every ad you run for the duration of your current campaign will carry your tag line, in order to achieve your primary objective, you will also want to develop specific content for your ads which accomplish your secondary objectives.

Rotating Benefits. Once the tag takes care of identifying you in order to create awareness, you can concentrate the advertising copy on making people aware of certain specials you might offer, or you might need to develop special ads to compete with similar businesses during heavy seasons.

Marjorie Allen, for instance, might want to run a set of newspaper ads aimed at familiarizing the public with different aspects of her business—information that she could not include on the business card that was her first and only advertising medium. She might create an ad with the specific secondary objective of telling about the intimate dinners for two that she will supply for Valentine's Day or wedding anniversaries. During wedding season, she might need to advertise her special (trendy and sophisticated) reception dinners. When there is no particular special occasion, she will use her ads to expand on her primary theme—the variety and quality of her catering. No matter what the subobjective, the ad will include her primary tag line.

Each ad that she develops will inform people of new aspects of her business—benefits that she could not fit into a single ad. Rotating your benefits throughout a series of ads, specifically developed to meet your needs, keeps your ad interesting, even in a small space.

Addressing Specific Audiences. Besides subobjectives, remember that you have subaudiences. While you created your tag line to appeal to all your potential customers, your individual ads must be written with a particular target audience in mind. Going back to Marjorie, she might have a secondary target audience of women, 30–45, who give social parties such as bridal showers, office parties, etc. While most of her specific ads will be aimed at the business audience, some of them should be written with this smaller audience in mind. Her ads aimed at businesspeople would feature occasions and information pertinent to them; her ads aimed at the female clientele would feature exactly those showers and parties that they demand most often. The tag remains the same, but the central feature of the ad changes according to what is most appealing to its intended audience.

Checklist for Coordinating Ads with Objectives

In the last chapter, you made a list of your benefits, divided according to the audience that they appeal to, and the occasions that they might help to promote. Now we're going to refine this list a bit further.

- Make a list of every objective and subobjective that your advertising must accomplish in the coming year. Make a note of which target audience the specific ad will be directed toward.

- Take a look at your media plan. How large are your print ads? How many benefits can you use in each ad without overcrowding the space? (Remember, your ad must have room for your logo and tag line, an illustration if used, a headline, and subbenefits that help to prove that head-line.)

- For each ad objective and subobjective, list one major headline benefit, and as many subbenefits that prove your headline as your space will allow. The headline must be a benefit aimed at convincing your audience to help you to achieve the advertising objective. For instance, if your objective is to persuade your seasonal audience of young husbands to buy their wives some of your gold jewelry at Valentine's Day, your head benefit might be "Nothing says I Love You Like Gold." Subbenefits that prove that your gold will say "I love you" might include "personally engraved with your special message," "encased in a reusable jewel box," and "our easy credit plan makes this special gift affordable now."

- You do not have to write a different set of ads for every single day of advertising, nor for every different medium. You should, however, have enough ideas to keep constantly changing to meet the specific objectives of the season and audiences.

- Check to make sure that you have incorporated the benefits most mean-ingful to your target audiences into these ad plans.

COMMON CREATIVE TECHNIQUES

Professional advertisers have developed several general techniques that help to ensure a cohesive advertising campaign. The use of devices like the testimonial, the threat/promise technique, or the principle of association each help to channel your theme into a specific format that can work across media.

The Testimonial

The *testimonial* ad features a spokesperson for the business—someone that the public is likely to identify with. Sometimes, this person is a celebrity. People in the target audience look up to this celebrity, and will be likely to use the product or patronize the business because someone that they admire uses it. There is an emotional benefit in being associated with people that we esteem, even in this limited and distant manner.

Choosing a Spokesperson. The trick in choosing a spokesperson for tes-timonial ads is, first, to choose someone that your target audience truly looks up to. Since we all have a natural resistance to being persuaded, only the most inse-cure of us will follow the suggestion of someone that we don't particularly care for. Second, and perhaps equally important, your audience should believe that this spokesperson knows something about the kind of service or product that he or she is endorsing. If a local socialite widely featured on the society pages for her beautiful gowns appears in your ads endorsing your dress shop, people who admire her style are also likely to want to shop with you. Similarly, if the local Lothario says that he prefers women dressed by you—well, if we think he's attractive, we women might also want you to supply our wardrobes. However, if your spokesperson is a woman who has just emerged on John Blackwell's list of the Ten Worst Dressed Women, then your shop will have very limited target audience appeal.

Celebrity vs. "Real People." Celebrity endorsements can backfire if your business is one that we look toward to solve problems. We rarely believe those ads that cast prominent actresses, who rave about their favorite floor wax, because we find it hard to believe that these stellar figures ever do such mundane work. We would, however, believe an ordinary, real housewife, who claims that she has tried the product and found it better than any other. The service businesses, especially, can benefit by featuring real, satisfied customers in their campaigns. If we are afraid to call a roofer, in case he does a bad job, the ad featuring a local man whose roof has been sound for the ten years since John Mansard put it up is likely to quiet a lot of qualms.

Checklist for Using Testimonials in Advertising

- Is the spokesperson one that my audience can identify with?
- Will the audience believe that this spokesperson knows enough about the subject to make an authoritative recommendation?
- Will the spokesperson be easily recognizable to the audience as one who has some expertise in this area?
- If I use the spokesperson in print, will audiences recognize the face? If on radio, can this spokesperson sound believable on microphone?
- Does my product demand the testimony of an expert celebrity? Or would the audience be more likely to listen to a real person from their own ranks?

The Principle of Association

Another good technique is that of *association*. With this, your advertising message links your business with a place, a segment of society, or even a feeling, that people want to be associated with. Make your restaurant the place "For the Ultimate Yuppie." Tell us that shopping in your boutique is like "Rummaging through the Left Bank in Paris." Assure us nostalgia seekers that in your linen shop we can "Return to the Romance of Yesteryear."

Checklist for Effective Association Advertising

- How does my target audience like to picture themselves? What ambitions and aspirations might they have that I can identify?
- With what type of group would my typical customers like to associate themselves?

- Can I identify a certain feeling that my customers would like to get when they do business with me?
- How can I associate my product or service with those aspirations?

The Threat/Promise Technique

Another principle often employed by advertisers is that of *threat/promise*. They begin by warning against impending social unacceptability, looking stupid, paying out money unwisely, being out of style—whatever they think we are likely to want to take steps to avoid. Then they promise us that this will never happen to us, if only we do business with them.

Origins of Threat/Promise. One of the most famous threat/promise ads of all times, and one of the earliest, was done for Listerine Mouthwash. It showed a formally gowned woman, kneeling before an open hope chest and looking off into the distance as a tear rolled down her cheek. The headline? "Often a bridesmaid but never a bride." The threat was that, because so many women suffered from the dreaded halitosis, they were doomed to be old maids. The promise? Well, the real promise was that Listerine would cure that halitosis. The implied promise was that we could then get married and live happily ever after.

There has been a rumor in the history books that the term "halitosis" was invented by John B. Watson, father of behavioral psychology and, incidentally, head of an advertising agency. Watson and his behaviorists believed (and with good reason, it appears) that people could be conditioned into wanting things, by making the advertising stimulate our fears. Watson did not, in fact, invent the term *halitosis*—this is a valid, scientific term supplied to the ad's creator, Milton Feasley, by Listerine's chemist. But the principle of threat/promise has remained effective throughout the 20th century.

Pitfalls of Threat/Promise. Unless you use it carefully, I find two basic problems with the threat/promise approach to advertising. While it is true that we will sometimes act or purchase products to calm our fears of social or business inadequacies, this is not always the case. Witness the vast numbers of people who continue to buy cigarettes despite the massive fear campaign waged in the last two decades. Death might be too remote a fear to have any lasting effect. Finding a fear that will truly threaten your advertising market is a tricky business. You don't want to be in the position of creating bogeymen.

Another problem with using the threat/promise technique is that you are opening your ad with something negative and unpleasant. These depressing thoughts, rather than your promises of relief, might be what makes the most vivid impression on your target audience. Advertising studies have shown that those ads for cleaning products that begin with references to the drudgery of housework often leave the shopper cold. When she gets to the supermarket, she remembers only vague negative ideas about those products rather than the exalted promises that came later in the ad. So, to open with a negative can back-fire.

Pointers on Effective Threat/Promise Ads. As a rule, openings that instill real fear or real guilt in your target audience are effective. Mere threats of drudgery or simple unpleasantness do not have enough emotional impact to create anything but a vague, negative impression.

You might try a variation on threat/promise. Instead of threatening your customers with drudgery or social ostracism, try to raise in them a need for ease or popularity. Instead of having your ad dwell on all the misery, begin by focusing on a desire for relief. In other words, don't spend a precious ten seconds of your radio ad describing the fears that accompany a trip to the repair shop: fear of being bilked, fear of ungodly repair bills, fear of incompetent repairs, and so on. Instead, dwell on our hopes for a place that is reliable, fast, and honest. Then tell us that our dreams have come true.

Checklist for Using the Threat/Promise Technique

- What real concerns motivate people to use my business?
- What emotional factors are involved in using my product or service? List both positive and negative factors.
- Of the negative factors you listed in 1 and 2, which are real threats, that people will take action to avoid? Eliminate any that are only vague worries or any that we're unlikely to believe will happen.
- Of the positive factors, which seem most likely to remove the real threats?
- Can you make the promise without first dwelling on the unpleasantness? Or do you need to remind people of unpleasant consequences before you promise them relief?

Whatever technique you choose, be it testimonial, threat/promise, principles of association, or some other design, stick to it. Using one particular technique in developing all your ads goes a long way toward assuring campaign consistency.

THE ADVERTISING FORMULA

Creating a need, raising a hope, expressing a wish—these are things that good advertisements have created since the craft began. Every good ad person knows that you can't persuade people to buy things they neither want nor need, nor can you make them use services that they don't require. The purpose of advertising is not to convince people to buy products and/or services, regardless of need. More realistically, its purpose is to recognize a need, whether psychological, sociological, or physical, that people have and show them that doing business with you can help to satisfy that need. To do this, many professional advertisers rely on formulas that help them develop their advertising concepts.

The AIDA Formula

There are dozens of advertising formulae. One of the most popular is AIDA: Attention-Interest-Desire-Action. The idea is to begin your ad with an attention getting statement, action, or picture (Attention). The second step is to Interest the audience in your advertising message. Once you have their attention and interest, your ad must make them Desire what you have to offer. Finally, you urge them to Act—to come in today, or call now, or hurry to your sale, or whatever it is you want them to do when they see your ad.

The Motivated Sequence

I have had great success with a more academic version of the AIDA formula, borrowed from, of all things, a public speaking text. The aim of public speaking, like that of advertising, is to communicate ideas tailored to the needs and characteristics of an audience. Monroe's Motivated Sequence, the formula that I use to create effective advertising was developed to create messages that are tailored to our natural way of receiving or rejecting a message.*

I prefer Monroe to the AIDA sequence because it is more flexible. You can tailor the sequence to your audience, whether it is a friendly one, a hostile one, or merely indifferent. You can emphasize steps or downplay them according to your needs. There are five steps to the Motivated Sequence: Attention, Need, Satisfaction, Visualization, and Actuation.

Attention. Attention is self-explanatory. In order to have your message received and accepted, you must first attract the attention of your target audience to the ad. You can do this with headlines, sound effects, graphics, actions, or any other means that are appropriate to the medium and the message. Every good ad first gets the attention of the target audience. This step is essential.

Need. Need is also an essential step in the advertising process. Before people will be motivated to try a new product, to use a service, or to visit a new shop, they must feel some desire for the benefits that such an action can produce. Your job, as an advertiser, is to create a need for your particular product or service. It is not enough to convince readers that they need to buy gas when their tank is empty. They need to buy gas at your service station, because only there will they find what they really need or want.

Needs can be very real. If your basement is flooding at 3 a.m., you need a plumber who makes middle-of-the-night house calls. If someone sideswipes

---

*Ehninger, D., Gronbeck, B.E., McKerrow, R. and Monroe, A.H. *Principles and Types of Speech Communication*, 10th ed. (Glenview, Ill.: Scott, Foresman and Company 1986.)

your brand new Mercedes, you need a competent body shop, and good insurance.

There are few things that people need: clothing, warmth, shelter, transportation, and food. The rest are wants. We want a certain type of home because of our sociological and psychological characteristics. We want social acceptability, friendship, and physical attractiveness. We want to keep up with the Joneses, to express our individuality, and to have fun. We want these so much, sometimes, that they feel like needs. We also have problems that we must solve or that would make life more pleasant if they didn't exist.

The job of a good ad, then, is to look at your business and the ways in which it can benefit the customer. What need or want exists out there that you can address? If your ad can remind your target audience of this want or need, then that audience will be much more receptive to your message because they can identify with it.

Needs, of course, will vary with the target audience. The secret to a cohesive and effective campaign is to vary the need with the audience while keeping your solution to that need—your business and your identity—the same.

Satisfaction. Satisfaction is the third step in the motivated sequence. In this step, you show your audience how you can solve the problem that you have just reminded them of, or how you can fulfill the need that you have created. In this step, you can talk about what you do, and everything you have to offer. Here is where you offer evidence, including any proofs or guarantees that your business can, indeed, satisfy the need.

Visualization. Visualization shows the client enjoying the benefits of your business promises. Let them see themselves, happier and more satisfied, now that they have satisfied their need. This step is often used in broadcast advertising, but is rarely used in print.

Actuation. Actuation tells the audience what you want them to do in response to your message, and how to do it. In other words, along with a specific request for action, you give them your location, phone number, and any other information they might need in order to patronize your business. A good actuation step also includes a clincher—usually your tag line, which reminds us of who you are and what promise you made.

The Motivated Sequence in Action

In product advertising, Head and Shoulders provides a classic example of commercials written in the format of the motivated sequence. One TV ad opens with a girl seated on the bus, and a gorgeous guy climbing on and heading toward her. She looks hopeful and expectant. He looks eager. We have our attention step—the beginning of the classic boy-meets-girl story that has endured for centuries. We are also getting a hint about the universal need to be attractive to members of the opposite sex, to have romantic relationships, and to find love. Then, comes the real need.

The handsome young man pauses, a seat or two before our heroine, with a look of dismay clear on his face. We, the privileged audience, can hear his thoughts. "Nice girl," he thinks. "But oh, that dandruff." This raises two needs: the desire to solve the dandruff problem, but, even more obviously, the need to be socially and physically acceptable without embarrassing flaws. Never fear, though—the announcer steps right in with the satisfaction statement: this girl could have avoided all her trauma if she had only used Head and Shoulders. He tells us about its scientific ingredients, proving that it will help to control dandruff and make us socially acceptable. Back to the bus. We now get the visualization step, with our heroine enjoying the benefits of using Head and Shoulders. She looks brighter. Her hair is bouncier, her clothes are better, her skin is clearer, and, lo and behold, she's got her man. So, we proceed to the actuation, where the announcer returns to tell all us bedazzled viewers where we can purchase his miraculous product.

Applying the Motivated Sequence to Small Business Ads

The same procedure can work for the small business. Consider the following example.

Business: Picture frame shop; also offers selection of fine prints and posters. Specializes in unique matting—three color, special shapes, etc.

Target Audience: The affluent middle class. People who are ego-involved in their homes, decor conscious, but without the ability to invest in original art. The typical customer is female, about 30–45, employed outside the home, but very interested in creating a beautiful environment for those hours when she and her husband are home; she wants her decor to be a strong statement of individuality and personal style.

Advertising Objective (Overall): To encourage the current clientele to buy more artwork and have it framed here.

Advertising Objective (specific): To announce a sale of botanical prints.

Key Benefit: Unusual artwork custom-framed and matted to suit your decor.

Tag Line: Framemasters: Our images suit your style.

ADVERTISING PLAN: Newspaper ad in the morning paper to reach women at work. Supported by radio ads on an easy-listening station that is played in offices.

ATTENTION GETTER: (This will be the headline in the print ad, and the opening line of the radio ad.)

Empty walls and empty spaces.

NEED: (Aimed at these women's intense need for self-expression.)

Until you've put your mark on them, they could be just anyone's. Unless that mark is stylish—distinctive—your house is just a house. Make it a home. Make it yours.

SATISFACTION: (Aimed at proving to these women that, at Framemasters, the selection of special prints plus custom framing will help her to fill her home with art that is also self-expressive. The satisfaction step not only satisfies that need, but also fulfills the particular purpose of the ad: to announce the sale on botanical prints.) Fill those spaces with art that suits your image with a special selection of botanical prints, on sale this week at Framemasters. Express your taste, your style, your love of beauty and nature. Framemasters offers over 1000 different florals, in every color, from the real to the surreal—and Framemasters will frame and mat your selections to suit your personal style to perfection. Choose from our selection of over 200 frame styles and thousands of color combinations.

VISUALIZATION: (Designed to show the customer how much more personalized and tasteful her home will be if she takes advantage of your sale; she can now visualize herself enjoying the benefits of doing business with you.) With your taste and our selection and styling, you can leave your own, personal mark on those walls, and make them yours.

ACTUATION: (Telling the women what they should do, and how to do it.) Make your house a home. Visit the Framemasters gallery at 200 Linden, across from the courthouse. Our botanical print sale will only last a week. Make your mark with Framemasters. Our images suit your style.

NEWSPAPER AD:

HEADLINE: LEAVE YOUR MARK! (Attention, and to a degree, need.)

SUBHEAD: Beautiful botanicals to suit your style. (Satisfaction)

VISUAL: A blank canvas, with a partial painting of a flower in one corner. (Need—we have a need to see things completed.) Body Copy: (NOTE: To the person motivated by self-expression, the attention step also creates a need. Anyone who wants to express themselves is automatically attracted to a blank slate where they can leave their mark.) Make them your own. (More Satisfaction) Choose from over 1000 botanical prints, in colors and styles that suit your individuality.

Frame them your special way with one of our 200 frame styles.

Mat them, in mats custom-cut and colored to your special needs.

(Actuation) Sale ends Saturday.

Framemasters: Our images suit your style.
200 Linden Street, Peoria

Monday – Saturday, 9 – 5.
Mastercard and Visa accepted.

DIFFERENT SEQUENCES FOR DIFFERENT AUDIENCES

As you will notice in the preceding examples, the sequence does not necessarily have to be in an exact order. It is possible, for instance, to raise a need, to offer satisfaction, to raise another need, to offer another way to satisfy it, in the body of the ad. The attention step can also create a need, while it gains our attention.

The visualization step that strengthens the persuasive appeal of the ad by reminding us of our need and how nice it is to have it satisfied, is not always necessary. While I used it in the Framemasters radio ad, I did not use it in print, due to space limitations.

Perhaps the greatest flexibility that the motivated sequence offers the advertiser is in the way you can adapt an ad to differing audiences by expanding and contracting the steps in the sequence.

The Hostile Audience Variation

If you have an audience who is hostile to your message, you can sometimes at least make them give your ad a fair hearing by spending most of your ad creating a need. New products and services often face the hostile audience problem; since your service has never existed before, we have gotten along without it. Why should we spend good money on it now?

Let's say that you have just opened an under-age teen night club. Your target audience, at least those who are not still sneaking into bars with fake ID, might think your new place is unnecessary. They have movies, pizza parlors, and parties at home. Why should they pay a cover charge to sit in your place, sip Coke, and listen to a live DJ when they could hang out at the pizza parlor, with no cover charge, sip Coke and listen to the piped-in radio? Here, your ad needs to spend most of its effort convincing people that while they did get along without your service in the past, they would have been much happier or successful, if you had been there. In other words, the bulk of your ad must be aimed at convincing people that there is a need for what you are offering. Having spent approximately 20 seconds of your 30-second radio ad creating a need, (in this case for privacy, a place of your own where adults aren't welcome, a place to dance, etc.) you then spend the remainder of the time briefly stating that you can satisfy the need, and how (satisfaction and actuation).

The Neutral Audience Variation

Many businesses face a neutral audience. We tend to be neutral about those things that we know very little about. If we knew a lot about something, we'd be sure to have formed an opinion. A new health care center, dedicated to preventive medicine, is likely to find itself with a neutral audience. Most of us are far too accustomed to running to the doctor after we're sick, instead of taking steps to prevent getting sick in the first place. So, when we hear about one opening in our area, we are likely to feel neutral about it. We don't know enough, yet, to be for or against preventive medicine.

Here, you need to extend the satisfaction step. To reduce ignorance, and to create awareness of who you are and what you do, your ads at this stage need to dwell on exactly what your business is about. Explanation, rather than need stimulation, is the key to successful ads aimed at neutral audiences.

The Loyal Audience Variation

Finally, if you are very lucky, you have a business that already appeals to a large and satisfied audience. Then, you might ask, why even advertise? Because once your advertising ceases, a lot of your not-so-faithful customers no longer see and hear your name in the media so they forget about you. Even your best customers need occasional reminders about how satisfied they are since they've become customers, and how well you've tended to their needs. What you're doing is encouraging your customers to keep the faith and stick with you.

For instance, as we head toward April, many Americans feel a pressing need for a tax preparation service. Moreover, most people will return over and over again to the same tax preparer, because they feel that the individual is familiar with their finances and will benefit them most. Therefore, you have a built-in, loyal audience, with a particular need that you can satisfy. You need to advertise mainly to remind them to bring in their work now and avoid the rush, and to remind them of the past benefits they have enjoyed by using your service. You also need to be advertising because your competition is. You don't want your faithful customer lured away simply because you weren't adequately visible. Here, your ad emphasizes visualization, reminding people of the misery they are saving themselves and the assurance and possible monetary savings that your service gives them.

Whatever your objectives, then, you can design advertising that addresses them by varying the steps in the motivated sequence.

SUMMARY

The major aim of an advertising campaign is to achieve consistency throughout the media and across all our ads. We can accomplish this with a consistent theme and the development of a tag line that appears in every ad.

The adoption of a specific advertising technique, such as the testimonial ad, the threat/promise structure, or the principle of association, if used in every ad can also contribute to cohesiveness.

Finally, the use of an advertising formula such as Monroe's Motivated Sequence can help you to create ads specifically designed to reach a specific target audience with a particular message.

13

Creating a Look
for your Print Ads

WHEN JIM CASEY OPENED HIS MONUMENT COMPANY, HE DID WHAT MOST NEW businesspeople did. He went to the printer and ordered business cards. He wanted a distinctive look, rather than a generic card, so he had an artist friend draw a monument to go next to his name. When he went to the newspaper, he asked them to use the monument shape as a border for his ad. This looked good, and Jim thought he had his ad style.

When he began to develop a direct mail brochure, the monument shape didn't fit the brochure cover, and when he had it sized to fit, there was scarcely any room for copy. So he abandoned it. When he went to buy a Yellow Pages ad, he discovered, much to his dismay, that three of his competitors already had monument-shaped ads. So Jim was back to square one.

What Jim's ads—and every good ad—needed, was a workable format, which could be used on every form of ad that he created, and which set him apart from his competitors.

The total look of your ads, no matter which medium they appear in, can convey a lot to your target audience, even if they never read the content. A typeface can convey personality, youthful, friendly and inexpensive, or dignified, exclusive and expensive. The border you choose can help you to stand out from other ads on the page, and can also convey personality and price range. The amount of white space that all your ads contain convey definite price and quality messages to your audience, as do the types of illustrations.

Not only is your advertising format a good conveyer of image, but it also works to make your advertising recognizable. It will give you a distinctive look so that the reader will think of you, even if she just catches your ad out of the corner of her eye (or his eye, depending on your target audience).

In this chapter, we will help you to devise a workable, recognizable format that not only conveys your image, but also separates you from your competition. Tips on type styles, and sources for shapes, borders, and corners will help you to create a personal look. We'll learn how to put a format together so that newspaper ads, direct mail, billboards, and even your shopping bags have a look that says "You." Finally, we'll learn which elements are permanent, and which can change so that your format will see you through any number of advertising situations for many years to come.

THE TOTAL LOOK

Professionally designed advertising campaigns all have the consistency of type, layout, and design that I described above, and for a very good reason. Ads that all have similarities in their design become recognizable. We know that few readers will take the time to carefully scrutinize every ad that you place. Some days they just aren't in the market. If your ad format is distinctive to you, you will at least force the reader to call your company name to mind as he or she sees your ad. This enhances your frequency, and keeps your name in the public mind.

Choosing a Look for Your Audience

Your look—the one you adapt for your business—must be just as consistent as these professional campaigns. You have to make important decisions about the elements that go into your ads, and the impression that these will make on your target audience. A too-formal look might alienate your fun-loving, casual market. Too much white space around your message might cause people to think you are too expensive for their budgets. An ad that is too crowded with information might cause people to think that you are a discount store—and if you are not, you will alienate a lot of people who come in expecting knocked-off prices, even though your merchandise is very reasonable.

Choosing a Look to Suit Your Media Placement

You also need to take a good look at the places where your ads are likely to appear. If your best newspaper location is on the entertainment page, then you know ahead of time that you will be crowded in with 50 other ads for similar businesses. This means that your ads must be designed in a way that will help them to stand out from the crowd. In other words, if your advertising will consistently appear in a clutter of other ads, then your format must not only differ from that of your primary competition, but also have a look that will separate it from all the businesses that advertise with you.

By now, you should have a good idea about what your ads need to communicate. You should also have a good idea about what types of print ads you will be using, and how big your newspaper ads will be. Now it is time to begin to translate that information into a look that communicates to your audience.

THE RIGHT LOOK FOR YOUR PRICE RANGE

Flip through your daily newspaper. You'll see dozens of ads for hundreds of places—some bad, some good. You might also notice, as you flip, that whether or not you read the individual ads, they communicate something to you. Without knowing anything concrete about a business, you form impressions about how expensive each place is just because of the look of the ad.

The Bargain Look

Take an ad for K-Mart or Woolworths. These places are known for reasonably priced, bargain merchandise. Their ads have a certain consistency. The store might feature as many as 15 items per ad, along with the price of each item. Grocery stores do the same thing. There is very little white space in the ad; they've used every inch to show you a wide sampling of merchandise and the very low prices of these items.

This crowded look, even if exquisitely organized, is one we commonly associate with bargain pricing. Even a small store, with a 2-column inch ad, conveys an idea of low pricing when it packs the ad with information, leaving little or no white space. Most of us have had the experience of perusing an advertising circular, chock-full of little pictures, lots of small type, and a generally crowded look, assuming that we will be getting bargains. When we see a higher price than we expect, we feel betrayed. We tend to instantly classify the store as expensive, even if the pricing is moderate (but not discount). We are wrong in this assessment. The store is only overpriced for its advertising look. We read cluttered ads to mean low pricing. If a business violates the expectations we get from its advertising, we turn away, indignant.

This might be the biggest pitfall for the small business advertiser. Hampered by a limited budget, we often try to cram a lot of information into a very small ad—thus unintentionally creating a bargain look. The customers that we do draw in are not getting exactly what they expect, even if every word in the ad is literally truthful. So, many potential customers leave disappointed, no matter how reasonable your prices are.

If in laying out your ad, you find that you are in this trap, either ruthlessly prune your advertising copy to leave more space, or redo your media plan until you can afford bigger ads. There is nothing worse than a disappointed potential customer.

The Medium-Priced Look

Now look at ads for medium-priced products and services. A medium-priced department store ad might feature no more than three items, all related. They might, for instance, show us a dress, shoes, and a scarf. Price is probably given, along with information about the product categories featured. The ad is less cluttered than the bargain-basement ad, but uses much of the available space. You'll see more white space—but not much.

Once again, the reader has learned to perceive ads with a moderate amount of white space as representing a medium-priced category. Even an ad without illustrations, which leaves its corners and logo area clear, will be perceived this way. So a moderately full ad, or a well-spaced, but copy-heavy brochure will convey your message about price without words.

The High-Priced Look

Then there's the high-priced category. These ads almost never give information about cost. At most, they illustrate or feature one item, amidst a sea of blank space. The implication here is that, if you have to wonder about cost, you can't afford to do business here. The more space you leave, the more likely you are to be perceived as belonging to the expensive category of businesses.

You can use this perception to your advantage if you are in a moderate price category, by designing wonderfully spacious ads that give pricing information. People will see your classy look—lots of white space, a clean, sparse layout—and think, "a place with class and quality." When they see your price, however, they will think, "Plus—affordable!" For whole groups of people out there, this becomes an immensely appealing message. Beware, however, of using too much white space without giving prices, unless you fall into the Tiffany's and Cartier class. People will stay away in droves, assuming that they can't afford you, and those who do come in might find your pricing suspect.

Knowing this, you might want to make some modifications to your media plan. If you need lots of white space to convey the right image to your public, you might want to adjust your advertising frequency to allow for fewer but larger ads. However, you might do better to concentrate on honing your advertising message down to the essentials, and allowing your ads to change often so that you can convey a lot of information sequentially. At any rate, you should have a better idea about how much information you can put into your print ads without misleading your target audience about your pricing strategies. (See Figs. 13-1, 13-2, and 13-3 for sample layouts for each price category.)

Your key to finding treasure for all occasions

Laki's Gift Boutique

Special Christmas Sale
Everything 20% off

* Precious Moments  *Wreaths

* Hummels * Hats

* Potpourri

All holiday Gifts
Attractive Wedding and Shower Accessories
All-Year Christmas Room
European Imports

1618 Dickson
Mesa, Arizona
579-9873

Fig. 13-1. This ad for Laki's Gift Boutique, with several different blocks of copy, many different illustrations, and a generally crowded layout, is typical of ads for a business with low pricing strategies.

Fig. 13-2. Petit Paris uses a lot of its space, but also leaves enough white space to keep the ad from seeming cluttered. The single illustration and moderate amount of copy convey the idea that this is a business with moderate prices. (Ad design courtesy of Matthew Brown. Clip art from Carol Belanger Grafton, *1001 Spot Illustrations of the Lively Twenties*. Border taken from Ted Menten, *Ready-to-Use Art Nouveau Borders*, both courtesy of Dover Books)

Dazzle Him

With
Compliments

finishing touches for your wardrobe

1151 Grove Street
Clarks Summit, PA 587-1414

Fig. 13-3. The ads for With Compliments use a lot of white space and a minimum of copy. This communicates a high price range to us. (Clip art from Carol Belanger Grafton's *1001 Illustrations of the Lively Twenties*, courtesy of Dover Books)

Checklist for Determining the Best Look for Your Price Category

You need an ad that is either crowded with type or with several pictures if:

- Your image is one of very low prices and convenience merchandise.
- Your policy is to discount merchandise.
- Your selling strategy is based on frequent sales and price breaks.

You need an ad with moderate white space and only two to three pictured items (if using illustrations) if:

- Your goods fall into the shopping category.
- Your goods are competitively priced, and people tend to comparison shop.
- You do not want an exclusive, high-priced image.
- Your ads typically reflect prices, but your normal policy is not one of constant sales events.

You need an ad with a lot of white space, and no more than one picture if:

- Your goods or services fall into the luxury category.
- You carry high quality goods, with price tags that reflect such quality.
- You carry one-of-a-kind merchandise that, while not exorbitantly priced, is higher than its mass-produced equivalent.
- You are striving for an elite image for the people who can afford to spend disposable income.

TYPE STYLES AND YOUR LOOK

Another important factor that you need to consider in designing print ads is type style. The style of lettering you choose will affect the way that your target audience perceives your ads. Therefore, before the reader even looks at your message, he or she will have formed some impression about the kind of business you are, your price range, image, and whether they want to do business with you.

The Right Letters for Your Look

Typefaces create images. Script lettering, for instance, conveys an impression of elegance. There are, however, script type styles that look as though they have been done with a brush. These create a slightly more casual, personal impression on the reader. Other script styles look like handwriting, calligraphy, or the lettering used on wedding invitations. Each of these lend a slightly different flavor to the ad. (Figure 13-4 illustrates three styles of script, each with its own distinctive personality.)

Thick, heavy letters look bold and generally informal. The thinner the letter, the more expensive it tends to look (see Fig. 13-5). Some type styles look very streamlined and modern. Others have a distinctly old-fashioned look. Some are almost pictorial with wood-graining or a rubber-stamped effect. There are round bubbly styles, and severe, sharp no-nonsense ones. Some styles look high-tech, others almost hand-crafted. (See Fig. 13-6 for an assortment of type styles with personality.)

Any printer can supply you with a chart of available type styles. Some printers, however, have a wider choice than others. If your first advertising efforts will be mainly brochures, flyers, or business cards, don't settle for the cheapest printer. Go to one who can provide you with typefaces that suit your needs. Once you have an established well-printed style of logo, you can use this in all other print media. When you want a newspaper ad or a billboard, the representative will simply photograph your original and reduce or enlarge it as needed. So when having your first print work done, go for quality and clarity.

Fig. 13-4. Three styles of script that each convey a different personality. Troubador Light, with its engraved look, is as formal as a wedding invitation. Bank Script, also formal, gives a staid and old world impression. Hughson, on the other hand, looks informal enough to be a handwritten note. (Type styles taken from *Script and Cursive Alphabets* by Dan X. Solo. Courtesy of Dover Books)

Thin letters look expensive

The same type, bold, looks less expensive

Fig. 13-5. Thin lettering tends to convey more of a high priced, elegant look than does thick, bold type.

The Right Style for Readability

A few words of warning. Some styles of type are better than others if you want people to read your ad. Most of us, for instance, find it much easier to read *serif type*—the type found on the standard typewriter than *sans serif* (the type found on a dot-matrix computer). This is because standard books, which for most of us were our first contact with the printed word, use serif type. The eye is more

Fig. 13-6. You can convey your image by choosing a type style with personality.

accustomed to this style, and so finds it easier to deal with. (Figure 13-7 illustrates the difference between serif and sans serif types.)

Sans serif lettering is good for headlines and logos, because they are short enough to read easily and quickly. Any body copy, picture captions, etc., that go into your ad should be set in a serif typeface.

We also find it easier to read dark lettering on a light ground than to read *reverse type*—light lettering on a dark ground. Because it is different, and seems to stand out on the page, it might be tempting to have your newspaper ads done in white type on black. Most people find this to be fatiguing to the eye. This means that the average reader, who is not, after all, waiting with bated breath to see what you have to say, will not read as carefully as you might wish. Besides,

This is <u>sans serif</u> type.

This is <u>serif</u> type

Fig. 13-7. Sans serif is harder for people to read than serif type. Serifs are the small, ornamental strokes at the tops and bottoms of letters.

Normal, black and white type is what we're
accustomed to reading

Reverse type is harder on the eyes.
People don't like to read big blocks of
reverse type.

Fig. 13-8. Reverse type is harder on the eyes than normal, black printing on a light ground.

most newspapers charge an extra production fee when you run an ad using reverse type. A small-budget advertiser doesn't need this. (Check Fig. 13-8 to see for yourself which style is easier to read.)

Another common temptation is to use either all capital letters or all small letters in an attempt to look stylish or stand out from the crowd. Avoid this temptation! You will be more readable and credible if you only capitalize those letters that need it—proper nouns and words at the beginning of sentences. We are accustomed to reading words that use standard upper- and lowercase letters; any change in this standard affects readability.

One of the difficulties with this rule of thumb is that not every typeface is available in both upper- and lowercase letters. If the style you want belongs in this category, then you had better confine it to your logo. Or choose something else.

Choosing Available Type Styles

Another problem that you will have to consider is that many newspapers have now gone to a computerized typesetting system. This means that, while your friendly neighborhood printer can offer you 50 or 60 choices of type styles, your newspaper might only have 15 or so available. This leaves you with two options. You can either have every ad you run typeset at the printers before it goes to the newspaper, or you can make one of your type choices from the available newspaper styles at newspapers.

Styles for Logos. Notice that I say to choose ''one'' of your choices from the newspaper selection. Don't make the mistake of limiting yourself to standard newspaper type when choosing your logo. You want to create a personality, not suppress it. Most standard newspaper typefaces are not very exciting, although they are excellent for readability in body copy. So choose your logo type at the printer or have one done by a graphic artist. Despite the seemingly high initial cost, this investment will pay you back a thousandfold in the end.

Styles for Changeable Copy. Your second type style should be something fairly standard, easily available, and easy to read. Get type style charts from any newspapers you plan to advertise in, and choose a style that is available from all them. Or, as I mentioned before, have your ads type-set at your friendly printer, before you go to the newspaper office. This last option leaves you the freest reign with creativity, and guarantees consistency in every medium. It is, however, more expensive.

Expanding Your Selection

There are hundreds of type styles to choose from. A visit to any good art supply dealer will gain you a look at catalogues full of transfer and rub-on lettering, which feature type styles for almost any personality and look you might want. If you are careful, and have a steady hand, you can use these to create your own ads, thus maintaining complete control over their final look. Or you can use these letters just for logo creation, or to ensure that your headlines and logo are in the style you want. If you can give the newspaper camera-ready, press-typed headlines and logos, then you are only at their mercy for the fine print—body copy, address, etc.

The Final Choices

While you have hundreds of styles to choose from, you should limit your personal typefaces to no more than two. Any more than two different styles in an ad creates a cluttered, disorganized look. Even if you want clutter, to convey your bargain price range, you want your ads to be attractive. Avoid looking like a patchwork quilt. Be firm. Choose two compatible type styles, and stick to them. Everywhere.

Your logo is one style. If the typeface you choose for this is simple and easy to read, then you can use the same type style elsewhere in your ad. For instance, if you have chosen a logo done in calligraphy, you can also use this for your headline or price information. If your logo looks like someone's handwriting, and is easy to read, then you can use that same handwriting for the copy in the body of your ad. However, if your logo type is very distinctive, with lots of curlycues and ornamentation, then you might be well advised to discard that style in the rest of your ad. You want things to be easy to read.

Your second typeface must be compatible with the first. An ad using a script logo and computer-style body copy would appear to have a split personality. Make sure that your two styles have similar personalities.

Don't think that because you are limited to two type styles, your ads will be boring. Type styles usually come in families. The typeface Bodoni, for instance, comes in light, medium, heavy and bold, condensed, poster, and italic. So you have several variations within this one type style, and you can use all of them without creating chaos. Figure 13-9 shows some of the variations you get with a single, readily available typeface. Even the more distinctive styles have at least

ZAPF CHANCERY LIGHT

ABCDEFGHIJKLMNOPQRSTUVWXYZ
abcdefghijklmnopqrstuvwxyz
ABCDEFGHIJKLMNOPQRSTUVWXYZ
ß fi fl Ø 1234567890 $ ¢ £ / & % § † ‡
. , : ; ? ! ¿ ¡ ' ' " " * - – — ( ) [ ]

ZAPF CHANCERY DEMI BOLD

ABCDEFGHIJKLMNOPQRSTUVWXYZ
abcdefghijklmnopqrstuvwxyz
ABCDEFGHIJKLMNOPQRSTUVWXYZ
ß fi fl Ø 1234567890 $ ¢ £ / & % § † ‡
. , : ; ? ! ¿ ¡ ' ' " " * - – — ( ) [ ]

ZAPF CHANCERY LIGHT ITALIC

ABCDEFGHIJKLMNOPQRSTUVWXYZ
abcdefghijklmnopqrstuvwxyz
ABCDEFGHIJKLMNOPQRSTUVWXYZ
ß fi fl Ø 1234567890 $ ¢ £ / & % § † ‡
. , : ; ? ! ¿ ¡ ' ' " " * - – — ( ) [ ]

ZAPF CHANCERY BOLD

ABCDEFGHIJKLMNOPQRSTUVWXYZ
abcdefghijklmnopqrstuvwxyz
ABCDEFGHIJKLMNOPQRSTUVWXYZ
ß fi fl Ø 1234567890 $ ¢ £ / & % § † ‡
. , : ; ? ! ¿ ¡ ' ' " " * - – — ( ) [ ]

ZAPF CHANCERY MEDIUM

ABCDEFGHIJKLMNOPQRSTUVWXYZ
abcdefghijklmnopqrstuvwxyz
ABCDEFGHIJKLMNOPQRSTUVWXYZ
ß fi fl Ø 1234567890 $ ¢ £ / & % § † ‡
. , : ; ? ! ¿ ¡ ' ' " " * - – — ( ) [ ]

ZAPF INTERNATIONAL LIGHT

ABCDEFGHIJKLMNOPQRSTUVWXYZ
abcdefghijklmnopqrstuvwxyz
ABCDEFGHIJKLMNOPQRSTUVWXYZ
ß fi fl Ø 1234567890 $ ¢ £ / & % § † ‡
. , : ; ? ! ¿ ¡ ' ' " " * - – — ( ) [ ]

ZAPF CHANCERY MEDIUM ITALIC

ABCDEFGHIJKLMNOPQRSTUVWXYZ
abcdefghijklmnopqrstuvwxyz
ABCDEFGHIJKLMNOPQRSTUVWXYZ
ß fi fl Ø 1234567890 $ ¢ £ / & % § † ‡
. , : ; ? ! ¿ ¡ ' ' " " * - – — ( ) [ ]

Fig. 13-9. Limiting your choice to two type styles can still give you a lot of variety in your ads. Many type styles have several available variations that will give you a lot of choices. For instance, this figure illustrates only about half the available variations on Zapf.

two variations. So your logo might be in the fancier of the two options, with headlines in the less elaborate style.

Remember—choose two type families. Your headline and logo type can be sans serif, but your body type should be serif type. Check with your local papers before choosing to see if the styles you want are readily available. Make sure that the styles you have chosen reflect the image and personality that you want for your business.

Checklist for Choosing Your Type Styles

- Is your logo done in lettering that is easy to read? Could you also use this style in the headline? Is it readily available at the newspaper, or at your printer? If so, you might want to use logo type wherever you want emphasis in the ad.

- If you are using your logo type for headlines, etc., is there another, easy-to-read typeface that has the same personality and image as your logo, and which would be suitable for body copy?
- If you cannot use your logo type elsewhere in the ad, can you find one typestyle with enough variations to keep your ad interesting?
- Is the type style you chose for body copy available at your newspaper? If not, are you prepared to have every ad typeset before it goes to the paper?
- Is your logo type available from the printer? If not, would you save money by using this style only for your logo, and choosing a readily available typeface for headlines and body copy?
- Do the typestyles that you have chosen seem to reflect the image and personality that you want to convey to your public?

BORDER STYLES

One element of print advertising that is often overlooked is the border. If you leave it to the newspaper, you will get a standard square or rectangular box surrounded by a medium-heavy black line. Just like everyone else.

You want your ad to stand out. To get noticed. You also want your ad to reflect a certain image. Perhaps the standard black box will suit the image you want, but you probably have better options. There are hundreds of different border styles available to you, if you only take the time to look.

In the first place, your newspaper can provide you with that same plain black line in varying thicknesses, from hairline to so bold that it looks like the edging on a funeral card. Often you can get a double-lined border—either two lines of the same thickness, or one thick and one thin.

Second, you can go to other sources for your borders. Both the Dover Clip Art Series of books, and the manufacturers of press-on lettering offer a variety of border lines that can give you a distinctive look.

Corners for Creative Looks

Varying the corners of your ad can give you a distinctive look. Corners don't have to be square. They can be rounded. They can be inverted. They can be cut off at the point. You can put a small box in each corner, or a scroll. All of these will give your ad a different look.

Using Clip Art to Personalize Your Look

Don't overlook the possibilities that clip art and press-type books can provide you with. Dover Books publishes several collections of copyright-free decorative borders and corners, which can help you to create everything from holiday themes, to a prim, Victorian look, to rustic. For a complete (free) catalog of copyright-free borders, lettering, corner motifs, and clip art, write: Dover Publications, Inc., 31 East 2nd Street, Mineola, NY, 11501. Most Dover books cost under $5.

Transfer-lettering companies make border tapes that look like leafy garlands, herringbone chains, or strings of Christmas lights. You don't have to settle for plain lines. (Figure 13-10 shows a few of the corner styles available from Dover Books Clip Art Series.)

A jewelry store might choose a border that looks like a fine gold chain. A gift shop might stick to a plain, black borderline, but use corners that look like gift-wrap ribbons. An electrician could use a border that looks like wiring, with a plug in one corner. Be creative, but restrained. I once saw an ad for a telephone installation service that used a coiled phone cord as a border. This was so heavy and thick that it took up valuable advertising space. The advertiser could never have run an effective small ad because there was scarcely any room left for copy.

Checklist for Effective Borders

- Is the border style that you have chosen distinctive enough to make your ad stand out on the page?
- Is your border style compatible with the type styles that you have chosen?
- Is your border style small enough to leave sufficient space for your ad copy?
- Is your chosen style readily available at the newspaper or printer? If not, can you prepare a sample border to leave with your print media salespeople to shrink or enlarge as the contents of your ads require? (Note: This means that all your ads will retain the same aspect ratio—wider than they are tall, taller than they are wide, etc.—a good idea for consistency.)

THE SHAPE OF YOUR AD

Once you have chosen border and corner styles, you are ready to create the general shape of your ad, as it will appear from now on.

Vertical vs. Horizontal Ads

First, choose the shape that you want your normal ad to be. If you are buying one-column inch ads, you have no choice—your ad will be one column wide by one inch high. Depending on the newspaper, this will either be two inches wide, or one and a half inches wide. So your shape is predetermined. But once you get into larger ads, you have choices.

You could run vertically oriented ads—longer than they are wide. You could buy ads designed in a perfect square. Or you could choose horizontal ads, which stretch across one or more columns, wider than they are high. Most advertising

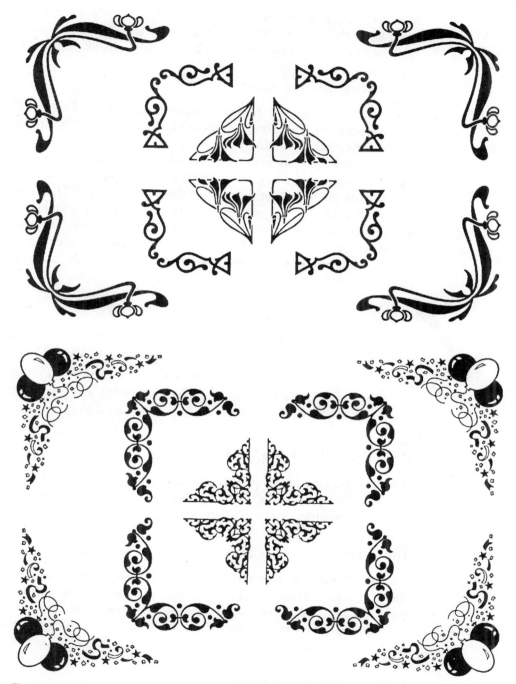

Fig. 13-10. Clip art services, such as Dover Books, offer a wide selection of corners that can give life and personality to your ad format. Above is a small sample of corners available from Ted Menten, *Ready-to-Use Decorative Corners*, Dover Books.

salesmen recommend this horizontal orientation, since it tends to be more eye-catching to the reader. Since, per column inch, you get more width than height (1½ inches wide, 1 inch high), you get a larger look for your advertising dollar.

Shapes that Set You Apart

Once you know your orientation, choose a general ad shape. Will all your ads have rounded corners? Or will you cut off the upper right-hand corner? Will you have a border within a border?

One furniture store in town chose to buy a vertical ad—two columns wide by six inches high. The border he used created the shape of a house with a peaked roof. His theme was "Furnishings for the whole house." The only problem was all the space around that peaked roof—the rest of the column inches that he paid for, but couldn't use. He would have been better off to draw his house shape within an outer, rectangular border. Then he could have used the upper corners for copy. The moral: Don't create amusing ad shapes at the expense of ad space. If you pay for it, use it.

Checklist for Effective Ad Shapes

- Does the general shape that you have chosen give you a large look for your ad? Single vertical columns do not show up as well as horizontal ads.
- Does your ad shape complement your type styles and image?
- Does your ad shape make efficient use of the space you will be purchasing—no wasted corners or odd lines that crowd out valuable content?

PUTTING THE FORMAT TOGETHER

Now that your ad has a general shape and style, you can begin to think about formats. We won't worry about content yet—just the general placement of the words and pictures in a consistent, coherent look that will work for you.

The Elements of a Large Ad

A major ad has several elements: headline, subheading, illustration, caption, tag line, and logo, plus any pertinent information about location, credit cards, phone, etc. A professional ad uses these elements in a consistent manner. The headline and logo are always in the same place; the illustration is always in the same style and location from ad to ad, and so is the copy.

The Small Budget Version

With a small advertising budget, you might not be able to afford enough space for all these elements. If so, you can eliminate subheadings. You can choose to eliminate the illustration, and let your logo and type style create graphic interest. A good ad will always contain a headline, your logo, and tag line. Don't forget directional information: address, phone number if needed, hours of business, etc.

Putting the Parts in Proportion

If your ad is using the full complement of elements, you can use a simple rule of thumb about sizing. Your headline and logo type should be roughly the same size. So should your subheading and tag line. Headlines and logos should, together, use up about 30 – 40 percent of your ad space. Subheads and tag lines should take up anywhere from 20 – 30 percent. The remaining space is for copy, or for copy and illustration.

Should you choose to eliminate the illustration, the remaining space is for copy. You can also increase the size of your headline, logo, or both.

Drawings, or Photographs?

If you are using an illustration, you have choices. You can use a drawing or a photograph. Research says that photographs are more memorable—but they don't reproduce very well in the newspaper, especially in small ads. Nor do they look very clear in a two-color brochure, although they're great if you can afford a four-color brochure with high-quality paper. If you do decide to go with photographs, though, experts say the larger the photograph that you give to the newspaper, the more clearly the details will emerge when it is reduced to fit your ad. So when having pictures taken, always ask for 8$1/2$- × -11 prints.

Illustrations, on the other hand, either require an artist, or a great source of clip art. Even though you might use a different illustration in every one of your ads, they must all be done in the same style. So if your first illustration is a silhouette, then every following picture must also be a silhouette. The advantage to using illustrations is that once you have found a source for artwork, you have total control over the image and look of your ad. Once again, Dover Books' catalog that I mentioned previously is a great source for this clip art. Ordering two or three books in a similar style (silhouettes, advertising art of the Twenties, old-fashioned woodcuts, etc.) can give you a large array of pictures to choose from, all of which will be stylistically consistent.

Basic Considerations for Illustrations

At any rate, whether you use photographs or illustrations, there are a few basic content considerations. A good picture will generally depict one of two things—the product or service that you offer, or the kinds of people who use your product or service. If your business has nothing very visual about it, either stick to showing people enjoying your benefits, or create your visual interest with typefaces. If you have something to show the public, do. Ads with pictures get more attention than ads without.

With these decisions in mind, you can begin to play with these elements, pushing them around the paper until you have a look you like.

Creating the Layout Format

To begin creating the format for your advertising campaign, draw several boxes the size and shape of your average ad. To make sure that they are accurate, measure from the newspapers that you will be advertising in, making sure your column widths are accurate. Adjust your box so that it fits the general shape (including corners) that you have chosen.

Assembling the Pieces. It would be helpful, at this point, if you could get access to a copy machine that can reduce and enlarge. This would help you to get type and pictures in the size that your ad will actually be when it appears. Cut out headlines that you see in the paper that are the general style and size that you think would be good for your ad. Then take these to the copy machine, along with several lines of type in your chosen typeface. (Don't worry about words—copy the alphabet several times, if you want. You are aiming at creating a look.) Have your typeface shrunken or reduced until it matches the size of your sample headline. Make several copies of your chosen typeface. Do the same with your logo. Have it copied in the size that best fits your ad. Ditto for your tag line.

If you haven't got access to a machine like this, then you will have to rely on yourself. Don't worry about real artistic ability—just try to copy your typefaces in the right size to the best of your ability so you can get an idea of what the finished ad will look like with the typefaces all in place.

Putting the Elements Together. Go back to those boxes you drew. Cut up your headline type, logo, tag line, etc. Lay them out so that they fit into the box. Try putting the headline at the top, centered. Put the logo at the bottom, also centered. Do you like the look? If not, move them around until you find a placement that satisfies you.

If you will be using an illustration, find one in a style similar to the one you plan to use. Add this to your box. Where does it seem to fit best? Do you have room for copy? Draw in straight black lines to show where the copy will appear.

Ideally, your copy should be in one place in the ad layout, rather than scattered all over. This gives the ad a coherent look, and makes it easier to read. So if your elements don't give you much room for copy, you might need to do some more shrinking. Also make sure that there is room for your address, phone number, and any other required information.

If you find a look you like, don't stop there. Stick it down with rubber cement, and try a few more arrangements. You might find two or three good layouts, and you'll want to be able to compare them. After all—the format you design today is the one you will be using for several years. You'll want a good one that you can live with. Make sure you have the proper amount of white space for your price category. And make sure your tag line is there. Your tag line must appear in every ad since it is your campaign theme.

It's important to work with the actual size ad that you will be printing. Many people begin by creating ads on 8 1/2- × -11 sheets, and are dismayed to find that, when shrunk to proper size, their work is no longer readable, or that an ad that looked airy and graceful is now cluttered. Figures 13-11, 13-12, 13-13, and 13-14 are samples of popular layout styles. Use them as guidelines, not gospels.

ADAPTING YOUR FORMAT TO OTHER MEDIA

So far, we have been working to create a newspaper ad format. I began with this because it is the most common form of advertising for the small businessperson. This same format, however, should be adaptable enough to work in other print media.

The Business Card

For instance, your business card should use the same typefaces as the ad. It should also carry your logo and tag line. Your layout might differ from the newspaper ad, since business cards have a standard format, but you will have retained enough of your recognizable advertising basics to promote consistency. Figure 13-15 shows a business card adapted from the format of a newspaper ad, also shown in Fig. 13-16.

The Flyer

Now let's say you decide to do a flyer. How do you maintain the same look? It's easy. Take the border you have chosen, and enlarge it to fit the paper you are using for your flyer. Now, put your headline, tag line, and logo (adjusted for size) in the same places on the flyer as they are in the ad. You will end up with a lot more white space then you had in the newspaper, but that's good. You can use that for copy—lots of it. (All the copy, of course, will be set in the same type that you use in your newspaper ads.) The flyer is your chance to give people a lot of information, rather than the bare minimum that your newspaper ad communicates. (Figure 13-17 shows a postcard flyer, compatible with both the print ad and business card, for With Compliments.)

Brochures

Three-fold brochures? Your front page should use your border style, logo, and tag line. The typeface for the brochure copy should be the same as in all your other ads. Illustrations throughout the brochure should be consistent with your advertising style.

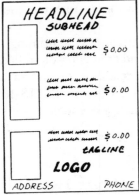
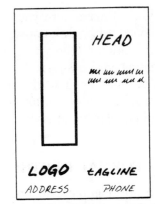

Fig. 13-11. Here are a few simple layout styles that convey a low-priced image. Notice how little white space is left, and how many different elements appear in each ad. Once you have chosen a basic layout pattern, you should stick to it in all your print ads.

Fig. 13-12. These layout styles, which feature two illustrations and a moderate amount of copy, convey a mid-price range image. There is more white space left open in these ads than in those with the bargain image.

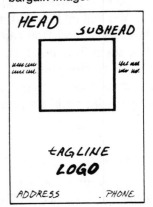
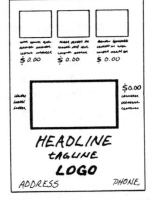
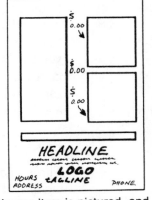

Fig. 13-13. Notice how much white space these three layouts leave. Only one item is pictured, and there is no mention of price. This sort of layout is used to convey a high-class, expensive image.

HEADLINE, HEADLINE

SUBHEADING

· COPY POINT ·COPY POINT

ADDRESS, PHONE

LOGO TAGLINE TAGLINE

Fig. 13-14. You don't need to use an illustration in your ads. Above is one of dozens of possible layouts that use only type to convey the message.

Flatter yourself . . .

**With
Compliments**

finishing touches for your wardrobe

1151 Grove Street
Clarks Summit, PA 587-1414

Fig. 13-15. Notice how the business card keeps the same general typeface, layout style and look as the print ad (Fig. 13-16).

Make His day

**With
Compliments**

finishing touches for your wardrobe
1151 Grove Street
Clarks Summit, PA 587-1414

Fig. 13-16. All ads for With Compliments feature several unvarying elements—the two-line logo in Times Roman Bold type, underscored by a double line, with the tag line, "finishing touches for your wardrobe." The ads also feature a very short copy line, some with a line art illustration. (All illustrations for this campaign come from Carol Belanger Grafton, *1001 Spot Illustrations of the Lively Twenties*. Courtesy of Dover Books)

With Compliments cordially invites you to attend our
Anniversary Celebration during the week of July 25
    Everything will be at a special, anniversary price. Our
distinct, quality merchandise features everything from antique
perfume bottles to the most modernistic of gift items to compliment
your wardrobe.
    During our anniversary, gift wrapping is free.
    So are the food and beverages.
    With Compliments offers the ideal alternative for corporate
gift giving. We cater to those who have a taste for quality and
distinction.

With
Compliments

finishing touches for your wardrobe

1151 Grove Street
Clarks Summit, PA 587-1414

Fig. 13-17. This postcard-flyer might have more copy than the newspaper ads for With Compliments, but because it uses the same typeface and general layout style, it is consistent and easy to recognize as part of a coherent advertising campaign.

Billboards

How about billboards? These are easiest of all. You don't have room for much on a billboard, because any more than 14 or 15 words would be unreadable at high speeds. If you are new, a billboard might include just your tag line, logo, and address, plus (maybe) illustration. Your tag line can be used as the board's "headline." If you keep your established border shape, type, etc., your outdoor advertising will be immediately recognizable. Later, when your business has more visibility, your tag line can move down with your logo, and you can steal headlines from your best newspaper ads for the billboard. (Figure 13-18 shows a billboard, using the format established in newspaper, from With Compliments.)

    Once you have a format, take a look at your bags, stationery, etc. Can they make use of some of the elements in your format, too?

Checklist for a Usable Advertising Format

- Do you have no more than 2 type styles (including your logo)?

- Are the type styles compatible with the image you want your business to convey?

- Is your second type style compatible with your logo?
- Have you used serif type for your body copy to make it easy to read?
- Are your type styles easily available—or have you budgeted both money and time for having them typeset?
- Do you have a border that sets your ad apart from the competition, without using up valuable copy space?
- Have you used the corners of your ads in a way that sets your ad apart?
- Do the border and corner styles complement the type styles you use?
- Are you using an illustration? Do you have a readily available source for illustrations of this kind? Does the style of the illustration go well with your type style?
- If using photographs, can you get them made into large prints that will reduce with enough clarity for newspaper?
- Have you chosen the elements (headline, copy, tag line, illustration, etc.) that will always appear in your ad?
- Have you arranged these within your border in a manner that is easy to read? Does it leave enough white space to convey your correct price category?
- Did you make sure to leave enough room for your address, phone (if needed) and any other pertinent information that people look for in your ads, such as charge card information, maps, hours, etc.?
- Is your format arrangement one that could easily be adapted to other forms of print media?

Say it Best. . .

With
Compliments

finishing touches for your wardrobe

1151 Grove Street   **Clarks Summit**

Fig. 13-18. Even the billboard looks like the basic print ad format.

SUMMARY

The first steps in creating an advertising format are to choose type styles that convey your image, and a border that will help give your ad a distinctive personality. You must also determine how much white space you will need in order to convey the proper price category of your store. With these elements in mind, you can then choose a general shape for your ad, and arrange the headline, illustration, copy, logo, and necessary information in a manner that pleases you. This is your ad format. Regardless of the content of your ad—changing headlines, copy, and illustrations—the format that you have created is the overall look that your advertising campaign will have from now on.

This format should be flexible enough to work in all print media. Using your distinctive type, logo, and tag line, plus your established border style will allow you to move among the print media with professional consistency.

Because consistency of format is so important to an advertising campaign, make sure that you choose type styles and forms of illustrations that will be easily available to you. Drastic changes in the look and style of your ad could mean that you lose recognizability.

14

How to Write
Effective Print Ads

"MY NEWSPAPER REP AND I HAVE A NICE ARRANGEMENT," SAID CLAUDIA. "I decide what I want in the ad, and I phone it into him. We've got a format all worked out, so he knows what border to use, and where the logo goes, and what goes in which type style. But things never seem to look the same anyway. Sometimes I have headlines in teeny, tiny type. And sometimes there's no white space left. Sometimes the ads seem too general, but sometimes I don't think I said enough. Isn't there some formula to make things come out right?"

One of the most important things that an advertiser needs is a copy platform. A copy platform will tell you exactly what your ad needs to say, and how much space you have to say it. Chapter 14 explains how to create a copy platform that will specify how long your headlines and copy can be, and what each element in your ad needs to communicate in order to accomplish your objectives.

How many words can I use for my headline and still keep my format? Can this ever change? How do I write a good headline? How can I make sure that readers understand what I want if they don't take time to read the copy? If I have a special event, or a sale, how do I convey that and still stick to my format? And, if I'm writing copy for direct mail or a flier, how can I make that follow the format of my basic print advertising? Chapter 14 will explain how to write headlines and copy that will fit your format, with any medium you choose.

THE COPY PLATFORM

Let's begin, once again, with your newspaper advertising. We have already, in previous chapters, discussed the general messages that you need to get across, the benefits that will most interest your potential customers, and the differences in benefits that appeal to your different target audiences. You will need to review these before you begin to write specific ads.

Professional advertisers do not plunge right in and begin by simply filling in the blanks on the advertising format with words. They begin by creating a copy platform, which tells them specifically who they are talking to, what the purpose of the ad is, and what benefits it needs to convey. The copy platform will also specify about how many words you have to work with in creating the specific ad, and whether you need a headline, subheading, picture caption, etc.

The reason for calling all this information together on one sheet of paper, even though you already feel that you have a good grasp on what you are doing, is two-fold. First, it serves as a pointed reminder to you about every specific that must be used in the ad. Second, it functions as a checklist so that when you have a rough draft of your copy you can determine whether you have covered everything in a manner best suited to your audience and image you wish to project. So, although creating a copy platform seems like a lot of tedious, extraneous work to the eager-beaver advertiser, it's not. It is a map that keeps you from getting lost in an overabundance of creativity. Or, sometimes, it is a prod that shows you the right way to go when you aren't feeling very inspired.

Contents of a Copy Platform

What, specifically, goes on your copy platform? First, the size of the ad, and its newspaper placement. You will want to be very clear about whether you are writing for a 3-inch space, or an 18-inch space. You'll also want to remember whether this particular ad goes on the financial page, or in the sports section, because this can make a big difference in the approach your ad takes.

How do you determine what the ad placement is likely to be? Easy: look at the intended audience for the ad, and figure out what section they are most likely to be reading. This information should already be in your media plan.

The third thing your copy platform should list is a brief, demographic and psychographic description of your target audience. An ad aimed at up-and-coming young executives will be written differently than one aimed at arm-chair sports fanatics.

Write down the specific purpose of this particular ad including 1) what you want to feature in this ad, and 2) what you want the potential customer to do when reading the ad. This will help you to decide what benefits this particular ad needs to feature, and what type of copy you will need, i.e.: Hurry down while they last, vs. keep us in mind. Your general advertising (that which runs whenever you are not featuring a seasonal sale, service, etc.) will normally inform people of who you are and what you do. Or, (referring to your long term objectives) you might be trying to change an image, or attract a new target audience. Usually, you also have a subpurpose of highlighting those benefits meaningful to your chosen target audience that you might not have used in previous ads.

Specific advertising can make people aware of a major sale or a new service; it can invite customers to your first anniversary celebration, or inform customers that you've added parking. Subpurposes should rotate benefits throughout your advertising campaign to inform the consumer about your regular products, services, and advantages. Since few of us can buy enough space to feature every benefit in every ad, we instead need to choose the benefits that best suit the specific audience that we are trying to reach with a particular ad. If you broke down your benefits as suggested in chapter 12, you should already have a good idea of which benefits each ad for each audience should feature.

Next, list the image that you are aiming to create for your business. This will determine the general tone of your ad. A business that wants a sophisticated image will not use ad headlines and copy full of sick humor, nor will a service that wants a very businesslike, no-nonsense reputation adapt a romantic, nostalgic tone.

If you are using an illustration, make a note on your copy platform about what will be pictured. Since your headline and copy must work together with your illustration, this becomes an important constraint on your advertising content.

In addition, it doesn't hurt to put your tag line up at the bottom of your copy platform, and any other essential information (address, phone number, map, if needed, etc.) so that you don't forget to include it in the finished product. You'd be surprised how often these get left out.

Sample Copy Platform

Outdoorwear ad for The Casual Man

Size ad: three columns by four inches (12 column inches)

Placement: Lifestyle Section, Sunday's *Times*

Target Audience: Men and women, 25–45, upper-middle class who care about quality clothing and classic styles.

Feature: Outdoor clothing, very classic cashmere coats

Other features: Imply that the reader can be a part of the picture.

Audience response? Headline: ''You've managed to Make it This Far.'' The reader should associate with this ad by agreeing with it (Yes, I did, didn't I?). Then, seeing that the right clothes can get him one step further, they will rush down and buy at the Casual Man. I hope.

Image: Quality and tradition

Illustration: Photo: a man and woman walking down a country road. Man wears cashmere topcoat, woman's coat is cashmere with mink collar, alligator belt.

You've managed to make it this far...

The right clothes will take you one step farther.

The casual man

214 Adams, Kingston

Where Tradition is the Trend

Fig. 14-1. This ad, for a high-priced men's store, uses only headline and subhead to convey its message—elegance that is not overstated either in the copy or in the merchandise. (Ad by Tracey Burns)

Tag line: Where Tradition is the Trend

Other musts: Logo, address.

Word Count: Headline 35 spaces; copy 10 words (app.) Figure 14-1 shows the ad that resulted from this copy platform.

Sample Copy Platform 2

General reminder ad for The Casual Man

Size: 2 col. by 3 inches

Placement: Page 3, Thursday *Times*

Target audience: Professional males, 25 – 45, upper-middle class with classic style. These men are not trendy.

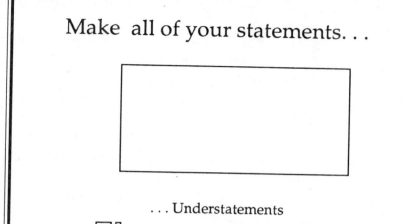

Make all of your statements. . .

. . . Understatements

The casual man

214 Adams, Kingston

Where Tradition is the Trend

Fig. 14-2. This ad for the Casual Man uses the exact same layout as the previous ad (Fig. 14-1). The picture has changed, as has the headline and subhead. Yet the image conveyed by the copy is the same—an appeal to the young executive on the move up the corporate and social scale. (Ad by Tracey Burns)

Feature: Formal wear

Other features: The Casual Man's clothes are classic and understated.

Audience response: If I buy this clothing, I will look as though I had "old money," as though I had arrived at a successful life. I will show very good taste.

Image: Classic elegance

Illustration: Man in tuxedo (head shot) looking as though he were romancing an unseen woman across the table.

Tag line: Where Tradition is the trend.

Necessary info: logo, tag line, address.

Word Counts: Headline, 31 spaces; copy one word. Figure 14-2 shows the resulting ad.

Checklist for Creating Your Own Copy Platform
- What medium is this ad for? Does it need to coordinate with any ads in other media?
- What size is the ad (number of columns wide by number of inches high). What does this work out to in inches?
- Where will the ad appear?
- Who is my main target audience, and to what specific characteristics of this audience must my ad appeal?
- What is the main benefit that this ad will feature?
- What other benefits will I offer that both interest this particular audience and help prove the main benefit?
- What do I want the audience to do when they read this ad?
- What image must the ad project?
- Is there an illustration? If so, what will it picture, and what style will it be?
- What necessary information must go into the ad? (Logo, tag line, address, phone, credit cards, maps, etc.) What are my word count and headline count? (See below.)

WORD COUNTS

Once you have a copy platform, and know generally what you want to say, you need to know approximately how many words you have to work with when saying it. Don't just assume that the printers will somehow shrink your headline and copy to fit the required space. They can, but this can play havoc with your format. It can also result in type too small to be readable. Once you have your word counts figured, they should be added to the information in your copy platform.

Headline Counts

If you followed the checklists for developing a format (chapter 13) you should have a sample of a correctly sized headline, which fits your space. Count the number of letters in that headline. This should give you a rough estimate of how many letters and spaces your headlines can run. Don't take this as a hard and fast rule—sometimes you might want to run a two-line head, where your current layout only shows one line. Then you can double your count. (Of course, if you do this, you must either use smaller type, a smaller illustration and less copy, or a larger ad.)

Subhead Counts

The same principle will apply to your subheading. Since you will always be working with the same typeface for these, your usable letter and space count remains about the same for every ad. Should you enlarge or shrink your ad drastically, you might have to recount, but minor reductions and enlargements shouldn't affect you.

Ad Copy Counts

To figure out how much copy your ad can handle, look to your layout again. How large a space have you left? Measure it carefully. How many column inches do you have for copy? (Remember—one column wide by one inch high.) Find an ad or article using your preferred typeface, in the correct type size. Measure out one inch of that, and count the words. This will tell you how many words will fit into one column inch of your own ad. If you are lucky enough to find an ad the same size and type as the one designated in your layout, you can simply count the words in the similar ad, and write yours to about the same length. If not, you will have to figure out how many column inches your copy is using, and multiply the word count of that similar column inch by the number of inches you need.

Your headline letter and space count must be fairly exact, since you have only one or two lines to work with, which leaves little room for error. Your copy word count is only approximate, however. You can be several words longer or shorter without ruining the look of your format.

HEADLINE AND COPY FUNCTIONS

Remember that every element of your ad must perform a specific function. You can't afford to waste space on trivialities, especially now that you know the limit to the amount of information you can convey. When you begin to write your actual ads and headlines, make sure they work in the most effective manner.

Headlines

Your headline must attract attention. It should be big enough and interesting enough to at least stop readers until they see your name and promise. Better still, it should interest them enough to read the rest of your ad and find out what you have to offer. A good headline attracts attention by offering a benefit, offering news, or summarizing a selling message.

If your layout calls for a subheading, then this should work to further prove or explain the headline. If your headline shouts "Save!," your subhead should tell readers what they are saving on. If it says "Indulge yourself," your subhead should explain how. When using a subhead, your headline can be short and sweet. If you don't use a subhead, then your headline must convey the entire message, and attract attention on its own.

The subhead, and the opening copy should be used to sustain interest in your business and the offer that your ad is making. It should create a need or desire for your offer, as the need step in Monroe's Motivated Sequence (chapter 12) implies.

Copy Functions

The rest of your copy, and your tag line, must show that you can satisfy the desire that you have just created. If you've promised savings, the copy must show how customers will save with you. If you have promised glamour, your copy should prove that doing business with you will help to achieve that end. Ideally, so should your tag line. In a good, consistent campaign, your headline and tag line will always work together (along with the illustration, if used) to create that single, dominant personality that you have chosen for your business.

Your copy should also call for action. If you are having a grand opening special, tell your reader how long they have to enjoy it. At the very least, make sure that your audience has the necessary information to help them act—your name, hours, phone number, and location.

Checklist for Organizing Your Headlines and Copy

- Is your headline an effective attention step?
- Do your subheads and/or opening copy stimulate desire or need?
- Does the remaining copy and the tag line show how you can satisfy the need?
- Does any ending copy, and your business-operating information encourage the consumer to act?

CREATING HEADLINES

Once you have an approximate idea of how long your headline can run, you can begin to create one. Look at your copy platform. What news are you announcing? What is the new benefit that you are offering? What is the main point that you want your ad to convey? These should lead you to some idea of what your headline needs to say.

Stylistic Choices

There is a lot of debate about whether a headline should be long or short in order to be effective. So far, the evidence seems to suggest that either way will work for you—as long as the headline catches the attention of the target audience. That is the whole point of your headline; it is the flag that will signal your desired audience that they want to know more, and that they want to do business with you.

Benefits. For this reason, the best headlines present benefits to the target audience. You have already had a lot of practice in turning your selling points into benefits. Do any of these fit your purpose for this ad?

Don't announce a sale, if you want to convey benefits. Announce that your customer can save, or can buy three for the price of two. Don't announce that your new employee is the best financial planner in town. Say, "Finally—the Advice You've Been Looking For!"

News. "Finally!" You see that word a lot in ads. Other common words are "Announcing, New, New and Improved, At last, Here, Today, Now. . . ." They're common headline words for one good reason. They work. Especially when reading the paper, people are attuned to looking for news, and that's what these words promise. They work well for the advertiser, because they alert readers, who like to be up-to-date, that your business is changing. A headline that promises news gets read. A newsy headline that also offers a benefit is even better. Sometimes, however, your headline count just won't let you use a benefit-oriented headline. Then, a news announcement alone functions effectively.

Advice. So does an offer of advice. In your ad, you become an expert who can solve problems, or inspire creativity in your reader. They need your product or service to get the whole effect. Headlines that tell the reader how to do something, or why they are having a certain problem are good attention-getting devices. "Five Ways to Dress Up Dinner" just might stir the creative impulses of your reader, just as "Ten Good Reasons to Call Barry's Tree Service" might get people looking for sick shrub symptoms.

Superlative Claims. Another tactic is to make a strong, superlative claim about yourself. People might read the rest of your ad just for the sake of argument, but if you can prove your claim in the body of the ad, you might have won yourself customers. A bank might tell its customers "We Do More For You." Many of us noncustomers will read the ad just because we don't believe the claim. We might be surprised, and we might switch banks if the copy proves the statement.

Humor. Humor also attracts attention. Schumacher's headed one of their ads "Fulfill your WURST Desires." The pun, and the double entendre, attracted chuckles—and a lot of attention. Be careful not to try too hard, or you'll merely provoke groans. A good natured, humorous headline is memorable. The catch? Humor wears thin fast. You'll need to be able to change your ads often.

Signaling Your Audience. Another way to get attention is to call your customer by name. A nursery headline could begin by signaling "Lilac Lovers!" A cooking teacher could call for "Cooks Who Care."

Questions. Finally, you can open your ad with a question. This is a deceptively simple and over-used technique. Opening with a question is easy—but opening with a good question—one that gets your readers involved, is tough. Ask your audiences if they are "Looking for a Really Good Apple Pie?" and they'll say "Well, yeah, but. . . ." and drift off to another ad. You haven't exactly given them a thought-provoking inquiry. You seem to be implying that you have a good pie, but "Really Good" isn't much of a benefit when you think of it. Ask "Are there more hairs on your pillow than on your brush?" You might get a response. You have singled out an audience—balding people—and asked about a problem that threatens them. The target audience will read on, because they hope you can offer help. A good question implies a problem that you can solve, or asks a question that people want an answer to.

Keeping Headlines Consistent

Whichever headline technique you use, remember that ever-present need for consistency. In a good campaign, every ad will make use of the same technique. You will invariably, in all your general information ads, use humor, or advice, benefits, or questions, throughout the duration of your campaign. So choose carefully, making sure that your chosen technique is one that you can sustain across several ads.

The one exception to the consistency rule is with sale and special event ads. Ideally, your headlines for these will be similar to all your general ads, but in reality, most advertisers end up with announcement ads for special events, using either a benefit or a news-oriented headline. Before you violate your format, try out a few headlines to see if you can work with your general campaign technique. If not—c'est la guerre. Just make sure your layout, border, and type styles are the same, and you won't lose any credibility.

Checklist for Good Headlines

- Does my headline attract attention?
- Does it make the target audience want to know more about what's in the ad?
- Does it offer a benefit? Give the reader new information? Tell them how to do something? Signal out my target customers by name? Make a startling, attention-getting statement? If it does none of these, try again.
- If I have asked a question, is it one that will make people want the answer? Or will they care about the answer? If not, try again until you find a really provoking question.
- Is this headline consistent with headlines you have used in other ads?
- Does the headline work with the illustration to communicate my message quickly and accurately?
- Does the headline lead us right into the information in the subheading (if used) and body copy?
- Does the headline fit my word count?

DETERMINING BODY COPY NEEDS AND STYLES

Body copy can vary from a few words to describe price and style, to long, news-paper-style columns of information. The copy you need is determined by your ad size, your product or service type, the presence or absence of an illustration, and your format.

Copy Length

Short copy ads (price, size, colors, etc.) can be used when your ad features an illustration, and when the product or service featured needs little or no addi-tional explanation. Long copy might be necessary if you have a new service or product that people are unfamiliar with. Remember that the size of your ad limits copy length. A business that demands long copy also demands ads large enough to present that copy readably.

If your budget limits you to very small ads, then you might not want to write blocks of copy at all. Instead, you might be wise to content yourself with listing the information that you want the ad to convey. In a general informative ad, this information will include some of your benefits—always remembering to choose those that best suit the audience most likely to be reading the newspaper, and section of the paper where your will place your ad. Remember, too, to change those benefits at regular intervals so that your audience will become acquainted with as many of your benefits as possible within a short period of time. (Figure 14-3 shows an ad that changes the copy points to feature new aspects of the business. Notice how the format remains the same. Also, see Fig. 11-1.)

If your ad budget allows you to buy some large ads at infrequent intervals, you should still use the general arrangement and copy style in these larger ads that you use in your small ads. To go from lists to long paragraphs will only con-fuse your look.

Copy Content

If you are writing a sale or special event ad, then your headline, of course, will refer in some way to the occasion. Your copy points must then explain the neces-sary details, always phrasing them as benefits if possible.

General Information Ads. For example, a small, general informative ad for a mom and pop grocery store might include a headline, tag line, logo, the address and hours, plus room for a very few copy points. One week, in the heat of summer, the ad might feature deliciously cold Smith's homemade ice cream, the cut-to-order meat counter, and 24-hour convenience. The next ad could fea-ture beat-the-heat cold-cuts, the chilled soft-drink cooler, and convenient park-ing.

Each of these would be presented as separate copy points, each highlighted

Worried about her style versus yours?

Let us restyle your comfortable bachelor furniture into a look she'll love. At a price you'll love. Our staff of experts can make your sofas, chairs--even beds look new and stylish while they retain the feel that you've come to cherish--almost as much as you cherish her.

Give your furniture a Facelift

the Restoration Shop
Route 6, Tunckhannock 587-0574

Fig. 14-3. Copy points should change from ad to ad in order to acquaint the public with different aspects of your business. This ad for the Restoration Shop highlights furniture restyling. Other ads, in Fig. 11-1 featured furniture stripping, custom finishes, and reupholstering. (Clip art from Carol Belanger Grafton, *Love and Romance*. Courtesy of Dover Books)

by an asterisk, or a bullet (a small darkened-in design) to set them apart from each other. No other copy would be necessary.

Special Event Ads. Your format remains the same in a special event ad, but the content changes. For instance, when that same grocery ran a sale, the ad would feature home-made Italian sausage, this week only $1.99; fresh green peppers, 39 cents each; and Mom's free recipe for sausage and pepper sandwiches. Once again, there is no need for paragraphs of explanation. The items and services speak for themselves.

The Large Ad

Large, spacious ad can accommodate a lot of information. People will read long copy. However, readability increases if the copy is broken up into short paragraphs. Better still, people seem to be unable to resist reading lists—so you can use several copy points, each numbered, or set apart from each other with bullets. Figure 14-4 is an example of a long copy ad, which uses the list format to make copy points stand out.

Special Considerations for Service Businesses

Service businesses often do better by using their ads to acquaint the public with the range of services that they provide than by attempting paragraphs of convincing copy. If you have found that your service requires a rational, rather than an emotional approach, then you might be able to use a fairly complete listing of those services as your copy. If, however, you have discovered that the public has some emotional investment in your service, then you might want to write copy that evokes those emotions. If you, as a hairdresser, realize that your typical customer wants to feel very up-to-the-minute and chic, then a short paragraph assuring her that your stylists attend regular training seminars to give her the very latest looks would be worthwhile. If your realty understands the intense hope that goes along with searching out the perfect nest, you will want to let your copy show that you understand.

Don't forget, though—the higher the investment, the more need you have for factual material along with the emotional. Especially if your business is one that the public is not very well informed about, your copy must work at informing people not only about why they should come to you, but also about exactly what it is that you do and why it is beneficial.

Copy for Retail Ads

Retail advertising rarely calls for long copy. Retail ads either aim to communicate benefits about using a particular store, or about buying particular featured products. Low priced featured items rarely require more than price information;

What Shall it Be?

The Restoration Shop can help me make changes:

1. stripping old finishes
2. Lacquering
3. faux finishe
4. reupholstering
5. reshaping
6. repairs

plus--they pick up and deliver--free. I'll call today!

Give your furniture a Facelift

the Restoration Shop
Route 6, Tunckhannock 587-0574

Fig. 14-4. The Restoration Shop could have also used this tactic for its copy—the list format that enumerates different reasons for using its services. To suddenly change to a list style when all of the other ads are straight copy would be to change the format. But if all of the other ads had been lists, then this would be an acceptable format to follow. (Clip art courtesy of Dover Books)

higher priced items, however, often call for some convincing copy that describes rational and emotional reasons for purchasing those items. Retail ads, however, almost always include price information.

Copy for Ads with Illustrations

If you have an illustration, then your copy should function as a cutline for that illustration. See the ads for the Casual Man (Figs. 14-1, 14-2) for an example of how this works. Don't just plunk in a picture and then ignore it. Both words and pictures must function as a unit. So if your restaurant ad features a giant lobster in a bib, then your copy should explain that your lobster dinners are so juicy and generous that diners must wear bibs.

With these points in mind, take a look at your format. How much copy do you need? What does it need to communicate? Once you have that firmly in mind, you can begin to write your copy.

Checklist for Determining Copy Needs

- How much copy can the ad use?
- Does my format suggest that I write copy in paragraphs, or in lists?
- If I am using an illustration, must the copy explain more about the illustration than the headline has already given?
- Given my target audience, do I need to write factual copy, or do I need to offer emotional benefits?
- Does the headline suggest points that my copy must include?

WRITING COPY

Perhaps the easiest way to begin writing copy is to do just that. Sit down and write a simple sentence that communicates your most important benefit. If you have already done that in your headline, then write one that tells us something specific about you, or your product or service. When I say specific, I mean just that. Don't tell us you're selling plants. Tell us what size plants, how many varieties, what kinds, whether they're for indoor or outdoor use, and, if it's important, where they came from.

Answer the Customer's Questions

Think about what you have written down. If you were a customer, hearing about this for the first time, does this copy answer your most important questions? Does it give you a reason to come in and take a look, or to pick up the phone and call?

If you think so, then take a second look. Did you tell them what you want them to do, or did you merely give them a reason to do it? While the response you want may seem obvious to you, you have to make it clear to your potential customer. So add an action phrase to your copy. Tell the customer what to do. This can be as direct as ''Rush on down before supplies run out,'' or as gentle as ''Keep us in mind.''

Keep Your Language Simple

Use simple language in your ad, no matter how sophisticated your desired customer. Pretend that you are explaining your product or service to someone with the personality you envision for your customer, but who has only reached the seventh grade. This is not intended to insult your customer. It will only help you create a clear, direct selling message. Advertising expert David Ogilvie claims that a few of his early ads, which used difficult words, totally bombed. The same ads with simplified vocabularies were unqualified successes. An ad is no place to show off your education. We don't read ads with the same concentration with which we read the news. The messages have to be clear, simple, and to the point.

Remember Your Objectives

In creating your copy, keep three things in mind—the persons to whom you are writing (as typified in your target audience profile), the ideas you want to communicate (expressed as benefits to that person), and the response you want them to make. If your first attempt at ad copy doesn't speak to all three of these points, then try again. Be careful, too, of your style. Is your image sophisticated? Humorous? Folksy? Then your ad copy should read that way.

Remember Space Limitations

Finally, be careful of word counts. Make sure your message fits the available space. If your copy is too long, be ruthless. Cut out any extra words, or any ideas that do not contribute directly to the aim of the particular ad. Or separate your copy into specific points and benefits, eliminating all transitions.

Write with the Right Style

Nothing says that advertising copy has to fulfill all the rules that you learned in grammar school. Yes, you should use correct grammar. No—advertising copy does not use all the rules of conventional writing that you learned in composition class.

Avoid Formal Transitions. First, because of limited space, advertising copy does not always make use of traditional transitions. If you need to move from one point to another, do it quickly. Rather than wasting time and space tying two dissimilar ideas together, use one handy word—"and" or "plus." People are used to this in advertising.

Write Conversationally. Second, advertising can be conversational, which is not always compatible with "written" style. If you want an ad that is easy to read, and especially if you want to establish a friendly or informal type of image, then you can be colloquial in your writing style. Read your copy aloud, if you are taking this approach. If it sounds like a friend talking, rather than someone writing a letter, then you have achieved your aim. If it's not strictly grammatical, that's OK. Conversational, however, is only one copy style. Your advertising might call for one of several approaches.

Alternate Approaches to Copy Writing

General Categories. The *general category* approach is one that you might use whenever your ad is featuring several related products or services. If you have five items featured in your ad, or are introducing three separate services, then your copy must tie these together in some manner. It must talk about all items featured in some manner that makes then logical and desirable. This can be a brief piece of copy, as short as one line, which also leaves room for more information beneath each featured item. For example, a private security agency might feature three types of service: private parties, security check-in at apartment houses, and regular after-business patrol service. The main body copy must tie these services together to point out that your agency offers peace of mind no matter what your security needs. Then you can go on to detail these needs, and your solutions specifically.

The Involved Style. Another approach to copy style is the *involved style*. You can use this if you have a lot of space to write in. The idea here is to give your audience the details. Explain each product attribute, and then the benefits that this creates, in as much detail as you need. That way, we'll know everything we need to know about what makes it desirable.

Bare Facts Advertising. For short-copy ads, you might be better advised to stick to a *bare facts style* of advertising. Here, you don't worry about creating a personality. Your sentences (or even phrases) are very short, relating only the most important points.

Make it Personal

Remember, any good ad makes a benefit claim, proves it, and tells the customer what response they need to make. If your headline promises a benefit, your copy needs to prove it.

Whatever style you choose, try to write your copy as though you were talking to a single person. Use the words "you" and "your" to make your message personal. Write in the present tense. And don't be afraid to use contractions. "A sale you do not want to pass up," sounds stilted in an ad. It's OK to use "don't."

Most of your sentences should be short, but beware of choppy copy. A long sentence or two is fine. However, beware also of the semicolon. While it looks impressive, it is also a bit formal for advertising. Better to use periods.

If you keep the reader, purpose of the ad, and desired response in mind, and remember to keep it simple, you should be able to produce good advertising copy time after time.

COPY FOR OTHER PRINT FORMATS

Not every advertiser uses newspaper. Sometimes you will want to write copy for brochures, directory advertising, or a sales letter.

The same rules apply to these as to newspaper copy. Be simple; convey benefits; put yourself in the readers' shoes and make sure that you answer any questions they might have. Call for action.

Directory Advertising

In directory advertising, you will follow the same rules that you used in your general newspaper ads. If you have chosen to buy a display ad, you need to feature your key benefit (which can make a good headline in this instance), hours, phone number, and products or services. Include anything that a directory reader might want to know, that will persuade that person to call you ahead of the competition. Remember to keep the same format that you used in newspaper.

Brochures

A brochure also follows the same rules for effective copy. The major difference is that you will have room for a lot more of it. Remember, never fill your brochure with long paragraphs. To the reader, these look gray and intimidating. It's better to write short blocks of copy, perhaps following these with a list of benefits that support and explain the copy (see Fig. 14-5).

Sales Letters

Even a sales letter follows the rules. In fact, this might be the easiest type of advertising copy of all. For one thing, it is easy to write a letter as though you were talking to an individual customer. For another, you don't have the same space limitations that other forms of print media impose. You can write in traditional paragraphs, and use conventional grammar and punctuation.

However, although an interested customer might read your entire letter, many people will only skim. To make sure that even the casual reader gets your

Why Us?

To keep worries off your back!!

Our years of experience in security assure you of maximum acceptable protection at minimum cost.

"Bring Our Maturity to Your Security"

What does Senior Security Service offer?

Round The Clock Protection........

...from Villains like these ...

...and we are diversified:

* Car Dealerships
* Department Stores
* Factories
* Warehouses
* Inventory Control
* Museums
* Cemeteries
* Apartment Complexes
* Construction Sites
* Social and Public Events
* Uniformed or Undercover

Who are we?

O ld Dogs

Who still know a few good tricks!

The Members of Senior Security Service are:

* Mature
* Healthy
* Dependable
* Experienced
* Semi-Retired
* Ex-Military
* Fully Bonded
* Flexible and
* Affordable

Fig. 14-5. This brochure uses a question and answer format for leading the reader through the copy. Instead of writing long paragraphs, which tend to look grey on the page and discourage reading, the important features of the service are listed, separated by bullets. (Clip art from Carol Belanger Grafton, *Silhouettes* and *Old Fashioned Mortised Cuts*. Courtesy of Dover Books)

Clinton A. Wallace, President

5342 Fallwood Dr. Suite 114
Indianapolis, IN 46220
(317) 253-3922

July 30, 1988

Dear Business Owner:

Who's in charge when you leave work at night? Is your current
security service giving you peace of mind? Do their employees
seem experienced, and well versed in protection work? Or must you
constantly worry about safety? And is the high cost of that
security making you wonder if a good old-fashioned burglary
wouldn't be less damaging to your wallet?

Good security means a service which uses veteran employees, with
mature, level heads and a lot of experience in protection work.
Good security also means security that is cost-effective.

And that's what Senior Security Service can offer you. Round the
clock protection for your business, by mature, experienced
personnel at the lowest price around.

Senior Security Service employees are war veterans --they fought
to make our country secure. They also worked to make their
families secure. And, now that they've retired, they're ready to
make your business secure, whether you're a bank or a bakery.

Senior Security Service employees began their retirement by doing
part-time security work for others. And now we've founded Senior
Security Service in order to offer you their expertise full time.
We are fully licensed and bonded, so whether you need temporary
guards for a private party, or a full-time person for your office
complex, you can rest assured that you will get dependable
service from us.

And we guarantee that Senior Security Service rates will be the
lowest in town. So sure, that if you find another service that
operates at a lower rate, we will refund the difference. Just
another one of our ways to assure you total peace of mind.

When you leave work, we know that you want to relax, assured that
everything is under control. We want that for you too. So call
Senior Security Service today--and leave the worries to us.

Sincerely,

Clinton A. Wallace
President

caw/rdw

"Bring Our Maturity to Your Security"

Fig. 14-6. The direct mail letter (enclosed with the brochure) explains the Senior Security
Service in detail. The important benefits are underlined, so that people too impatient to
read the whole letter will still notice the real selling points.

most important points, you might want to use your brochure style—incorporating a list of key benefits, set off by numbers or bullets—into the body of the letter. You will notice that direct mail advertising letters also use underlining fairly heavily. This also draws the reader's attention to certain key points in the copy (see Fig. 14-6).

Remember—the rules for effective copy never change, only the length. And remember, you are writing to a specific person, who might be interested in doing business with you. Your main concern should be in giving that person the information that will convince them to take the final step.

Checklist for Advertising Copy

- Does my copy fit the available advertising space?
- Are there any wasted words that can be pruned away?
- Have I directed my message directly to my target audience, using ''you'' and ''your'' to keep it personal?
- Is my copy written in the present tense?
- Does it convey an important benefit?
- Does it tell the readers what they should do in response to your message?
- Have I kept the message simple and clear?
- Does my copy, along with the rest of the ad, answer any important questions that my readers might have?
- Is my style consistent with that used in other advertising?
- Does my copy follow my copy platform, and communicate all the necessary information? Does it accomplish my objective?

SUMMARY

Headlines, subheadings and copy must all work together with the tag line and illustration to create a unified ad. They must all project an image—the one that you want people to have of your business. Whether long or short, your headlines and copy must be aimed at communicating benefits to your target audience.

The best way to keep a check on your ads is to begin with a copy platform, which details all the ideas that a specific ad must communicate. Then, keep in mind the space limitations of your format; you can create headlines, subheadings and copy that concentrate on communicating those ideas clearly and succinctly.

15

How to Write Effective Radio and TV Ads

DIANE AND MIKE WERE THRILLED WITH THE PRINT FORMAT FOR THEIR SPEAK-easy-styled cocktail lounge. They found clip-art books with Art Deco borders and type, and a whole book of flappers and gangster-style men for illustrations. The problem was translating all that into radio and TV. "We like our look, and we want to keep it," said Mike. "So how do we make sure that our broadcast ads sound like our print ads look?"

While Mike and Diane might not have time to write all their radio scripts or to make storyboards for television ads, they did take time to learn how to put these ads together. By understanding the various elements of radio and television advertising, they were able to develop an idea, using character voices, music, and sound effects that tied their broadcast ads right in with their print.

They specified that all their ads would use dialogue—a popular format—featuring characters who were easily identifiable as gangsters and flappers, with names like Babyface and Zelda. They chose roaring twenties style music. And they made sure that they used the tag line from their print ads on radio.

Because they were careful to specify that all the dialogues took place right outside the door of their restaurant, with Babyface looking through the peephole protesting that Joe sent him, Mike and Diane were able to produce their TV commercial cheaply. Cameras showed two characters at the peephole, and used the radio script as a voice-over while the TV screen showed viewers slides of the restaurant interior, lounge, and service. The commercial looked the way the radio ad sounded, and both broadcast ads were consistent with the print ads—all on a small business advertising budget.

Mike and Diane have mastered the tricks to creating effective broadcast ads that will fit their small budget. While broadcast ads are trickier than those for print, they are within the capabilities of most people, if they watch out for pitfalls.

To the average person, writing for broadcasting seems more exciting than mere newspaper writing. There is something glamorous about the broadcast media. Plus, there is the stimulating opportunity to use sound, rather than just words, to create your images.

However, writing for the broadcast media also brings special problems. Broadcasting is impermanent. Your message is here one second, and gone the rest. Plus, people tend to use commercial time to escape to the refrigerator, or to temporarily tune out. Therefore, any advertising you do in these media must be especially well done. It must signal a target audience; it must be interesting enough to make that audience want to pay attention; and it must be memorable enough to stick in the minds of the audience once it has ended. Plus, it must be simple. Because of time limitations, a good broadcast ad can only make one point. Anything more, and you come across muddled.

This chapter will discuss the techniques for writing successful broadcast commercials. We will look first at consistency—ways that you can tie any broadcast commercials in with your print ads. Then we will look at the elements of radio advertising: voices, sound effects, and music. All these combine to create a specific advertising format, which will determine your on-the-air personality. Finally, we'll examine ways that you can extend your broadcast personality to television.

If the following discussion of techniques seems technical and overwhelming, rest assured. You will not have to drag out your cassette recorder and make your commercial come to life. A production studio can do this for you. Many radio stations will both script and produce your radio spots, and, for a fee, will distribute them to other stations with whom you are advertising.

You will, undoubtedly, require these services; you also need to keep enough control over your ads to assure that they remain consistent with your advertising in other media. For this reason, no matter who does the actual production work, you, as advertiser, must determine your basic elements, format, and style.

KEEPING CONSISTENT WITH YOUR PRINT ADS

Face it. People don't really listen to radio. They tune in with half an ear, and then absent-mindedly push the button when a commercial comes. Yet, with all this lack of attention, radio continues to work successfully for thousands of small business advertisers. Why? One of the main reasons is consistency.

Few advertisers use radio as their primary medium for selling. Usually, radio commercials function as back-up media that increase the reach and frequency of a print advertising campaign. The first consideration then, when carrying that campaign over to a nonvisual medium is consistency. How can we connect the print ad, which relies totally on sight, to radio, which appeals solely to the ear?

In the first place, there are certain elements of your print ad that also appear in any radio spot you do: your store name, address and phone number, and your tag line. These are musts!

Second, however, are other less easily recognizable elements that can also translate from print to broadcasting. One is image. If your print ads are very no-nonsense and businesslike, then this determines the style of your radio spots. If you have used print to project a romantic image, then your radio ads must also be romantic in tone.

Another print element that can carry over into radio is your key visual. If your ad has been consistently using a cartoon character as part of the logo, then your radio ad can give that character a voice, and let him speak for you. If your print ads regularly feature a bird hatching from its shell, then your radio ad should let us hear an egg cracking, and a few feeble cheeps. In other words, if you have used any one visual consistently in print ads, and that visual is capable of being translated into sound, then those sound effects should be used in your broadcast ads.

If you have consistently used a spokesperson in your newspaper ads, then get that person to do radio. Or if your ads generally portray sophisticated women at lunch, then your radio voices must portray those same personalities and activities.

What if you don't use a visual? Well, you still have an image. That image must carry over into your broadcast ads. You are still featuring a consistent set of benefits to a particular audience. Remember, make sure you carry those copy points over to your broadcast ad.

Checklist for Creating Consistent Radio Ads

- Have I used my tag line in the radio spot?
- If I normally use a visual, is there any way that I can translate this into sound effects? Can I make it the theme of my radio ads?
- What image does my print advertising present? How can I translate this into sound and copy?
- Have I used a spokesperson in my print ads? Can I use that person in radio?
- Have I followed a headline format that lends itself to radio copy, such as questions, lists of advice, reasons to shop with me?

BROADCAST ADVERTISING'S SPECIAL NEEDS

Because of its ephemeral nature, radio advertising has certain peculiar rules of its own. These include single point copy, repetition, and the need to signal a target audience.

Single Point Copy

Single point copy means exactly that. Your radio ad should have one, single point that it wants to communicate. Therefore, a copy platform for a radio ad will single out one, specific, meaningful benefit, and use that as the basis of the ad.

This doesn't mean that you can't run a sale ad that features several items. The main point of a sale ad is, after all, that you are reducing prices to help your customers save. The specific items are only the details.

What it does mean is that radio is not the place to write ads that try to convince the public that you are the place to go for homemade pasta, and also that your bar is the friendliest one in town. Pasta is one radio ad. Your bar is another.

Need for Repetition

Once you have determined what single point you want to make, you need to repeat it. Since your listener only has a short time to grasp your message that he or she isn't interested in, the only way you can make your message stick is through repetition and restatement.

Your name and the featured benefit should appear in your ad at least three times. In a 30-second ad, this means that we should hear them once in the first 10 seconds, once in the middle, and once in the final 10 seconds of the ad.

Repetition is not a perfect word for this constraint. You will repeat your name, but restate your promise. Word-for-word repetition gets dull. Restatement can show great creativity. So if your main selling point is a huge selection, you can open with "No need to run all over town looking for the right dress. At Calvey's you'll find over 1000 styles to choose from." In the second ten seconds, tell the customer that "Shopping at Calvey's is like finding five specialty boutiques under one roof." You can close with "Calvey's—Your every style for every occasion dress shop."

You can see, with at least three mentions of a single point, why you can't cram too many ideas into a single ad. In the Calvey's example, I have already used almost half of my 30-second ad restating the name and promise. That leaves very little time for other benefits, details about featured brands, or address. Yet three is a minimum for memorability. Anything less, and you miss the chance to make an impact.

Signaling the Target Audience

Finally, radio advertising must signal the target audience. If it doesn't, then their fingers will hit that radio dial before you get a chance to make your point. There are several ways to do this.

Using their Names. One way to signal your target audience is to call them by name, just as you might have done in your print headline. So a spot that opens with "Attention all Dodge drivers" just might stop that dial.

Using their Music. Another method is by using music that is meaningful to your target audience. If we like the tune, we might sometimes stick around and listen, even if you are just another commercial.

Using Attention-Getting Devices. Finally, you can signal your audience with a good attention-getting device. These can include sound effects, or simply a very intriguing or exciting opening statement.

Whichever device you choose, make sure that your ad opens with something that will make the listener want to know what comes next. Make sure that you quickly follow the opener with a name and a promise, which can be effectively restated three times throughout the ad.

THE AUDIO ELEMENTS: What You Hear

In putting together the radio ad, there are three major elements that must be carefully chosen: the spokesperson, the sound effects, and the music.

The Spokesperson

The spokesperson will help to determine the personality and credibility of your ad. The type of voice, dialect, the perceived age of the speaker, and even the choice of male or female will all affect the audience's perception of your business.

Sex. First, look at the sex of your spokesperson. Do you want a male? If your primary target audience is male, then this is the logical first choice, mainly because studies have shown that people feel that ads featuring persons of their own sex are aimed at them. Logically, males would be more likely to tune in and pay attention to radio spots with a male announcer. Females will listen more quickly to females, unless they don't perceive the speaker as a logical authority for the product or service you are featuring. Men describing the expertise of the local electrician are likely to seem authoritative, even if the ad is aimed at women. Women describing their feelings of reassurance when that electrician enters the house could be just as credible. So, depending on the content of the ad, your speaker should be of the sex that the audience is most likely to believe.

Age. The age that we perceive the spokespeople to be can also affect listen-ership. An elderly sounding voice is likely to attract the attention of the senior citizen; a voice that sounds like a 16-year-old Valley girl will signal to the young folks. The one exception to this rule is that almost anyone except teens will lis-ten to ads using young children. Other kids will listen, because their peers seem to be speaking to them. Adults (at least those who are parents) have learned that, very likely, the child has a message for them.

Quality of Voice. Quality of voice is also important. A breathy, sexy voice is an unlikely choice for a family diner. Nor would you choose a rough, gravelly voice to sell your stock of fragile glassware. Voices convey personality; choose one that matches your chosen image.

You can also use voices to convey character. Studies have shown that Ameri-cans give greater credibility to spokespersons with a British accent than to the plain old U.S. sound. They also tend to perceive French accents as romantic and/or sexy; Italians as sexy but a bit naughty, Bostonians as very prim and proper, etc. A gift shop featuring European imports might want a spokesperson with a European accent. So might a local brewery, but they might want an accent that sounds almost like cartoon-image of a rotund little braumeister. If your ad features a cartoon dog, then a growly sort of voice can convince listeners that your dog is speaking to them over the air. Try to visualize the character you want to speak for you as a voice, then try to use that type of voice in your ads.

Children as Attention-Getters. Children, as I mentioned earlier, are possible voices—either real children or adults who are very skilled at imitation. The sight and/or sound of young tots performing well amazes people. Be careful, though. All too often, the advertiser also gets overcome by that same amuse-ment, and lets his young talent steal the spotlight from the product or service that he should be advertising. Get your sales message across first.

If you are using a mixed cast of children and adults, it might be wise to let the child give the selling points, while the adult asks questions, or reacts. Since the young actor tends to grab the spotlight, this will focus attention on your sales message.

Using Your Own Voice. One last possibility—yourself as spokesperson. If your business relies heavily on your personal identity, then you might be the most credible person of all to make promises about the benefits you can offer. If you can sound at all alive and warm on the air, then give this option a try. It worked wonders for Frank Perdue.

Whatever spokesperson you choose, make sure he or she sounds like the personality that your ad wants to convey. Don't be misled by the looks of a potential speaker—shut your eyes. People on radio almost never look the way they sound. And the sound is all important here.

Remember, once you have found a spokesperson, stick to that person for all future ads. That voice becomes part of your identity. You don't want to muddle it.

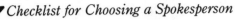

Checklist for Choosing a Spokesperson

- When seeking advice about my products or services, will my target audience be more likely to listen to a male or a female voice?
- What type of voice will best convey the image that I want to create for my store?
- Will my ideal spokesperson sound old? Young? Middle aged?
- Do I need a particular personality for my spokesperson—comic, sophisticated, lively?
- Do my print ads use a visual that suggests what my spokesperson should sound like?
- Would a foreign accent or cartoon voice best convey the style I need?
- Is my own name so strongly associated with the business and my reputation that I would do best as my own spokesperson?

Sound Effects

It's surprising how few advertisers take advantage of sound effects as a way of enhancing a radio commercial. These effects are what make radio such a creative medium. They can take us anywhere, to different eras in history, different continents, even different planets. They can create moods. They can even convey us quickly from one time or place to another, without having to waste scarce air time on words. Sound effects function as a shorthand that conveys information and image wordlessly.

Creating Moods. Assume that your ad needs to convey intimacy. The announcer could ask us to close our eyes and picture a special moment (very dangerous for those listening from automobiles). Or you could create the effect with sound. A crackling fire, the soft clink of crystal, the popping of a champagne cork, accompanied by soft strains of violin music will tell the listener instantly what the mood is.

Identifying a Situation. If your store is featuring cellular phones, you can set up the situation (driver in traffic, needing to get in touch with his next, urgent appointment) easily. Sound effects of engines running, cars passing, and horns honking will effectively convey the idea of rush-hour traffic.

Creating Time or Place Transitions. If you want to convey the passage of time or a change of place, you can do that by simply fading out one set of sounds and bringing in a new set to establish the new atmosphere.

Tips on Using Sound Effects. Be careful of getting carried away. Some sounds don't carry well over radio—we hear them, but we don't know what they are. Your radio script might read "SFX (which indicates a sound effect in radio) BABY CLIMBING DOWN FROM HIGH CHAIR." If you make sure to have the baby gurgle, we might get half your message. But how do we know what those other bumps and scrapes are?

A few sound effects can be done manually. Bring in crystal glasses to clink, for instance. Door knocks are easy, and so are foot steps. Crumpled cellophane held in front of the microphone sounds just like a raging fire to the audience at home. But you needn't rely on these for your commercials. Most radio stations have huge libraries of sound effect recordings for you to choose from, ranging from sounds of war to office sounds, jungle noises, and even an orchestra tuning up. Be as creative as you need to be, without getting carried away.

Checklist for Using Sound Effects

- What atmosphere do I want to convey with my ads? Are there any sounds that will immediately suggest this to the listener?
- Do my print visuals suggest any sound effects for radio?
- What about the setting? If I want the listener to picture a situation or place, are there sounds that they would expect to hear in those situations?

Music

Music, too, is a great conveyer of mood and image. Better still, music can signal to your target audience that "This one's for you." Feature music that appeals to a segment of the audience, and they start to pay attention. Make a mistake, and put punk rock music behind an ad for a gentleman tailor, and no self-respecting adult will even notice the ad. Punk rock is generally a signal for teenagers to tune in, and adults to go to the refrigerator.

Choosing the Right Sound. Choosing the correct type of music is important; so is choosing music that conveys the right mood. Normally, the beat determines the mood, so look for fast paced music to convey cheerfulness, and slow music for dignity, three-quarter time to communicate a waltz-style romanticism, and jazz or disco for trendiness.

Avoiding Distraction. Be careful not to choose songs with words. Even if you want to convey the idea that your pastries are flown in fresh daily from New York, resist the temptation to use the old Frank Sinatra song as a background. Who do you think your listeners would rather hear? You? Or Frank? Why try to compete? Also, avoid songs that are now, or even recently, popular. People tend to get disturbed when you start talking over their favorite song.

Avoiding Copyright Problems. Another good reason for avoiding popular songs is a legal one. Much of today's music is protected by copyright. Before you can use this music in your commercial, you will have to secure permission from the owner of that copyright, and probably also fork over a hefty ''use'' fee. Why pay, when your friendly radio station (or production studio) can provide you with yet another whole library of copyright-free music?

Need for Consistency. If you choose one tune, and use it consistently, it might come to be identified with you. As soon as people hear the opening bars, your name will come to mind. If it's a catchy tune, people might even find themselves humming or whistling your theme. What a great way to improve your frequency!

Just because you have a company song doesn't mean you have to give up signaling your secondary target audiences. Just change the beat. I once reviewed a record put out by Oscar Mayer, which played about 12 different versions of their famous jingle: straight, waltz-time, bossa nova, polka, marching band, and even madrigal. If you plan to use a lot of radio, it's worth getting a musician who has one of those electronic synthesizers to record several versions of your theme song for you. If you're only doing a little, try to choose a song that has a couple of different recorded versions—one suited to each of your target audiences.

Using Music as a Sound Effect. You can also use music within the commercial for emphasis. Angelic harp music can signal a transition from confusion to calm. Your company's 70th anniversary music can begin with the Charleston and segue into something modern to denote the passing of time.

Even little bits of music can be effective. The dum da dum dum of the Dragnet theme effectively conveys suspense. The crashing of piano keys sounds like a tension headache. A couple bars of pipe organ music can create a soaplike ending for your commercial. Once again, the possibilities are limited only by your imagination and the needs of your commercial format.

Checklist for Choosing Music

- What type of music does my target audience prefer?
- What type of music best suits the image I want to portray?
- Of the above music, what type will best suit both my image and target audience?
- Of these, are there any songs that will immediately suggest to the listener any of the qualities I want to convey? (Ex.: the theme from Superman to suggest that your plumbing service can save the day for leaking cellars.)
- Do the songs that I am considering have words? Can I either get instrumental versions, or fade this music out before the words interfere with my copy?

- Are the songs that I am considering covered by the blanket copyright agreement of the stations on which I will advertise?
- Are there different versions of my music available, with beats that will appeal to my secondary target audiences? If not, is there a song or style of song that will appeal to all my audiences?

Voice, sound effects, and music, then, have an important function in radio advertising. They not only help to establish the specifics of an aural format for your business, but also convey a definite image and personality. Use them wisely. And have fun.

FORMATS FOR RADIO COMMERCIALS

Your print advertising has a certain format that helps your readers to recognize your ads immediately. Radio ads also fit into format styles. There are fewer formats to choose from; you can use a straight sell, a hard sell, a dialogue; an interview; a testimonial, a slice-of-life, a drama, or a fantasy format. As with print, once you have chosen a basic format, you need to stick to it. The variations that make it yours come through your spokesperson, music, sound effects, and script. The format is merely the basic structure that holds these together. Appendix E gives examples of ads using these formats in proper script form.

Straight Sells

A *straight sell* radio commercial is probably the easiest to write. Straight sells involve only a single spokesperson who talks, straightforwardly, about your business. Many of the ads using this format don't even use music. The pace for this format is relaxed and conversational. Your spokesperson is simply explaining to the listening audience why it pays to do business with you. Here is an example of a straight sell commercial, written for The Casual Man, including its copy platform—a concept we will get to later in this chapter. Notice how the theme of the ad matches the print ad in Fig. 14-2?

COPY PLATFORM FOR THE CASUAL MAN

Copywriter: Tracey Burns

Stations: 93, 101.5, 104 (soft rock)

Timing: 30 seconds during afternoon drive time (4 – 6 p.m.) and on weekends.

SPECIFIC PURPOSE: To relate the listener to the Casual Man style where a wide selection will suit all tastes.

Spokesperson: Anncr w/ a soft New England accent.

Format: Straight sell.

Style: Simple, direct, elegant.

Music: Soft jazz by Earl Klugh.

SFX: None.

Key Benefit: Quality clothing made from natural fibers that makes all statements understatements.

Tag: Where tradition is the trend.

Other Benefits: Clothing for work or play.

Client: The Casual Man   **Structure:** Straight Sell

Product: Men's Clothing   **Length:** 30 seconds

SFX: SOFT JAZZ MUSIC BY EARL KLUGH UP AND UNDER

ANNCR: (with soft New England accent) Make all of your statements understatements. (PAUSE)

Like yourself, the Casual Man cares about the way you look. That's why all of the clothing is made only from natural fibers. If you can picture yourself wearing a crisp white oxford, charcoal pleated slacks, a navy and red tie, and a navy sportcoat then you have pictured yourself as the Casual Man. The wide selection of Polo by Ralph Lauren, Woolrich, and B.D. Baggie will help you make a statement from morning until night. At the Casual Man you never have to try to make a statement again.

The Casual Man—where tradition is the trend. Located in the United Penn Plaza, Kingston and N. Washington on Courthouse Square, Scranton.

SFX: MUSIC OUT

A *hard sell* is a variation on this, which uses a faster pace and a more insistent demand that the listener rush right down to the shop, or race right over to the phone.

Dialogues

A *dialogue* involves two people discussing your business. One of these people tends to be ignorant of your great benefits, while the second person is always very glad to tell the first one all about you. These ads can be done straight—two friends enjoying a serious give and take of information. Or they can be very funny. Your characters can be theater critics, allegedly reviewing your latest extravaganza, or two absent-minded professors struggling to compare their research on shopping strategies. Your business image determines the choice of serious vs. humorous as does the tone set by your other advertising. If your print ads are serious, better pass up the temptation to get funny with your radio spots.

Slice-Of-Life

Slice-of-life is an interesting variation on the dialogue format. In this format, you must imagine that your microphone just happened to pause at an open window, overhearing and recording people discussing your business. Generally, one person will focus on some item and ask where it came from, and the proud owner will respond with your name. A give and take of information that manages to convey all your benefits ensues. This differs slightly from the straight dialogue in that it conveys real people in real situations, while the straight dialogue can fictionalize, exaggerate, or dramatize.

Man-On-the-Street Interviews

The *man-on-the-street interview* is another variation on the dialogue where an interviewer asks a supposedly innocent bystander where they bought their fabulous poodle (or umbrella, or bouquet of flowers, etc.). The bystander, of course, bought it at your shop, and proceeds to tell the interviewer all about how wonderful you are.

This is an easy format to use—maybe too easy. So many advertisers have used it that it has become predictable and stale. Unless you can bring fresh humor or a new twist to the supposed interview, better try something else.

Testimonials

A *testimonial* ad is one alternative. This format can feature a celebrity who is meaningful to your target audience, explaining why he or she prefers to do business with you. Or you can take your microphone to real, average customers, who can testify that your business has helped them to find happiness, solve problems, or achieve a certain style. Finally, you can feature several letters from different customers, each bolstering the claims that your ad wants to communicate. The key to choosing a testimonial spokesperson lies in identifying the types of people that your audience is most likely to listen to.

Drama

Drama is a format that presents a tiny playlet to the audience. A problem is encountered, a crisis reached, a solution is found, and everyone lives happily ever after. Dramas can be comic; they can be written in a melodramatic soap opera style; or they can employ a story-teller format, with a narrator and almost no dialogue. The problem, of course, is one that you can solve—making you the hero of the hour.

Fantasy

Finally, we have the *fantasy* format. This can be a combination of many of the other formats I have discussed. It can be a drama, a mock-testimonial, even a staged slice-of-life. The difference is that, in a fantasy, we go all out. Our characters can be Martians, or werewolves. We can stage our ad in an anthole in the Grand Canyon, from a cloud floating overhead, or from the drainpipe in the sink. We can make the whole package sound like an audio cartoon.

Undoubtedly the fantasy is the most fun format to work with. It is also the most dangerous. Too often, the advertiser gets carried away by the possibilities, and creates a fabulous 30-second feature that fails to impress the listener with his or her name and selling message. Make sure you work the basic message in before you begin to fantasize.

As with newspaper, you need to establish your format and basic elements before you can begin to write your actual ads. Just like newspaper, you need to begin your actual ad writing with a copy platform.

THE RADIO COPY PLATFORM

Radio copy platforms differ slightly from those made for print. For one thing, you are writing copy for particular radio stations, and these stations have their own formats that you need to consider. Since different radio stations could have different target audiences, each one might require adjustments in your ad—music, spokespeople, additional benefits featured, etc. For another, your copy platform will be more specific, since it must list those very requirements: kind of spokesperson, type of music, specific format, and so on.

Once again, the copy platform is there to remind you of every detail that must be taken into account when the actual copy is written. A sample platform will illustrate this best.

SAMPLE COPY PLATFORM FOR JOE'S PLACE

Time: 30 seconds

Stations: WWXX, WWYY (Both soft rock stations)

Timing: To be aired during afternoon drive time (4 – 6 p.m.)

SPECIFIC PURPOSE: To establish an image for Joe's Place as a roaring twenties speakeasy.

Spokespersons: One male, gangster-type voice, to give sales message; one female (gum-chewing flapper type).

Format: Drama

Style: Melodramatic; almost like an old gangster film.

Music: Charleston

SFX: (sound effects) distant machine guns, roaring motors, cocktail crowd noises.

Key Benefit: Our customers can escape from the modern world and fantasize about being gangsters, flappers—in other words, have a good time in an old-time atmosphere.

Tag: There's no prohibition against fun at Joe's Place.

Other benefits: play roulette for a free meal; all drinks served in tea cups; silent films projected on rear wall.

Special Feature of this Ad: If you knock and say Joe sent you, you'll get a free drink.

As you can see, the copy platform specifies every important aspect that must be considered in writing the particular ad; it also specifies the types of sounds that will be used to establish atmosphere, the types of characters that you are writing dialogue for, and the music, and the necessary content. With this platform, a radio station or production studio should be able to produce ads that fit your requirements.

Many people, however, prefer to maintain complete control over their advertising process, including the actual writing of the script. Keep your copy platform points in mind, and you can write your own.

Checklist for Radio Copy Platforms

- How long will the spot be? (60 seconds, 30 or 10?)
- What stations will air this spot, and what type of format do they have?
- When will this spot be aired? (Time of day and season if helpful.)
- What is my objective in running this ad? (Remember—you can only communicate one main point with radio.)
- What type of spokespeople do I want to use? What vocal characteristics should they have? (Age, accent, type of voice, etc.)
- What format will I use? Is this consistent with my other radio ads? Will it work with the style of print ads I have used?
- What style of ad would I like? (Dramatic? Lively? Sophisticated? Cartoonlike? Romantic?)
- What music am I using in this particular spot?

- Will there be any sound effects? If so, what?
- What is the key benefit that this ad will offer?
- What other points must I include to make this benefit clear and believable?
- Have I included my tag line?
- Have I included necessary information, such as location?

WRITING RADIO COPY

Radio stations normally offer you a choice of 30-second, or 60-second ads. This will determine the length of your script. Seventy-five words is the maximum length for a 30-second commercial, while a 60-second ad has a 135-word maximum. This is, of course, assuming that you don't need time for music, sound effects, and dramatic pauses. However, these word counts offer you a general guide to length.

Structuring the Ad

Your radio ads should follow Monroe's Motivated Sequence, as presented in chapter 12. Remember that your ad must open with an attention-getting device. It must then focus on creating a need or desire for your product or service. You must next prove that you can satisfy this desire or need. In many ads, you can then visualize the benefits of doing business with you. Finally, give a call to action that suggests what you want the audience to do upon hearing your ad, and tells the listener exactly how to go about responding.

Be careful of creating a negative-sounding need. If the opening of your ad dwells too much on the woe and misery of a certain problem, then that woe and misery rather than the bright promise of your solution will be what sticks in the customer's mind. Create desire, want, and need, but do it positively. Make us say "I want that!" rather than "I need to be relieved from oppression."

Wording the Ad

Watch your wordings carefully. Certain things that seem great in print fail abysmally out loud. If, for instance, your copy uses a lot of words beginning with the letter "s," your ad will tend to sound like one long hiss. Try saying "Saturday Sunshine Special for Size Sixes," and you'll see what I mean.

Avoid any too-obvious alliterations. While they might be catchy, they are very difficult for the announcer to pronounce successfully. For the same reason, avoid any wording that even hints of being a tongue twister.

Be sure you write in the present tense. Make sure that everything is in the active voice. Have people doing things, instead of having things done to them. Tell the customer that "We've stocked our store with hundreds of colors and sizes'' rather than saying ''Our store has been stocked. . . .'' For one thing, it's shorter to use active voice, and you need to cut out any spare words. Even more important, active voice lends immediacy and vitality to your ad.

Write the way people talk. Avoid long sentences that require a quick gasp for breath somewhere in the middle. Use contractions. Even slang is permissible, if it's in character. In a spoken advertisement, conversational dialogue is crucial. If you're unsure about your script, try reading it into a tape recorder. You'll soon hear the problems.

Remember that people only have this one chance to get your message. They will not be able to refer back to your ad. So information must be simplified. For this reason, you might not want to give your address in your radio ads, but merely indicate the cross streets. Mention a significant landmark that will help people locate you. If your phone number is important, repeat it. Or refer people to your newspaper ad or the phone book.

Checklist for Effective Radio Copy

- Does my opening grab the attention of the target market?
- Does the ad quickly create a desire for my product or service?
- Do I present the listener with proof that my product or service will satisfy that desire?
- Have I helped the listener to visualize how much better life will be if they take advantage of my offer?
- Have I told the listener what to do in order to satisfy the desire that I have created?
- Is the ad written in colloquial English? Does it sound like ordinary conversation?
- Have I used contractions? Would slang words help to make the ad sound more conversational?
- Have I avoided alliterations and tongue twisters?
- Have I tried to keep words beginning with ''s'' to a minimum?
- Have I mentioned the name of my business in the first ten seconds of a 30-second ad? The second 10 seconds? The third?
- Have I restated my key benefit at least three times?
- Are the sentences and phrases short enough to read without gasping for breath?

THE SCRIPT FORMAT

Radio scripts are written in a special, standardized way that indicates what is spoken, what is music, and what is sound effect. This method for writing copy and directions is called a *script format*. Because it makes the ad elements easy to decipher at a glance, and avoids misunderstandings, radio stations prefer that they get their scripts done in the correct manner.

A radio script begins with an identification of the advertiser. It specifies the length of the ad, and gives it a title that distinguishes it from other ads in your campaign.

Scripts are always double or triple spaced. Sound effects, musical directions, and any other directions for the use of sound are capitalized and underlined. They are always entered on a line separate from the dialogue, even if they occur in the middle of a speech. Character names are also capitalized, but not underlined. Dialogue itself is written in standard upper- and lowercase letters.

As already noted, the official script designation for sound effects is SFX. Music is also a sound effect, so that if you want a few soaplike organ chords at the end, you would indicate this by writing:

SFX: ORGAN MUSIC (5 SECONDS) AND FADE UNDER
Zelda: Gee, Babyface, I want to come to Joe's place every night.

With this direction, your music will continue to play softly under the dialogue.

SFX: MUSIC OUT indicates the place where music is to end. SFX: BURST OF MACHINE GUN FIRE indicates a conventional sound effect. If this sound effect were to come in the middle of a speech, you would indicate it this way:

BABYFACE: Come on, Doll.
SFX: MACHINE GUN FIRE
BABYFACE: We gotta go some place livelier.

Look at the sample scripts in Appendix E to see how a completed spot would look.

Remember, in writing for radio, you must maintain consistency. The image, key benefit, and tag line should carry over from other forms of advertising. You should choose a consistent musical style, and an announcer or announcers who fit your desired image. The music, spokespeople, and sound effect style that you choose will help to establish your image within a particular format, be it a straight sell by a single announcer or an out and out fantasy structure. The radio format you choose should be used throughout your campaign, even when your specific message changes.

KEEPING TELEVISION ADS CONSISTENT

If you want to create a professional looking advertising campaign and make use of television, then you would be well advised to choose a simple radio format—a straight sell.

There is one main reason for this. While television time might be affordable, television production is not. In a small market, you might be able to buy a 30-second early morning TV spot for $40. It might cost you another $500 to produce it, unless you keep things very simple.

Format Options

Even with a small budget, you still have some options for producing interesting television ads.

The Single Spokesperson. The simplest ad to produce is one where a single spokesperson appears on camera and simply discusses the product or service. This is known somewhat sarcastically as a *talking head* commercial since all the audience sees is a person sitting down and talking. TV is most valuable because it is so visual. There is nothing exciting about a talking head.

Spokesperson on Location. You can pep things up a bit by having the production crew come to your place of business and film the spokesperson talking while wandering through your establishment. Because this is known as *going on location*, it costs a bit more, but it is more visual and also gives your audience a chance to see what you are all about.

If you are a service, and there is nothing very visual about your location then you might dramatize things a bit by having the crew film you at work. A plumber might discuss his benefits while crawling out from under a sink. An insurance representative might give her presentation while standing in front of a burned-out building, or a heap of wrecked automobiles at the junkyard. Some local businesspeople have gone so far as to dress up in silly costumes while delivering their message in a highly dramatized manner. These gimmicks seem to have a certain camp flavor that makes up in memorability what it lacks in dignity. Any of these options would add visual interest to a straight sell—as long as they also fit the image created by your print advertising. This would allow you almost perfect continuity; in many instances you can use your radio script for the television commercial.

Testimonials. *Testimonials* also lend themselves to adaptation to television. The same rules apply to the testifier as to the anonymous spokesperson. Be somewhere and do something to make him or her worth watching. In other words, don't just stand there.

Simple Dramatizations. If you have very good talent, you might even be able to translate a simple dialogue or slice-of-life into a TV commercial. Bear in mind, it is harder for an amateur to sound and look convincing in front of a TV crew than in front of the anonymous radio microphone. If they can pull it off, and if you use your store, or some other convenient and already usable location as the setting, then this type of commercial should not cost much more to produce than the on-location straight sell. Check with your local college or university. You might be able to find actors and actresses in the theater or broadcasting departments.

Slides. Still another option is to use slides—still photographs that show various aspects of your business. This might sound dull on a medium that can show action, but a talented television producer can create action from your slides. By panning across a photo to highlight various key visuals, by zooming in toward a particular detail, then out again to give the bigger picture, and by dissolving from one shot to the next so that for a moment two ideas are almost superimposed on each other; still photos can appear to have a life and vitality of their own. Add music, and a voice-over (narration that is done off-camera), and you can create a relatively inexpensive but effective commercial.

With the new video equipment, your still photos—or even film shots—can be manipulated into special effects. The screen images can be rotated, doubled and tripled, thrown into reverse, or split into a prismlike effect. If you don't overdo it, these effects can add a glossier, more professional look to your TV commercial.

Options to Avoid

If you've dreamt of fantasy style ads with special set effects, animation, and lots of melodrama, better wake up. Those ads we take for granted in prime time costs hundreds of thousands of dollars to produce. Any attempt that you with your small budget might make to imitate them would only look amateurish. Keep your radio simple, and you can use TV consistently. Use a complicated radio format (and they sure can be fun!) and your television advertising will have little in common with the rest of your advertising.

Remember, though, that TV is visual. This means that you will not, if you are smart, overwhelm the viewer with words. In other words, you can't just hand in your radio script and expect it to work on TV. Television can show what you could only talk about on radio. So, where your radio script tells what we can instead depict on the screen, do some judicious cutting.

Checklist for Using Television

- Is there anything visual about your business location? Would seeing the location and merchandise make the ad more believable?
- If there is nothing visual at the place of business, is there anything interesting and visual about you when you perform your service?
- Is there any visual interest to seeing one of your customers either in need of your service, or enjoying the results? Would they be willing to show this on TV?
- Look at your radio spot. Can you use it for TV? Does it take place in a single, readily available location?

- If your radio spot requires actors, can you find people who would be believable? Will you need costumes? Props? Can you afford these?

- Can you use slides or still pictures to convey a vivid impression of your business and its benefits? Will your radio script fit this format?

- If you are using your radio script for television, are there lines that you can eliminate because we can see them for ourselves?

SCRIPTING FOR TELEVISION

Scripting for television can be difficult, at first. We have become so accustomed to putting words on paper to show what we mean that the idea of showing rather than telling can be challenging.

A good first step in creating a television script is to make yourself see what is happening at each point in the commercial. Write this out in story form. Indicate what someone is doing, and what they are saying while they do it. Indicate when anyone might be talking, but not seen on the screen. Once you have this sorted out, you can begin to turn it into a script.

Camera Terminology: Transitions

First, you will need to know a few basic camera terms.

Cut. To *cut* from one scene to the next means that the scene changes instantaneously. There is no transition. First we see the outside of the store, and then the next scene shows the inside counter.

Dissolve. To *dissolve* means that the scene changes slowly. The store exterior would slowly fade off the screen, and the interior would then slowly fade in. Dissolves are usually used in commercials to indicate that some time has passed between one scene and the next. They also help to indicate that we have moved to another, more distant location. They can be useful in communicating a romantic mood, if they are done rather slowly.

Supers. A very slow dissolve, where the first scene is faded out halfway, and the new scene is faded in halfway, and stopped, would create what is known as a *super*. Using this technique, the viewer sees both scenes equally well, but both are somewhat softened. A super can be used to show your product, large, superimposed over a shot of your store; it can also be used to superimpose lettering—key words from the commercial or your business name and address over the action scenes of your commercial.

Wipes. Another possible transition is a *wipe*. This means that one screen image is literally wiped off camera by the next one, either vertically or horizontally.

Split Screens. A *split screen* is a wipe that stops halfway. On screen, it appears that two images exist side to side—so that you could show both halves of a telephone conversation at once—or your service outdoing that of the competition.

Camera Terminology: The Shots

Aside from understanding camera transitions, you will also want to be able to call the shots. How much of the on-camera action do you want the camera to focus on?

Long Shots. A *long shot* (indicated in a script as LS) means that the camera is operating at a distance and will be able to take in a broad view of the action. Many commercials open with a long shot, because it can take in the entire scene, thus establishing the setting and situation.

Medium Shots. In a *medium shot* (MS), the viewer can still see the setting, but most of the extraneous detail has been eliminated. With people, the medium shot would frame them from the waist up. Often, after the establishing shot, a commercial will cut to a medium two shot (M2S)—focusing on the two people who will be giving the important commercial dialogue.

Close-Ups. A *close-up* (CU) zeroes in on the face of a single person, or shows an item in detail, excluding the background. This focuses the viewers attention on that face or item, and eliminates other details and actions that would otherwise distract them.

Finally, there is the *extreme close-up* (ECU). This moves the camera so close to the object that only a small part of it will fill up the entire television screen. Where a close-up might have focused on a toothbrush, the extreme close-up would show us only the bristles. Using these terms in your script indicates to the director what perspective you want for each shot.

Script Format

In a television script, the page is divided into two columns. The left-hand column is used to indicate what the camera is doing, and what is seen on the screen. The right-hand column designates the character who is speaking, and gives the dialogue—it is the audio column.

The Video Column. The video column is divided into scenes. A new scene is determined by a change in camera angle, or by a visual transition. So every time we need to give a camera direction, because we are showing something new on the screen, we must indicate a new scene.

The scenes in the script are numbered. Camera directions follow the number, plus a brief description of what is happening on-camera. All this information is typed in capital letters.

The Audio Column. Audio instructions are typed directly across from the camera directions, indicating what the audience will hear when the camera shows the scene. The speaker's name is designated in every scene, even if it is the same person who spoke in the previous scene. The name of the speaker is always capitalized. The dialogue, however, is typed in standard upper- and lowercase. Any sound effects are also indicated in the right column. As in radio, they are given their own separate lines and are capitalized and underlined.

If, during a particular scene, there is no on-camera spokesperson but rather an off-screen voice, indicate this by using the abbreviation VO, which means you are using a voice-over.

Here is a sample script for The Casual Man. Notice that it not only has the sound and feel of the radio and print ads, but carries over the tag line, address, and logo. This is a higher budget ad than most of us could afford, simply because of the actors—but a taxi and street might be manageable if you have a cooperative production crew.

Sample Script
Copywriter: Tracey Burns
Date: January 26, 1989
Structure: Dramatization

Advertiser: The Casual Man
Product: Men's Clothing
Length: 30 seconds

VIDEO	AUDIO
1. MEDIUM shot of a couple at dinner. The man is wearing a polyester plaid suit w/ an old-looking white oxford and a navy tie. Nothing about him says fashion. His date is wearing a cheap low-cut dress. She has bleached blond hair and is wearing lots of makeup and cheap jewelry. 4 seconds	SFX: a crowded restaurant
2. DISSOLVE to a black screen w/ white letters reading: DO YOU WANT TO GET A DATE? 5 seconds	VO: ANNCR: Do you want to get a date?
3. DISSOLVE to a man and a woman on a busy N.Y.C. street getting into a cab from opposite sides.	MUSIC: Jazz music under

The man is dressed in a camel-hair topcoat with tweed pants. He is also wearing a cream colored oxford and a rust silk paisley tie. He is carrying a leather briefcase. His hair is blond and parted on the side. He is wearing tortoise-shell glasses. The woman is wearing a suit from Chanel. 4 seconds

4.
DISSOLVE to a CU over the man's shoulder showing the Polo horse on his oxford. You can see him moving to get comfortable. 3 seconds

VO: CABBIE: "Where to"
VO: WOMAN: "Around the corner to 76th"
VO: MAN: "13 52nd."

5.
TILT down showing a CU of the woman crossing her legs and twisting her feet back and forth nervously. 2 seconds

SFX: Whispers from the woman

6.
TILT up to the man's oxford again. You can see the woman reaching to pay the cabbie. 4 seconds

VO: MAN:
Dom Perignon that's already chilled? I'd love to."

7.
CUT to a SUPER on black screen w/ white letters: OR ATTRACT ONE? 3 seconds

VO: ANNCR: Or attract one?

8.
CUT to the couples' back as she opens the door with key and then the door (wood and brass) shuts.

VO: ANNCR: Use tradition to break tradition. Start at the Casual Man where tradition is the trend.

9.
FREEZE and SUPER: The Casual Man Where Tradition is the Trend (in logo form) United

Located in the United Penn Plaza, Kingston and N. Washington Ave., on Courthouse

Penn Plaza, Kingston, 207
N. Washington Ave., Scranton.
5 seconds

Square, Scranton.

MUSIC OUT

THE STORYBOARD

One way to figure out where to cut is to storyboard your commercial. A storyboard is a way of visually depicting your script. It shows each scene that your script has indicated, but adds a pictorial element.

No—you don't have to be able to draw. If you can do stick figures, it will be enough to communicate your ideas. Or, use tracing paper, or cutouts. The idea of the storyboard is to show what you want, rather than trying to describe it.

A storyboard uses a sheet of paper divided into three columns. In the first column, you will see four or five little television screen-shaped pictures. These show the key action that occurs in each scene. The middle, very narrow column, indicates the scene number. The third column gives first the video description of the scene, plus camera actions (written exactly as it was in the script), and, immediately below, the dialogue and sound effect directions.

The storyboard is a good place to help you discover where you can edit dialogue. If your storyboard picture is already showing us what your announcer is describing, maybe you can cut down on the words and let the viewer focus on the pictures. If, however, you discover that the quality you want to communicate cannot be shown, then you know you need to retain the dialogue.

Once you are satisfied with your storyboard, you have done all you could to assure that your advertising campaign is consistent. Now you are in the hands of your producer. For local business, this will most likely be one of the local television stations, although you might be able to hire an independent producer who will make videotapes for you to use at any or all the stations in your area.

Take the time to sit down and talk to your producer. See what they can do for you. Their advanced knowledge of television techniques combined with your understanding of your advertising needs can help to lift your commercial from the average, run-of-the-mill homegrown ads we see on late night TV to something professional and effective.

SUMMARY

Good broadcast advertising concentrates on communicating a single point and repeating and restating that point until it makes some impact on the consumer. By a judicious selection of talent, music, and sound effects, broadcast commercials can create a distinct personality for your business—and one that is consistent with all your print advertising.

16

Publicity: How to Earn It and How to Get It

"I DON'T KNOW HOW HE DOES IT," MARVELED BERNIE. "HERE I AM, WITH THE only studio in town that offers aerobics, ballet, jazz, ballroom—heck, we're even starting walking-for-the-elderly classes. And my competitor gets a full page feature on his third-grade dance recital. That's not half as interesting as our walk program—or my student who got a part as an extra in 'Toe Shoes.' But no one ever writes about us."

"Have you ever thought of letting the newspaper know?" asked Veronica gently.

"Well, yeah," nodded Bernie. "That neighbor of Joe's is a reporter. Last time we were over, I told him all about it. He didn't even nibble."

"Joe's friend is a sportswriter, isn't he?"

"Oh—yeah. I guess he is."

Just knowing that your business is interesting won't get the word out to other people. Even knowing people in the media might not help. To get publicity for your business, you need to actively seek it. You need to learn what makes a good story, and then you must learn how to sell it to the local media. You don't have to be a writer, but knowing how to put together information for the press won't hurt.

KNOWING WHAT'S NEWSWORTHY

Many businesspeople don't think there's anything newsworthy about them until they're burglarized, or until a woman gives birth in the dressing room. Newsworthy doesn't have to mean earthshaking. Newsworthy only means that you have done something new, or made changes in your business that the public is entitled to know about. Newsworthy means that there is something about you that the public might find interesting. Or, newsworthy could mean that you are offering a benefit to the public, which they might not appreciate until you call it to their attention.

Take Bernie's walking classes for the elderly. They might not sound very exciting to you, but think of all the senior citizens who go to the mall to walk. At Bernie's, they learn to do it correctly to get the most from their outing. They do it with others so they can enjoy an outing with friends, at an appointed time. And no one else in town is offering this service. It's interesting—to every senior citizen, and to every concerned relative of a senior citizen. It's also interesting to the newspaper, which knows that it has readers who will want to know about those classes. They will tell the readers—if Bernie will tell the newspaper.

Before we get into the hows of publicity, though, let's take a look at the whats. What about you might be worthy of publicity? If there's nothing inherently interesting about you right now, what can you do to make yourself publicity-worthy?

"Natural" Publicity Items

Some things about your business are always worth notifying the press about. They might not be earthshaking, front-page events, but the newspaper is there to serve the community, and routinely covers certain stories about people and places that you can use to your advantage.

Employee News. Whenever you hire a new employee, tell the press. Many newspapers run columns devoted specifically to people in the community and their hirings, promotions, etc. If there is no citywide column, most dailies cover neighborhood news, and the neighborhood editor might be interested in finding out about your new employees.

Promotions also get space. So do any awards that you or your employees might win. What about record-breaking orders? Maybe you give an annual party for your employees. You might think this is between you and your staff, but the newspaper often sends out a photographer just to tell the community what a good employer you are.

Business Changes. Are you making any changes in your business? Whether you are increasing the size of your staff or the size of your store, tell people about it. Are you bringing in new product lines, especially of things that people have been asking about? Let them know.

Customer News. Maybe you've had some celebrity customers. If these customers are not locals, but rather people who wouldn't normally be in your area, then the press and public might be interested in hearing about their visit. Better still, listen to your own customers. They might have uses for your products that are unusual. Several years back, a funeral director found that his embalming fluid made a great deck sealant for his boat. He told the manufacturer, who told the mortuary science trade journals. They got a nice story out of the discovery, and so did the funeral director who made the discovery.

Unusual Services. Even services can be used in novel ways. As a very novice glass etcher, I looked all over town for someone who would sandblast my glass panels once I had cut the design pattern. The local monument company was very cooperative, and soon had an interesting sideline in glass etching.

If you learn that one of your customers is using the copper tubing from your plumbing section to make pot racks, notify the paper. You might get a story on a clever customer, with credit going to your store.

Location News. How about your location? Is there anything newsworthy about your building? The area on which you built? How long have you been doing business there? One of our neighborhood butchers won a feature article simply because he's been doing business in the same shop as his father and grandfather—and was still doing things in the same old-fashioned way. In this age of progress, that was news. Another got a whole series of articles about his shop, located in a salvaged and renovated historic building that had been threatened with demolition until he bought it. When an interest in trains seemed to surface in a northeastern community, a whole group of shops located in a former railroad depot got a story.

Business Differences. What about the business itself? How different are you from competing businesses? Do you offer something that no one else can? Do people want what you have to offer? For instance, now that the Baby Boomers are all grown up, you might become very newsworthy if your cosmetic counter has the only supply in the county of a new French wrinkle cream that you brought over yourself from a trip abroad.

Problem-Solvers. Can you solve a specific problem? Is there a need within the community that you think you can fill? They don't have to be desperate needs—when spring rolls around, your stock of concrete lawn ornaments can help people who need to create a garden this year. When it's snowy and cold, your snow-plow service is vital enough to rate a story.

Your Own Accomplishments. How about yourself? Modest as you might want to seem, there could be news in your own activities. If the local women's club asks you to be a luncheon speaker, notify the press. If you give speeches anywhere, that's news. Awards are worth reporting. So are incentive programs that you begin in your business, any training seminars that you take or send employees to—anything that reminds the public that yours is an active business that is learning and keeping up with the needs of the community.

Check with your newspaper to see if they have a special business progress supplement. Many newspapers issue these special supplements annually just to let their readers know about commerce in the area. You might have to buy advertising to rate a write-up—but it's worth a try. Here's your chance to spend lots of words and space telling people about your business. Your article can describe your line of products, your services, and even the people you want to see as happy customers. This is about the only time that most newspapers will let you do this. Your progress story is essentially an ad done in newspaper style. Any other press coverage that you get will have to have a "news angle."

✔ Checklist for Discovering Possible News Angles

- Are you a new business? Even if the daily paper does not consider this news, a smaller weekly might be interested in doing a feature on you.
- Do you offer a service that isn't available elsewhere in the community?
- Have you managed to stock products that are in high demand but difficult to obtain?
- Do you do things in an unusual way? For instance, are you still doing things by hand in an age of mass production?
- Do you or any of your employees have an interesting story to tell about how they learned the business, the way things used to be in the business, or new ways of doing the same old thing?
- Are you celebrating a grand opening? A landmark anniversary?
- Are you the last of your type of business in the area?
- Are you the first of your type of business in the area?
- Does your product or service solve a problem that is prevalent in the area?
- Have you hired or promoted any of your employees?
- Have you or your employees won any business-related awards?
- Have you preserved a historic building to house your business, or put a building to an unusual use?
- Have you made any speeches to civic or social groups?
- Have you or your employees gone to any special training seminars?
- Have you had any newsworthy customers?
- Do you know of any unusual ways to use your product or service that might interest the public?

CREATING NEWS

If you look around your business today, you might find that nothing particularly newsworthy is happening. This doesn't mean that you must resign yourself to lack of publicity. It merely means that you have to create your own news angle.

Unlike the natural news angle, which merely publicizes something that already exists about your business, the created news story could cost money. Not that you will have to pay for publicity—that is always free. But you might have to invest some of your budget to create an event or change worthy of publicity.

Special Events

You could decide to hold an open house. To make it interesting to the public and to give the newspaper photographer something to focus on, you will probably have to provide refreshments, maybe balloons for the children and special decorative effects such as flowers or plants. None of this has to be wildly expensive, but it will probably cost more than you would spend on your regular newspaper ad. Why go to all the trouble, then, of creating publicity events?

First, these events also bring people to your place of business. We all know that the most important first step is to get people through your doors. Second is that people read news stories in a different frame of mind than the one with which they approach advertising. We approach ads warily, with our sales resistance up. We read news stories with interest and are often unaware of the subtle persuasive message that is hidden in the publicity. So, you might get more impact from a few good news stories than you will with a few good ads.

Civic Involvement

One way to get publicity and the goodwill of the community is to get involved in civic events or charities. If your business sponsors a Christmas party for the local orphanage, the community will respect you, the children will have a good time, and you get a story (and a good feeling). If your restaurant routinely donates its left-over food to the local soup kitchen, you get the same results—as long as the story gets out.

You could also sponsor (or cosponsor with other small businesses) events to raise funds for charities. Sporting events, marathons, or tournaments get a lot of coverage—and once again, the fact that the proceeds go to a good cause gives you and your business a very good image.

Community Services

If your business is one that performs a service that benefits the community, you might hold a clinic for the people who need your service. For instance, if you sell water purifiers, you might offer a water testing clinic for local citizens. This is worth a mention in the media if water impurities are a prominent concern. Plus, you will discover a lot of potential customers when you are running your diagnostics.

Lessons and Seminars

Many small businesses gain both publicity and customers by holding in-store seminars. A gourmet food shop holds cooking classes and incidentally creates a market for her more exotic foods. A florist teaches flower arranging, and the demand for loose fresh flowers and greenery, or silk flowers soars. A local garage offers car care clinics. The press finds it unusual, because the clinic seems to be cutting into the garage's business, but instead it makes the customers more aware of the need for maintenance. So all these small businesses get publicity while also encouraging customers to make more use of their products and services.

Tips on Getting the Most from Your Coverage

Your special events and promotions will be especially newsworthy if you are creative about them. A local dairy bar celebrated its fifth anniversary with a lot of well-priced specials, balloons, and samples. They also had a cow in the yard and offered milking lessons to interested onlookers. Many businesses hire a hot air balloon for their promotions, and these always attracts a crowd—especially if you offer rides.

The best publicity for special days are those that offer something visual. Many times a newspaper will not want to use a lot of space and a reporter's time writing a story, but they will send a photographer if there is something worth seeing. Even better, you will probably be able to get the TV camera crew to come out.

When I did publicity for the Scranton Market Place, I devised a Christmas in July celebration. So did about twenty other businesses in town. Ours was the one that got the TV crews and photographers. Why? Well—Santa Claus might have visited all the other businesses, but only at the Market Place did he wear the traditional furred red jacket, patent leather boots, and a pair of wildly patterned, heat-beating Bermuda shorts. It was just different enough to give us an edge.

Both natural and created publicity stories require that you send out either a fact sheet or a press release to any media that you hope will carry the story. We'll look at ways to do both press releases and fact sheets later in this chapter. First, I want to look at a third type of story that might be easier to interest the media in.

Checklist for Creating Events for Publicity

- Do I have a natural celebration coming up—a grand opening, anniversary, or major sale?
- What can I do for this occasion to make it visual—worthy of a newspaper photographer and TV crew's time?
- Is there any way that I can make my celebration different from the typical celebration done by my type of business? Celebrities I can invite, events I can schedule, contests, demonstrations or lessons I can offer?
- Are there social service organizations in the area that can benefit from my business? Is there any way that I can offer them help?
- Can I (perhaps along with a few other businesses) sponsor a major fund-raising event for some local charity?
- Are there any clinics I can offer to help people uncover potential problems that my business can solve?
- Can I offer classes and demonstrations to show people how to make better use of my products and services?

TAPPING INTO TRENDS

Tapping into trends is not for publicity-greedy people who want a whole story to themselves. It is, however, a way to get the media to focus on your type of business, particular services that you offer, or lines of merchandise that you carry.

Identifying Trends

The idea is to listen to your customers, and read the trade journals and daily papers to see what fads, fancies, and concerns people have about your type of business. For example, you might have an art supply store. When flipping through *House Beautiful* one day at home, you notice an article on *faux* finishes—marbleizing, painting molding to look like stone, wood, or tortoise-shell. You begin to notice that several magazines feature these treatments. Several of your customers come in and buy supplies so that they can marbleize their own moldings. Hmmm—a new trend in decorating.

You carry the necessary paint supplies. One of your customers is skilled in the art and has done several beautiful pieces. A local unfinished furniture store carries a line of tables that are perfect for tortoise-shelling. So you call the home editor at the local paper and suggest they do a piece on the new fad for faux finishing since it can be accomplished right in your home town.

Naturally, the story will feature more than just your store and its supplies. But, it will mention that the needed supplies are available from you. Get the local expert to offer classes at your shop, and get another story out of the deal, plus a lot of customers for glazes, brushes, and colors.

Read your newspapers. What interests people? If you notice trends that your business can be a part of, then get busy. How can you make this trend into a story with a local angle?

This summer I volunteered to do publicity for a Lion's Club flea market. Besides the regular press releases announcing the time, place, and kinds of merchandise that the flea market would feature, I did two trend stories. The first featured an older man who had been manning the Lions Club food booth for years. Tying into what seems to be a burgeoning interest in ethnic cooking in our area, I wrote about Will's secret recipe, locked safely in a bank vault, and his offer to give that recipe and a six-month supply of the goodies, to anyone who could guess the secret ingredient. In this case, lucky for the Club, the paper ran my story word for word, and we didn't share the spotlight with anyone.

The second story was designed to create a desire for the kinds of merchandise available at flea markets. I got photos of my own living room, which looks lavishly furnished, but was created mainly from flea market finds that were lovingly reupholstered, refinished, and refurbished. The feature photo showed a vignette of our bay window, complete with antique chairs, tables, plants, and sculpture—at a cost of $124.

The accompanying article took the reader on a tour of area second-hand stores and flea markets—including the Lions Club annual event. We got our publicity, and so did a lot of other merchants. Plus we raised awareness of the real values to be found when buying second hand.

Using Trends for Your Own Ends

Trend articles are not limited only to fashion and decor oriented industries. New advances in technology make good stories for owners of appliance stores, office supply stores, or anyone who sells electrical or electronic supplies of any kind.

Books: who's reading what? Plumbing—what are the latest advances? Stationery—why are people going back to the fountain pen? Garden supplies—what are the fashionable flowers this year? Gas stations—what are the most frequent problems with the new cars we service? Groceries—what are the latest food trends?

The idea is simply to keep up with your field. When you see interests heading in a definite direction, you propose a story to the local media about that trend and how it can be followed in the local market. Yes—your competitors might also be featured in the story. Remember, the benefit from giving out information in this context might be greater than that from your ad, and you will have more space for explaining your business and what it has to offer. Even if you do have to offer a boost to the competition, your own gains should more than offset this.

Because I have spent many years doing publicity, I generally do the research and write my own trend stories. No one, however, expects you to do this. If you have found an angle for your type of business that will interest your community, you have already done enough of the media's work. Your next step is to interest those media.

Checklist for Tapping into Trends

- In looking at the trade journals and business oriented literature that you receive, are there any changes in your product or services generally that would particularly interest the public in your area?
- In looking at the newspapers and magazines, do you see a growing interest in products or services that you can supply? Can you supply at least a portion of the products or services needed to participate in the trend?
- Do you see problem areas within the community that you and other related businesses can help?
- If you have answered yes to any of these, try to see what is particularly interesting to your local community. What services, products and supplies can your area offer?

INTERESTING THE MEDIA

There are three traditional ways to interest the media in your publicity story. The first, and best known, is the press release. If you can write clearly and well, and have a clear perception of what the real news angle is for your story, then a press release is the way to go.

More simple, especially for the novice, is a fact sheet. This does not involve much writing, nor must you determine the news angle. You simply list pertinent information and let the newspaper fashion it into a story.

Sometimes, you can get publicity simply by making a phone call to the appropriate editor. Especially if you already know people in the local media, this can be an effective way to interest them in a trend story. Usually, a follow-up letter will help. Each of these methods has its own rules. Let's look at them individually.

The Phone Call

You have an idea for a trend story. Before you pick up the phone, take time to do a little homework. Who else might you feature in the story? How can you prove that this is a trend that interests your area? Who else might the editor contact for more information if they decide to do the story?

Get the Right Editor. Once you have the basic facts at your fingertips, dial the newspaper switchboard and find out who usually handles the type of story that you have in mind. Get that person's name, and contact them directly. Don't rely on leaving messages. They have a nasty way of getting lost. Your success depends entirely on your ability to talk to the person who makes decisions on stories, convincing them that your idea is worthwhile.

Be Brief but Thorough. Once you get the appropriate person on the phone, state your business directly. Begin with your evidence that there is an increasing local interest in the idea behind your story. Tell the editor what your idea for a story is. Then, if he or she has questions, supply all the information that you have collected. Then thank them and hang up.

Follow Up in Writing. If you are smart, you will then write a letter to that person, going over the same information that you supplied during your phone conversation. If you have ever seen a newspaper office, you'll appreciate how easy it is to mislay a memo; so your letter will not only make sure that the editor has the information in written form, but serves as a concrete reminder of the story.

Check in by Phone. A good publicity agent would call about three days after the letter is sent to make sure that the editor received the information. This keeps the story prominent in his or her mind, and creates an opportunity for more questions and information.

Don't pester the editor, or call more than three times. Be businesslike and brief in your conversations. If you annoy an editor, your idea is likely to go straight to the wastebasket. If you do not see your idea appear within a reasonable time limit, shrug and be philosophical. Even the professionals don't get every publicity story they dream up published. Get busy and dream up another angle, instead.

The Fact Sheet

For any of the publicity stories discussed earlier, you can send the local media a fact sheet. This is usually sufficient for a natural publicity story such as a new store opening or a promotion, but not quite as effective for a trend story.

The fact sheet simply answers the major questions basic to any journalism story: who, what, where, when, why. You do not have to write elaborate paragraphs of description. You don't even have to be able to write. You do need to supply good, accurate facts about the event that you want the media to cover.

For example, you want to announce to the public that your shoe store has hired a specialist in fitting children's shoes. Your fact sheet simply supplies the pertinent information. Who: Jim Craig. What: Specialist in fitting children's shoes. Where: Footnotes, in downtown Albuquerque. When: beginning on Friday, April 3, 1989. Why? Because poorly fitted children's shoes can cause permanent foot problems later in life.

You might want to send a photo of your specialist in with the fact sheet. You could also tell us How—describe the special equipment that Craig uses, or the special training he received with a prominent shoe company. Other than that, you only need to put your fact sheet into standard form.

The Heading. Standard form suggests that you type the name of the person to whom you are sending the fact sheet in the upper left-hand corner (TO: JANICE HARDING, CITY EDITOR). Once again, call the medium to find out who to address your fact sheet to. Face it; yours are very rarely earthshaking stories with a lot of news value. Your chances of seeing print if you merely address it to a hopeful "Editor" are pretty slim. Unless you can cure wrinkles or are now selling the fountain of youth, few journalists are going to waste time walking your envelope from desk to desk looking for a taker.

Under the editor's name, type the name of the newspaper or TV station. Both this and the editor's name should be in capital letters.

Next, give your fact sheet a short title (Foot specialist at Footnotes). Then skip two spaces, and type, in all caps, FOR RELEASE ON OR BEFORE _____ (fill in the appropriate date), PLEASE.

The Best Release Date. Make your release date long enough to give the editor time to fit the story in, but not so long that it hangs around the desk and gets lost. Generally a week's span from the time of the event is enough for a story about a past event.

For stories about upcoming events, specify a release date for the story on or about the day before the event. Thus, if your grand opening is on May 12, you will want to release the story on or before May 11.

"On or before" gives your editor a bit of leeway. Maybe there is no room for your story on your preferred date, but there is a hole to fill a day later. If you asked for release on May 10, and there was no room, your fact sheet would go to the trash. If you left it more open, the story might be held for later.

Never use FOR IMMEDIATE RELEASE. Editors tend to interpret this as "Either run it today or forget it."

The Information Contact. Once you have supplied the date, tell the editor who to contact for more information (yourself, or the employee who handles your publicity). In the upper right-hand corner, type in all caps FOR FURTHER INFORMATION: and the name. Beneath that, type your phone number.

The Facts. Skip at least ten spaces between this heading and the beginning of your information. Then simply fill in the blanks. Type WHO: in caps, and supply the information. Go to the next line and type WHAT: And so forth.

The Follow-Up. Once you have sent or delivered your fact sheet to the media, follow up on it. Once again, don't demand to know if it will be used. Simply call the editor to whom you addressed the fact sheet to assure yourself that they have received it. This call helps, because it forces the editor to sort through all the releases he or she receives in order to single yours out.

As you can see, the fact sheet does not permit you to describe very complicated stories. You can supply only the most basic information. You have very little opportunity to explain the significance of your story, or why you think that it might be of interest to the public. You might be able to slip a little of this into WHY and HOW; if you have a complicated story to tell, you might need to use a press release. Appendix F will show you a sample fact sheet, as well as the accompanying press release.

Checklist for Creating a Fact Sheet

- Check with the media for the name and department of the appropriate editor.
- Type name and title of editor in all caps in the upper left-hand corner.
- Beneath this, type the name of the medium.
- Give your fact sheet a short title, in all caps, on the next line. The title must suggest the main idea of the story.
- Below this, in all caps, give the release date.
- In the upper right-hand corner, type your name and phone number under the heading, FOR FURTHER INFORMATION:.
- Skip ten spaces.
- List the appropriate information under the categories: WHO, WHAT, WHERE, WHEN, and WHY. If a HOW will help you to explain the importance of the story to the community, add this to your list.

The Press Release

If you or one of your employees writes well, you can take advantage of the press release to tell your story in detail. Don't worry if you don't feel that you have a great journalistic style. If you can sort out your facts in the order of importance, and write clear sentences to explain these facts, you will be fine. Very few press releases appear in the paper exactly as written, even when done by professionals. Newspapers hire rewrite men and reporters to take care of this. The heading for your press release is exactly the same as for a fact sheet. Only the presentation of facts is different.

Beginning the Release. Your first paragraph should describe the most important, newsworthy fact. Ask yourself what the purpose of your press release is. Is it to let the community know about some new benefit they can derive from doing business with you? Is it the promotion of an employee? Is it to announce your involvement in planning a ''Beautify our Block'' program?

What the press release does is to answer, in prose, the same questions that you used in your fact sheet. Before you begin to write, list the who, what, where, when, why, and how of your story. The first paragraph of your story should explain most of these, very briefly. Study these. Which seems to be the answer most important and interesting to the reader? This is the fact that you should put down first. Go on to the second most important fact, the third, and so on, down to the least important.

At this stage, you are merely giving the bare facts, as they might be stated on a fact sheet. So, in our example for Footnotes, your first paragraph that includes all five questions might read like this:

Jim Craig, children's foot specialist, will offer custom shoe fitting for all children in the Albuquerque area. Designed to prevent the foot problems resulting from improper shoes, this service begins Friday, April 3, at Footnotes, 321 Main Avenue.

Explaining the Facts. Now, for the body of the release. Begin by explaining your first fact. In this instance, the story should explain who Jim Craig is, and what his qualifications are. The second will explain something about custom shoe fitting, and how it is done. Then you would explain more about the why— why should parents take advantage of this service. Finally, explain Footnotes and its exact location.

The least important facts are always at the bottom of the release for a good reason. Newspapers don't always have room for your entire story and will need to cut out parts to fit the available space. The easiest way is just to leave out the ending paragraphs. So, to protect the ideas that you most want to communicate, you put them at the top of the story.

One thing about the above example might puzzle you. Why is the paragraph about you and your location considered to be the least important fact? To you, of course, it is a critical piece of information. But put yourself in the mind of the reader. They care more about the service you offer, and its benefit. Until they understand this, they don't care about the where. Only when they are convinced that they should take advantage of the service will they look to find out where you are. Plus, your name and location is given in the lead paragraph—so even if your last paragraph gets chopped off in the newsroom, people will still be able to find you.

Proper Release Form. Once you have written out your story, you can type it into its final form. Yes—be sure to type it, double spaced, using clear black ribbon. Never write out the release in pen, and never use carbons, which smudge and annoy the media people who have to handle your release. If you are sending your release to more than one medium, you can photocopy it.

When typing, always leave one-inch margins, except on your first page. Here your copy should begin at least four inches down from the top of the paper. Remember to put the heading at the top of the first page.

If you use more than one page, indicate this at the bottom of page one by typing -more-. Put your short title and page number in the upper right-hand corner of the second page, and begin typing one inch from the top. At the close of your release, indicate that you are finished by typing either -end- or -30-. Appendix F shows a sample press release in proper journalistic form.

As with any information that you send to the media, follow up your release with a phone call. Once again, don't get discouraged if your story isn't used. Just keep trying.

Reasons for Failure. Sometimes a medium will reject a story for lack of space. Other times, a release fails because the writer failed to feature the right facts in the opening paragraph. It won't hurt to send out a second release, on the same topic, but beginning with a different fact than your first release.

For example, your local paper might not care about Jim Craig, who just got to town and is unknown in the community. But they will be interested in children's foot problems. So you might rearrange your lead paragraph to read like this:

Because properly fitted children's shoes will prevent foot problems in later life, Footnotes, 321 Main Avenue, is offering customized shoe fittings for children. Jim Craig, foot specialist, joins the Footnotes staff on Friday, April 3, to custom measure and fit all Footnote's young customers.

In this example, the WHY is featured because it is the angle most likely to concern the reader. Once people understand why a service is important, they want to know where they can get it, and when. The WHO is last since in your community no one knows Jim Craig, and therefore find this to be the least interesting fact. You might also try to rewrite your lead emphasizing what.

Custom shoe fittings to prevent children from developing foot problems begin Friday, April 3 at Footnotes, 321 Main Avenue. Foot specialist Jim Craig joins the Footnotes staff that day to offer customized measuring and fittings for all children under 12.

As you can see, there are many possible ways to present your story. The trick is to find the fact that will most interest your potential customers. If you fail on your first try, then rearrange your facts and try again.

Checklist for Press Releases

- Always call the medium to learn the name of the person who should receive your release.
- Always double space your releases.

- Always use a new typewriter ribbon. Photocopying is acceptable if you are sending out more than one release.
- Always leave one-inch margins—except at the top of the first page where copy begins four inches from the top.
- Always indicate -more- if your story takes more than one page.
- Always type your name and phone number in the upper right-hand corner of the first page.
- Always type the name and title of the editor on the first line of the upper left-hand corner of the first page, in all caps.
- Always type the name of the medium on the second line, using all caps.
- Always give your story a short title, in all caps, indicating the main content of your story. This goes beneath the name of the medium.
- Always include a release date, giving the media a span of several days in which they might use your story.
- Make sure that your first paragraph answers WHO, WHAT, WHERE, WHEN, WHY, and, perhaps, HOW, in the order of their importance and interest to the reader.
- Explain each successive fact in the paragraphs that follow. Give all pertinent information that explains each fact, in the order of their importance.
- Follow up your release. Phone the appropriate editor to make sure that he or she has received it. Don't demand that they use the release.
- If your release doesn't appear the first time, try following it with another release, suggesting a different angle.

CHOOSING THE MEDIA FOR YOUR RELEASE

Since it costs very little to send out a press release or fact sheet, you can send one to all your local media, including radio and television. Just remember to change the heading, addressing the release to the appropriate editor and medium.

Newspapers

Some stories, however, work best in a particular medium. Newspaper can handle almost anything. If they don't find your news worthy of an entire story, newspapers will often run a picture. Even a dull picture of a few people lined up and shaking hands will often make the paper. If you can offer something more exciting, your chances of publicity increase.

Newspapers can usually handle even color photographs, although they prefer black and white. Most papers can even use Polaroid shots, as long as the detail is clear and the picture itself looks reasonably professional.

If you are sending a picture, either alone or included with your release, it will need a caption. Type this on a separate sheet of paper, using the same heading form that you used for your release. Do not staple or clip it to the picture, or you might damage it. Simply put the caption beneath the picture in the envelope.

Your caption merely explains the picture. It will contain the same information that might be contained in the lead paragraph of a press release, identifying any people who appear in the shot. A picture of Jim Craig shaking hands with the manager of Footnotes might read as follows:

George Davis (left), manager of Footnotes, 321 Main Avenue, greets foot specialist Jim Craig (right). With Craig's arrival on the staff, Footnotes can now offer preventive foot care by making sure all children's shoes are properly fitted. This new service begins on Friday, April 3.

A picture of two people shaking hands is a very common one, and not as likely to attract reader attention as a more lively one. Get Craig to pose while measuring the feet of a cute little girl, and more people will read the caption to see what's happening.

Television

If the story has a really interesting visual angle, you might also want to contact the local TV stations. Television is a visual medium, and TV editors like stories that are interesting to look at. If you think your story is worth watching as well as reading about, contact the local stations. Send them a release or fact sheet, but attach a letter explaining what there is to see, and why you think your story would be good for television. Follow this up with a phone call.

Radio

Radio offers few opportunities for standard publicity. Many stations run five minutes of news an hour or less. Much of this highlights the major headline-making stories of the day. There is very little room for non-news, publicity oriented stories. However, some stations do feature talk shows and interviews.

A smart business person can take advantage of these programs by offering their expertise to the show's director. If you have a lot of knowledge about solutions to area problems, you might offer to share this with the station's listeners. For instance, Jim Craig might appear on a short interview program, explaining how improper shoes affect the feet, and how to prevent this.

Check out your local radio stations. See what types of talk and interview shows are available. Can you offer information that would be appropriate for the show's listeners? A phone call and discussion with the person in charge of that show might result in publicity for you.

Call the station to see who is in charge of choosing guests for the show. Write a letter to that person, explaining your idea. Tell them why you think your information would benefit the listening audience. Follow it up with a phone call. And good luck.

SUMMARY

Publicity is an art, not a science. The art lies in finding interesting news and features of your business that are worth publicizing. The small businessperson must find angles about his business that will interest or benefit the public. These ideas must be presented to the media in a way that will convince them that the public wants the information.

You can contact the media with a story idea in one of three ways: a fact sheet, press release, and a phone call explaining why your publicity idea is worthy of media attention. Once the written information has reached the desk of the appropriate editor, you should always follow it up with a phone call.

The media will not use every story you send out. However, the only way to get publicity is to keep trying. Remember, it costs less than advertising. People read it in an accepting frame of mind, because they feel that they are getting information rather than persuasion. The benefit to you is that you build an image in the mind of the reader that will carry over when they see your ads.

Checklist for Publicity Planning

- Check your local newspapers. Is there any local, state, or national news that in any way affect your business? Can you offer the public help or information about this news that is local in nature?

- In the same papers, are there any columns or departments that seem like natural places for stories about you, your business, or any of your employees?

- Check your local TV and radio programs. Do they have any interview programs where your expertise might be useful and interesting?

- Look at the list of benefits that you used to plan your advertising campaign. Will any of these make good stories?

- Figure out which of your stories are newsworthy, and which are essentially features (''trend'' stories). News stories demand a press release or fact sheet. Trend stories should use a letter.

- Look at the available media. Is WHO more important for one medium, and WHAT for another? If so, write two different press releases, emphasizing the facts that best suit the medium.

17

Advertising and the Law

TONY SENT HIS STOCK CLERK AROUND THE NEIGHBORHOOD WITH FLIERS ADVERtising his sale. He instructed the lad to make sure that he tucked each flier inside the door of each house. The next day he was cited for littering, in violation of a city ordinance.

Virginia wanted to capture the walk-by traffic, so she put a sign on the sidewalk by her luncheonette to advertise daily specials. The city immediately demanded that she remove it.

When Milton got a letter from an ecstatic customer that praised the great job he had done in painting her house, he used it in his ads. Then he found out that the customer was suing him for invasion of privacy.

Bill's advertised sale merchandise came in at the last minute—and it was hopelessly shoddy. When his earnest young clerk advised customers not to buy it, but to choose the higher priced and better quality model, a customer threatened to report him for using bait and switch advertising tactics.

That's right. Even if your advertising is honest to a fault, you can still run into legal difficulties. Chapter 17 will warn you of all the pitfalls—some obvious and some unexpected—that you can run into if you don't understand the law and all its implications.

FALSE ADVERTISING

False advertising is advertising that tells deliberate untruths, or advertising that inadvertently tells a falsehood because the ad writer didn't have all the facts. The Federal Trade Commission (FTC) has the power to regulate false and deceptive advertising, and to punish those who violate the regulations. Generally, false advertising falls into two categories: fraud and warranty.

Warranty

Warranty advertising has a certain form of wording that the law regards as a promise which must be kept. If your ad contains words such as promise, warrant, or guarantee, then you must be able to back up that promise. If you are selling a flashlight that you guarantee will run for 1000 hours, then you had better either be certain that this is true or replace those flashlights that do not live up to promise.

Even if you make your guarantee in good faith, you are liable if the promise turns out to be false. For example, the Ford Motor Company produced a safety glass guaranteed to be shatter-proof. They had done laboratory testing and believed that their guarantee was true. Mr. Baxter, however, bought the glass and found out differently. He took Ford Motor Company to court, and won. Even though they made the promise in good faith, Ford had to make restitution, and to withdraw its advertising claims. Warranty only applies to product sales, and to promises about qualities that the product has.

Fraud

Fraud, on the other hand, applies to both service advertising and products. Fraud involves a promise made by the seller that the seller knows to be false. So if your beautician claims that Sassoon trained her when she actually went to the local beauty college, she has perpetrated a fraud. If you claim that your clothing was made in Paris when in fact it was made in Peoria, you have also committed a fraud.

This is not only illegal—it is unethical, and bad business practice. Once your customers find out that you have deceived them, they will cease to trust you. And they will find some other place to do business.

The Penalties

If the FTC finds that your advertising is deceptive, they will first send you an order to cease and desist. This means that, if you withdraw the false advertising immediately, there will be no more questions asked. If, however, you persist in your errant ways, the FTC can pull the ads for you, and force you to issue a series of corrective ads.

The corrective advertising can involve devoting up to $1/3$ of your budget for a year to advertising that reveals the deception. So false advertising, if discovered, is not only expensive to correct, it can be humiliating.

DECEPTIVE ADVERTISING

No—deceptive advertising is not the same as false advertising. False advertising makes untrue claims, which can be proven. Deceptive advertising involves ads that tend to mislead the consumer, even though they do not make any outright false statements. The FTC also regulates this practice.

Supreme Court Guidelines

The Supreme Court has issued several guidelines to help you to avoid advertising that might deceive. In the first place, they suggest that you analyze your ads for the probable effect that they will have on the average and trusting mind. This means that ads written for a sophisticated audience, and fully clear to that audience, would be considered deceptive if they might mislead less analytical readers. Read your own ads as though you were a trusting child of 12. If they make a misleading impression on you, you'd better rewrite them.

An ad would also be deceptive if its dominant impression was misleading, even though every separate statement within the ad was literally true. To understand this, try to recall the impression you strove to create when you wrote your first resume. What did you leave out? What did you phrase in impressive sounding but true words to make it seem better than, in reality, it was? Ads are often written in this same way—not lying, but not telling the truth.

Furthermore, your ads must not leave out any information that might keep the customer from buying the product or using the service if that information were known. In other words, your ad for masonry cleaning must reveal that sandblasting can destroy some building surfaces. Similarly, cigarette ads must reveal the Surgeon General's warning. If you try to hide the facts, then the law considers that you have deceived the consumer.

Your ads must also be free from any fraudulent devices to lure customers into buying.

Common Deceptive Devices

Bait and Switch. Perhaps the most common fraudulent device is the use of bait-and-switch advertising. This offers a product for sale at some amazingly low price to lure the consumer into the store. However, if the customers should try to buy the product, they will find the process difficult. Either the last one was sold seconds before they entered the store, or the clerk will insist that the last remaining model—the floor model—is too hopelessly damaged to sell. The customer is then switched over to some more expensive version of the bait, and pressured into buying that higher-priced item.

The moral of that story is that, if you offer something for sale, it must really be for sale. If you run out, you must offer rain checks. And you must never, never refuse to sell the sale item, or try to tempt the customer up to a higher-priced, nonsale item if they attempt to buy the advertised special.

Free Items that Aren't. Another fraudulent device involves the advertising of free items. If you advertise that customers will receive something free with a purchase, then that item must really be free. There must be no reduction in the size of the original purchase to make up for the cost of the giveaway; no reduction in quality of the original; and, above all, no raising of the price of the required purchase in an attempt to recoup losses.

Deceptive Pricing Strategies. Pricing strategies can also be deceptive. If you advertise a sale, then the price reduction that the customer receives must be meaningful. One dollar off on a $40 item would be deceptive. If you advertise that an item is now available at one price, and give its former price (Now $16.98, formerly $19.98), then that former price must be the one charged at your place of business, rather than at some higher-priced competitors. If you advertise your price in comparison with those of your competitors (Our price, $1.99, elsewhere, $2.59), then "elsewhere" must refer to the pricing of bona fide competitors, not of the ritziest, most overpriced place in town.

When attempting to determine if your advertising might be deceptive, keep one more thing in mind. The FTC frowns on any advertising that might give you an unfair edge over your competition. Any advertising claims that you make that lure customers away from those competitors and into your own place had better be provable claims.

The main thing to remember is that, if you advertise ethically, then you will be safe. Your customers will appreciate your honesty and dependability; your competitors will refrain from trying to create legal problems for you. Your business will be better for it in the end.

COPYRIGHT

Another area where advertisers inadvertently get into trouble is through violation of copyright law. If you use any material in your advertising that is not your own work, or work specifically created for you, then you might fall into difficulty.

What is Copyright?

Copyright is a protection given to authors, artists, and composers, which insures their right to receive the profits generated by the works that they have created. If a work is protected by copyright, then anyone other than the holder of that copyright must receive permission before they can use it for commercial purposes.

Most commonly, advertisers run into copyright problems in two areas: artwork and music. In both cases, works protected by copyright must be cleared with the holder before they can be used. Failure to do so can result in a hefty fine. Permission to use copyrighted material must be secured from the holder in writing. Often, the user must pay a "use" fee to the holder. To determine who holds the copyright, you can write to the Register of Copyrights in Washington, D.C.

How Does it Affect my Advertising?

If you plan to use a popular song in your ad, or if you should decide that Snoopy would be a great character to illustrate your ad, then you must get clearance. Or, you could forgo the restricted material in favor of other works that are copyright free.

As I have stated in previous chapters, radio stations and production studios maintain libraries of music that are not copyright restricted. You can use any of this material freely. The same goes for artwork. There are hundreds of available books of clip art that are in the public domain—that is to say, they are available for anyone to use in any manner they please. If you cannot produce your own music or artwork, then you might be wise to use the public domain material. Otherwise, you must be prepared to fork over a copyright fee for every use that you make of the protected material.

PRIVACY CONCERNS

Many times, you will use photographs in your print advertising, or the voices and names of real people in your campaign. To protect yourself from an invasion of privacy suit, you should obtain a release from any individual whose likeness, name, or any identifiable characteristic appears in your advertising. To use any of these characteristics in your ads, without the permission of the person who is being identified, is against the law.

What Is an Identifiable Characteristic?

Identifiable characteristics include a recognizable voice, an identifiable profile, even if done in silhouette, a highly distinctive nose, or even an idiosyncratic walk that other members of the viewing public might identify with a particular person. Some people are identified by a particular trademark—their bushy eyebrows, a pair of rhinestone glasses, a particular way of dressing. If you use your mayor's handlebar mustache in your ad, and citizens will automatically associate that mustache with the mayor, he has ground to sue for invasion of privacy.

If your ad campaign uses talent, or employs any of the earlier-named characteristics of an individual, then you should protect yourself by obtaining a signed release that gives you permission to use that person's identity in your ads.

How Can I Protect Myself?

A good release will specify the exact purpose that the name, likeness, etc., will be used for. Your rights will only extend as far as the use specified in the release. So permission to use someone's picture in your newspaper ad would not extend to using a slide of that picture in a television commercial unless you also specified television usage in the release.

A release also must promise *consideration*. Allegedly, this means that the release promises some form of payment in return for permission to use a person's identity or likeness. In practice, however, a mere promise of the natural publicity that the person will receive as a result of appearing in an ad is considered to be sufficient consideration to make the release legal.

Finally, the release must have the bona fide signature of the person whose identity you are appropriating, or, in the case of a minor, the signature of a legal guardian.

No matter how minor an appearance someone might make in your ad—the picture of their crooked finger, beckoning, or a sneeze made on your cold-remedy sale commercial, get a release signed. Then you will always be assured of legal protection.

MISCELLANEOUS CONCERNS

To get the most out of a small business advertising campaign, you will often find yourself dealing with restrictions of which you might not even have been aware. Small things like your sign, or the way in which you distribute handbills, could get you into trouble if you don't know the law.

Signs and the Law

You might decide to put a *horse*—a standing sandwich board—or a yellow-lighted sign, outside your place of business. Unless you are familiar with zoning laws, you might find yourself firmly told to remove it.

Many cities require clearance before objects can be placed on sidewalks with pedestrian traffic. Still others restrict signage even further so that you must put your sign flat against the building rather than hanging over the sidewalk where it will be more visible to passers-by. Before you invest in any type of sign, check with your local zoning board to make sure that you will be able to use it.

The same goes for directional signs. In some cities, businesses with location problems often post small, weatherproof wooden or metal signs on trees or utility poles at intersections leading to their site. In some cities it is strictly forbidden; others might require a permit, where in still others there is no restriction on these signs except the permission of the utility whose pole you want to use, or the person who owns the tree.

Flyer Distribution and the Law

Finally, be careful of the way in which you distribute fliers. If you plan to distribute them in the downtown area, or any other public place, make sure that you don't require a permit. Likewise, if you wish to distribute fliers in a privately owned place, such as a mall, you will also need permission from whoever is in charge.

You are probably aware that you cannot put your flier in a mailbox, unless you have sent it through the post office. But were you aware that some cities require that you receive the written permission of anyone to whom you wish to distribute your fliers? Failure to get this permission can result in a fine for littering, should any disgruntled recipients of your flier complain to the authorities.

In short, it's better to be safe than sorry. If you have any questions at all about whether a permit or clearance might be required, get it. You don't need to tie up your budget paying fines.

SUMMARY

To ensure a successful campaign, the advertiser must be sure to abide by all legal restrictions that might be imposed on advertising. Ads that are truthful are good commercial practice; they help to build the trust of the consumer, and also avoid heavy penalties that might be imposed by the FTC.

Any ad that is using material not especially commissioned for that ad, such as music and artwork, must also abide by copyright restrictions, and the advertiser must obtain legal permission for use. Legal permission, in the form of a release, must also be obtained for the use of any person other than the advertisers themselves in all print and broadcast advertising.

The FTC, which regulates advertising, has the power to stop anyone who uses false advertising from continuing to run the ads in question.

Appendix A

Sample Demographic Profile: The Restoration Shop

My typical most frequent customer is a married woman, 35–55, with a relatively high disposable income, and at least some college education.

Because she is female, she will probably respond to an emotional appeal in my ads—the memories of good times when the furniture was new and strong, and the romance behind an antique find. However, because she is well-educated, I will also need to give her facts about my expertise.

In my typical customer's age group, I can appeal both to her own satisfaction with having beautifully finished furniture, and her family's pleasure in not having to worry about fragile pieces with easily marred finishes.

Because she has a fairly high disposable income, this customer does not mind paying to get quality workmanship, especially if my early ads convince her that there is value in saving older furniture rather than buying new.

SAMPLE PSYCHOGRAPHIC PROFILE

This typical customer sees herself as being a careful shopper who likes her home to be comfortable but elegant. She values antiques and the traditional look, but not to the point where they become hard to live with. She wants people to be able to relax and enjoy her home, but also to admire its tasteful look.

This customer often buys antique furniture at auctions, because she knows she gets good value for her money. Sometimes, if the piece is simple, she will refinish it herself. However, removing the old finish is a complicated and messy process that she doesn't have time for. I can save her that time, and still let her get the satisfaction out of putting on the new finish.

When she buys really valuable pieces, however, she wants them done in the most professional way possible. That's when she looks to me for a complete job. She wants to know that the piece will come home to her with all of its structural problems corrected. But she also wants it to look ''antique''—with the right, mellow finish instead of a bright, shiny coating. She also wants to be sure that I won't do anything to destroy the piece's value as an antique. If she feels sure that she can get this service from me, then she will come to me instead of my competitor.

Appendix B

Sample Research

Focus Group

BUSINESS: Compliments, a small shop that sells female accessories in a mid-price range ($5 – 75). The store owner wanted to reach a new, younger target audience, as she was already doing a good business with women over 30.

The focus group was conducted using eight women, four of them under 30 (to learn about the habits and wants of the desired audience) and four over 30 (to learn more about the perceptions of the target audience now being served).

QUESTIONS FOR FOCUS GROUP

1. What types of accessories do you usually buy?
2. How important are accessories to your wardrobe?
3. Do you buy accessories more often for yourself, or for gifts?
4. Where do you normally shop for accessories?
5. What would you change, if anything, about the place where you now shop? What do you like most about it?
6. Where else would you shop if that store were not available?
7. How far are you willing to travel to purchase an accessory?
8. What do you consider to be a reasonable price for a scarf, if you are buying it for yourself? What about for a gift?
9. How much would you spend on a pair of earrings for yourself? For a gift?

10. Have you ever shopped at either Looking Good or Compliments? How closely do you think these two stores are in competition? Which would you prefer to shop at, and why?

BASIC RESULTS OF FOCUS GROUP QUESTIONS

1. It is possible to attract a younger group to Compliments, since we carry the type of goods, and in the price range that this group considers desirable.

2. In order to attract them, it looks like we will need to rely on emotional appeals, and promises of a wide selection of unusual styles.

SURVEY FOR COMPLIMENTS

COVER SPEECH: Good afternoon. My name is Marry Goodhill, and I'm doing a survey about small accessory shops in the New Orleans area. If I could have just a few minutes of your time, I'd like to ask you a few questions about your own accessory buying habits. I promise that I'm not selling anything, just trying to get information that will help out the small businesses in our area.

1. How important are accessories to your wardrobe? (Note: This is your screening question. People who find them unimportant are not a part of your target audience, unless they tend to buy accessories as gifts, which should be your next question. If the respondent answers both questions negatively, thank them for their time, and go on to another survey.)
   __ Not important __ Somewhat important __ Important

2. How often do you buy accessories (scarves, belts, jewelry, perfume) as gifts for female friends and relatives?
   __ Usually __ Frequently __ Sometimes __ Rarely __ Never

3. What types of accessories do you most often buy for yourself? As Gifts? (Check all that apply)

   SELF
   __ jewelry
   __ scarves
   __ belts
   __ purses
   __ perfume
   __ hats
   __ cosmetics
   __ other

   GIFTS
   __ jewelry
   __ scarves
   __ belts
   __ purses
   __ perfume
   __ hats
   __ cosmetics
   __ other (please specify)

4. I'm going to give you four price categories. Please tell me which you consider to be a reasonable price for each of the following accessories, both as gifts and for yourself.
   a. $5 – 15
   b. $16 – 25
   c. $26 – 40
   d. Over 40

SELF	GIFTS
__ jewelry	__ jewelry
__ scarves	__ scarves
__ belts	__ belts
__ purses	__ purses
__ perfume	__ perfume
__ hats	__ hats
__ cosmetics	__ cosmetics
__ other	__ other (please specify)

5. Where do you usually buy accessories? (Choose the best answer)
   a. department store (please specify)
   b. Accessories Plus
   c. Compliments
   d. Looking Good
   e. Meredith's
   f. Other (please specify) _____.

6. Please rate the place where you shop most often on the following qualities. (Choose best answer)
   Service:
   1) excellent   2) Good   3) Fair   4) Poor
   Selection
   1) excellent   2) Good   3) Fair   4) Poor
   Reasonable Price
   1) excellent   2) Good   3) Fair   4) Poor
   Originality
   1) excellent   2) Good   3) Fair   4) Poor
   Ease of Shopping
   1) excellent   2) Good   3) Fair   4) Poor
   Location
   1) excellent   2) Good   3) Fair   4) Poor

7. Please rank the following qualities in order of their importance to you in choosing the place where you buy accessories, with 1 being most important.

___ personal service
___ reasonable prices
___ wide selection
___ unusual, original styles
___ convenience (location, ease of shopping)

8. How important are accessories to ___ your working clothes?
___ your dress clothes?
   a) very important
   b) somewhat important
   c) not important

9. How far are you normally willing to travel to buy accessories?
   a. less than 10 minutes
   b. 10 – 20 minutes
   c. 20 – 30 minutes
   d. more than 30 minutes

THE FOLLOWING QUESTIONS ARE DESIGNED TO TELL US SOME-
THING ABOUT THE KIND OF PEOPLE WHO USE ACCESSORIES.

10. What magazines do you read regularly?

   _____
   _____
   _____
   _____
   _____

11. Which of the following terms most closely describes the image you
    would like people to have of you?
   ___ elegant and sophisticated
   ___ casual and comfortable
   ___ a real individualist
   ___ competent and businesslike
   ___ very feminine
   ___ one of the guys
   ___ young but worldly wise

NOW WE NEED SOME DEMOGRAPHIC INFORMATION TO HELP US
TABULATE YOUR RESULTS. LET ME REMIND YOU THAT ALL
ANSWERS ARE STRICTLY CONFIDENTIAL.

12. Please indicate the category into which your age falls?
   ___ Under 18, ___ 19 – 25, ___ 25 – 34, ___ 35 – 44, ___ 45 – 54, ___
   55 – 64, ___ 65 or over.

13. Male ___ Female ___

14. __ Single __ Married __ Other

15. Occupation? _____
    Number of adults employed in household? ____

16. Other occupations _____?

17. How many children, and their ages _____?

18. Which of the following categories includes your total household income?
    __ Under $3000, __ 3 – 6999, __ 7 – 9999, __ 10 – 14,999, __
    15 – 19,999, __ 20 – 34,999, __ 35 – 49,999, __ 50 – 74,999, __ Over
    75,000.

THANK YOU FOR YOUR COOPERATION!

SURVEY RESULTS

As we began to tabulate the survey results, we noticed differences in the responses of two general age groups, and so we separated these to best illustrate the results.

18 – 30 Age Bracket—66% of Total

1. How important are accessories to your wardrobe?
   3% __ Not important   58% __ Somewhat important   39% __ Important

2. How often do you buy accessories (scarves, belts, jewelry, perfume) as gifts for female friends and relatives)
   64% __ Usually 21% __ Frequently 14% __ Sometimes
   0 __ Rarely 1% __ Never

3. What types of accessories do you most often buy for yourself? As Gifts?
   (Check all that apply)

SELF		GIFTS	
82% ____	jewelry	74% ____	jewelry
8% ____	scarves	6% ____	scarves
38% ____	belts	12% ____	belts
31% ____	purses	27% ____	purses
57% ____	perfume	65% ____	perfume
5% ____	hats	0% ____	hats
72% ____	cosmetics	21% ____	cosmetics
5% ____	other	4% ____	other (please specify)

4. I'm going to give you four price categories. Please tell me which you consider to be a reasonable price for each of the following accessories, both as gifts and for yourself.

a. $5 – 15
b. $16 – 25
c. $26 – 40
d. Over 40

SELF	GIFTS
a.____ jewelry	b.____ jewelry
a.____ scarves	b.____ scarves
b.____ belts	b.____ belts
c.____ purses	c.____ purses
c.____ perfume	c.____ perfume
a.____ cosmetics	a.____ cosmetics

5. Where do you usually buy accessories? (Choose the best answer)
   a. department store (please specify) 54%
   b. Accessories Plus 12%
   c. Compliments 3%
   d. Looking Good 17%
   e. Meredith's 2%
   f. Other (please specify) __ 22% (top contender—factory outlets)

6. Department stores tend to be chosen for convenience and wide selection; other stores seem to be selected because they have unusual styles.

7. Please rank the following qualities in order of their importance to you in choosing the place where you buy accessories, with 1 being most important.
    5% __ personal service
   34% __ reasonable prices
   33% __ wide selection
   25% __ unusual, original styles
    3% __ convenience (location, ease of shopping)

8. How important are accessories to __ your working clothes?
                                    __ your dress clothes?
   a) very important   work ____ 28%   dress ____ 67%
   b) somewhat important   work ____ 22%   dress ____ 22%
   c) not important   work ____ 50%   dress ____ 11%

9. How far are you normally willing to travel to buy accessories?
   a. less than 10 minutes 57%
   b. 10 – 20 minutes 21%
   c. 20 – 30 minutes 12%
   d. more than 30 minutes 10%

THE FOLLOWING QUESTIONS ARE DESIGNED TO TELL US SOME-
THING ABOUT THE KIND OF PEOPLE WHO USE ACCESSORIES.

10. What magazines do you read regularly?
    Fashion and appearance related magazines (82%)   fitness magazines
    (various) 34%
    Newsweek or Time (38%)

11. Which of the following terms most closely describes the image you
    would like people to have of you?
    4% _____ elegant and sophisticated
    47% _____ casual and comfortable
    21% _____ a real individualist
    6% _____ competent and businesslike
    2% _____ very feminine
    12% _____ one of the guys
    8% _____ young but worldly wise

31 – 50 Age Bracket—34% of Total

1. How important are accessories to your wardrobe?
   0 __ Not important 58% __ Somewhat important 42% __ Important

2. How often do you buy accessories (scarves, belts, jewelry, perfume) as
   gifts for female friends and relatives)
   37% __ Usually 32% __ Frequently 21% __ Sometimes
   6% __ Rarely 4% __ Never

3. What types of accessories do you most often buy for yourself? As Gifts?
   (Check all that apply)

SELF		GIFTS	
79% _____	jewelry	74% _____	jewelry
12% _____	scarves	12% _____	scarves
33% _____	belts	6% _____	belts
46% _____	purses	51% _____	purses
54% _____	perfume	61% _____	perfume
8% _____	hats	3% _____	hats
87% _____	cosmetics	23% _____	cosmetics

4. I'm going to give you four price categories. Please tell me which you
   consider to be a reasonable price for each of the following accessories,
   both as gifts and for yourself.
   a. $5 – 15
   b. $16 – 25
   c. $26 – 40
   d. Over 40

SELF	**GIFTS** (most common answer)
b.____ scarves	c.____ scarves
c.____ belts	c.____ belts
c.____ purses	c.____ purses
b.____ perfume	c.____ perfume
c.____ hats	____ hats
b.____ cosmetics	____ cosmetics

5. Where do you usually buy accessories? (Choose the *best* answer)
   a. department store (please specify) 46%
   b. Accessories Plus 4%
   c. Compliments 4%
   d. Looking Good 12%
   e. Meredith's 4%
   f. Other (please specify) 30% (most common: mail order; outlets)

6. Most choose department stores for convenience and one-stop shopping. Mail order because it offers styles not available locally, other competitors for service (1st), prices (second).

7. Please rank the following qualities in order of their importance to you in choosing the place where you buy accessories, with 1 being most important.
   21% ____ personal service
   12% ____ reasonable prices
   30% ____ wide selection
   25% ____ unusual, original styles
   12% ____ convenience (location, ease of shopping)

8. How important are accessories to __ your working clothes?
   __ your dress clothes?
   a) very important   Work __ 67%   Dress __ 64%
   b) somewhat important Work __ 31%   Dress __ 34%
   c) not important   Work __ 2%   Dress __ 2%

9. How far are you normally willing to travel to buy accessories?
   a. less than 10 minutes 7%
   b. 10−20 minutes 15%
   c. 20−30 minutes 73%
   d. more than 30 minutes 3%

THE FOLLOWING QUESTIONS ARE DESIGNED TO TELL US SOMETHING ABOUT THE KIND OF PEOPLE WHO USE ACCESSORIES.
   10. What magazines do you read regularly?
   Fashion Magazines (67%); Decorating (aimed at middle income, 31%;

upper income 39%), News magazines (54%); Hobby and crafts (33%) Women's mags (feminist type 43%)

11. Which of the following terms most closely describes the image you would like people to have of you?

27% _____ elegant and sophisticated
24% _____ casual and comfortable
 7% _____ a real individualist
26% _____ competent and businesslike
 3% _____ very feminine
 9% _____ one of the guys
 4% _____ young but worldly wise

ANALYSIS OF RESULTS AND RECOMMENDATIONS FOR ADVERTISING

Both of the surveyed age groups find accessories at least somewhat important to their wardrobes; the younger group are more likely to buy accessories as gifts.

The types of items purchased by the two groups are similar, although the older group buys more purses, both as gifts and for self. Neither group seems especially interested in hats or scarves, which suggests that these would not be good items to feature in sales ads or specials.

Reasonable accessory prices for the younger group range from $5 – 15 for most items, although they will pay more ($26 – 40) for perfume than the older group. As sexist as it might sound, this is probably because many of this group are still single. Interestingly, the older group, though, buys more cosmetics, and spends more for them. Their average reasonable price range was $16 – 40 for self; $26 – 40 for gifts.

Both groups tend to spend slightly more for gift accessories than they would normally spend on themselves, although the focus group revealed that both groups will occasionally splurge on a very high priced item for a special occasion.

The 18 – 30 age group most frequently goes to the department store to shop, mainly for convenience and a wide selection; they select other, smaller competitors because the store carries a particular style that they like. This indicates that wide selection and interesting, unusual styles would be a strong selling point for advertising.

The 31 – 50 group also favored department stores, though not as heavily. This was, once again, for convenience; most of these women are married with families and are in the store for other merchandise, so they simply buy their accessories there too. However, mail order emerges as a bigger contender than other area shops, mainly because women feel that they can order merchandise that they will not find here—they seem to want individuality, and things that no one else has.

For the older group, the qualities most instrumental in choosing a store are wide selection and unusual merchandise. For the younger group, price becomes a more important consideration, then both wide and unusual selections. The ability of accessories to create an individual look is an important aspect to emphasize in advertising; ads aimed at those below 30, your new target audience, should also feature lower priced but unusual merchandise.

Ads aimed at those over 30 can specify accessories for the working woman; these are not as important to the younger group, probably because many of them are still in school, or employed in jobs that require uniforms, smocks, etc. For this group, special occasion accessories seem to be most important.

Your area of trade varies widely with the two groups. Many of the younger group are students, without cars, and so the majority of your audience here will travel less than 20 minutes to buy a special accessory. In the older group, people will typically travel up to 30 minutes to buy a special accessory, indicating that this group can be reached with media that have a wider circulation.

As for the self-image of the two groups, your older audience falls into three main groups, almost equally strong: elegant and sophisticated; competent and businesslike, and casual and comfortable. An elegant but not frilly image might appeal to all of these groups.

It might also appeal to your younger target group, almost half of whom view themselves as casual but comfortable types, with 21 percent individualists.

Appendix C

Chapter 10 Sample Budget Breakdown for With Compliments

Percent of Budget to be Spent Each Month, in Accordance with Sales

JANUARY	1%
FEBRUARY	10%
MARCH	8.5%
APRIL	2.5%
MAY	13%
JUNE	13%
JULY	3.5%
AUGUST	6%
SEPTEMBER	2%
OCTOBER	2.5%
NOVEMBER	16%
DECEMBER	22%

Percent of Budget Broken Down by Target Audience

60% TO WOMEN, 35 – 55
40% TO WOMEN, 25 – 34

BUDGET BREAKDOWN ACCORDING TO MEDIA

Radio: $1344 (Roughly 60/40 among stations aimed at each group)
　　　WXXX (reaching 35 – 55)—$784
　　　WYYY (reaching 25 – 34)—$460

Tempo Magazine: $1560 (reaching women 35 – 55)
TV (Noncommercial sponsorship, reaching women 35 – 55): $1000
Philharmonic program: $300 (Women, 35 – 55)
Newspaper (reaching both audiences, placed in women's section): $7384

TOTAL: $11,488

MONTH	WYYY	WXXX	TIMES	TEMPO	TV	PHIL.	TOTAL
JAN.					83	25	108
FEB.	60	228	487	260	83	25	1143
MAR.	60	80	429	260	83	25	937
APR.	80	80			83	25	268
MAY	40	80	1014	260	83	25	1502
JUNE	40	80	1014	260	83	25	1502
JULY			312		83	25	420
AUG.			604		83	25	712
SEPT.			117		83	25	225
OCT.			195		83	25	303
NOV.	80	80	1254	260	83	25	1782
DEC.	100	156	1898	260	83	25	2522
TOTAL	460	784	7384	1560	1000	300	11,488

Appendix D

Examples of Selling Points Turned into Benefits

SELLING POINT	BENEFITS
Low prices	Save money. Get more for your money.
Big selection	Find everything you want. All your favorite styles; Something for every taste.
Luxurious decor	Shop in elegant surroundings.
Celebrity clientele	Shop with the celebrities; Shop with people in the know.
Air conditioning	Shop in cool comfort.
High prices	Buy the best, because you're worth it.
Quality goods	An investment in quality; Goods that will last; Get the best.
Expertise	Get the advice you need.
In business 50 years	Benefit from experience; A name you can trust.
Good location	Convenient.
Mass produced goods	Get on the bandwagon.
Unusual merchandise	Show your individuality.
Neighborhood store	Where everyone knows your name.

Appendix E
Sample Scripts

THE STRAIGHT SELL

ANNOUNCER: Feel like you're melting in this heat? Want something cool, smooth, and delicious? Want something creamy and packed full of flavor? You want a dairy fresh ice cream cone from Toner's. Visit our dairy, pet the cows, then come into our air-conditioned soda fountain and try one of our 25 varieties of home-made ice cream. We're on Route 6, right by the cider mill in Dalton. Beat the heat at Toner's, where our ice cream starts with the cow.

STRAIGHT SELL, DRAMATIZED

SFX; EERIE, SUSPENSEFUL MUSIC, UP AND UNDER

ANNOUNCER (HUMPHREY BOGART-TYPE DELIVERY): It was a dark and stormy night. As I shivered in the fog outside of Hillman's Book store, I knew my long search had come to an end. It was in there—no doubt about it. Everything I'd been looking for. Drama. Suspense. Sex and romance. Hard-hitting facts. Even the recipe for black-bottom pie that she used to tempt me with. Yes—at Hillman's Book Store—books on everything, for anybody—even a hard-boiled flat-foot like me. The biggest selection in town, and a great place to escape from the world and the dark and stormy night. Hillman's Book Store, in New Orleans French Quarter across from Jackson's Brewery. Find adventure tonight at Hillman's Bookstore.

DIALOGUE RADIO SCRIPT

SFX: RESTAURANT CROWD NOISES. MARSHALL'S MANOR THEME PLAYED BY 3-PIECE ORCHESTRA, UP THREE SECONDS AND UNDER.

WAITER: Is everything all right, ma'am?

WOMAN 1: Mmmmmmmm.....

WAITER: Is everything all right, sir?

MAN 1: Mmmmmmmmmm......

WAITER: Are you satisfied with your meal, madam?

WOMAN 2: Mmmmmmmmm....

WAITER: No matter what the event at Marshall's Manor—weddings, parties, business meetings—our dinners meet with a remarkably similar response.

CROWD: MMMmmmmmmmm!

WAITER: That's Marshall's Manor. Call us at 346-6540 for fantastic fresh food, wonderful atmosphere, and rave reviews. For all your catering needs, call Marshall's Manor at 346-6540.

WOMAN 1: At Marshall's Manor, the M stands for Mmmmmm.

SFX; ORCHESTRA, MARSHALL'S MANOR THEME, UP AND OUT.

SLICE-OF-LIFE COMMERCIAL

SFX: DRUM ROLL, EXCITED MURMUR OF CROWD FADING UNDER

ANNOUNCER: And this year's Prom Queen is. . . .

SFX: CROWD NOISE, UP AND UNDER

MALE: She's looking good!

MALE 2: She's looking great!

SFX: CROWD NOISES FADE OUT

JUDY: This year's prom has been a disaster. The Prom queen and I have the same dress on. But while she's turning heads, I'm getting turned down.

JEAN: You have to admit, her accessories really do make the outfit. I heard she got them at Looking Good—and she's looking great.

JUDY: You're right. I wish I'd known that before the prom.

FEMALE ANNOUNCER: Don't let it happen to you. At Looking Good, our wide selection of unusual styles in jewelry, belts, and other accessories can turn simple into simply sensational. Come to our new location, in Southfield, on Cranbrook Road near Evergreen. Because if you're on your way to Looking Good, you're on your way to looking great!

MAN-ON-THE-STREET INTERVIEW

<u>SFX: SOUNDS OF HEAVY TRAFFIC, UP AND UNDER</u>

ANNOUNCER: Excuse me, sir, but what's that plant you're carrying?

MAN 1: It's a philodendron for my darkroom.

ANNOUNCER: Your darkroom?

MAN 1: Yes. I spend a lot of time there, and I wanted to make it homey. The people at Floral Artistry knew what to recommend. Uh—excuse me. I have to get home before it's over-exposed.

ANNOUNCER: Ma'am? Is that bird cage you're carrying really made of ivy?

WOMAN: Yes—my lovebirds are getting married tonight, and I knew the people at Floral Artistry could make it perfect for them. . .

ANNOUNCER: Sir? I'm afraid to ask. . .

MAN 2: Yes—I'm proposing tonight, and thanks to the people at Floral Artistry, I can promise her a bed of roses. . .

<u>SFX: TRAFFIC SOUNDS FADE OUT</u>

FEMALE ANNOUNCER: Whatever your floral needs, see Floral Artistry, in downtown Iowa City across from the Pentacrest. At Floral Artistry, if you can dream it, we can make it.

TESTIMONIAL

ANNOUNCER: As an airline pilot, I have to travel a lot. I love my job, but hotel rooms get depressing. I like Detroit best, because I have a home away from home—Logan's Bed and Breakfast Inn. The Logan's are college professors who have opened their home to travelers like me. They're close to downtown, and the Renaissance Center, but sometimes I hate to leave their crackling fireplace and good conversation. Mornings, they serve breakfast—fresh baked pastry, fruit, juice, and real New Orleans coffee. I even have my own room, filled with Victorian antiques. Just like Grandma's house. It feels like home—and with a busy flight schedule like mine, Logan's Bed and Breakfast is a pause that refreshes—at lower prices than any hotel or motel in the city. That's Logan's Bed and Breakfast on Jefferson, just east of the Renaissance Center. Call 961-9042 and make Logan's Bed and Breakfast your home away from home.

DRAMATIC RADIO SCRIPT

<u>SFX; ORGAN MUSIC SWELLS UP AND UNDER</u>

ANNOUNCER (WITH A DEEP, FUNEREAL VOICE): Hillman's Book Store presents—The Trial.

<u>SFX; ORGAN MUSIC OUT. SOUNDS OF COURTROOM CROWD, JUDGE BANGING ON GAVEL FADE UNDER.</u>

MRS. HILLMAN: We were happy, your honor. He dabbled in business and finance, and pored over the city's finest collection of cookbooks. I had my art section, and the state's biggest selection of self-help books. And then . . . .

ATTORNEY: Yes, Mrs. Hillman?

MRS. HILLMAN: Then he discovered the Reference section. It seduced him. He ordered everything. He followed me, reciting facts and figures. He corrected my grammar. He set up a booth for kids taking college entrance exams.

ATTORNEY: Isn't it true, Mrs. Hillman, that your husband created the best reference book selection in town?

MRS. HILLMAN: Yes—but you try living with a walking encyclopedia.

ATTORNEY: And so you put it all on sale?

MRS. HILLMAN: Guilty, sir. I took 20 percent off. And they're selling fast. . .

ANNOUNCER: Hillman's Book Store, in the French Quarter across from the Jackson Brewery, is having a 20% off sale on all reference books. Hurry to Hillman's today—before Mr. Hillman changes his mind.

MRS. HILLMAN: Maybe he can turn to romance fiction. . . .

FANTASY RADIO FORMAT

SFX: TYPEWRITER KEYS, BANGING IN A TAP DANCE RHYTHM

MEHITABEL: (GROWLY, CATLIKE FEMALE VOICE) Archie—what kind of typing is that?

SFX: A QUICK TYPED BEAT, THEN TYPING STOPS ABRUPTLY.

ARCHIE: It's these new Canon electronic typewriters that Silver's got in, Mehitabel. They're a breeze, even for a cockroach like me. I can see what I'm typing on this little viewer—and I can correct whole lines with one touch. It's even got a ten-page memory. And look here.

SFX: ARCHIE'S VOICE TAKES ON AN ECHO EFFECT

ARCHIE: Silver's new Canon model uses a daisy wheel, so I can change typefaces ten times and do special effects. I might do a novel, Mehitabel. I might go back to writing columns.

MEHITABEL: Good luck, Archie. At these low prices, you'll have to write fast.

SFX: DOOR OPENING, MUFFLED TRAFFIC SOUNDS

ARCHIE: Mehitabel! What are you doing?

SFX: MEHITABEL AT A DISTANCE, TRAFFIC SOUNDS UP SLIGHTLY

MEHITABEL: Telling everyone to rush to the huge electronic typewriter sale this week at Silver's. That's Silver's in Downtown Des Moines, across from City Hall.

SHOUTING, SOUNDING EVEN FARTHER AWAY, TRAFFIC UP SLIGHTLY

MEHITABEL: At Silver's, you'll find everything for the office.

SFX: DOOR SLAMMING

ARCHIE: Even a typewriting cockroach.

Appendix F

Sample
Public Relations Plan:
Fanning's Dance Studio

TO: MARK HOGAN, LIFESTYLE EDITOR

IOWA CITY PRESS CITIZEN
WALKING CLASSES FOR SENIORS

FOR FURTHER
INFORMATION:
Bernie Fanning
326-9477

<u>FOR RELEASE ON OR BEFORE JULY 14, PLEASE</u>

WHO: Bernie Fanning
WHAT: Walking classes for senior citizens
WHERE: Fanning's Dance Studio, 606 Clinton, Iowa City
WHEN: Beginning June 20
WHY: To offer senior citizens an alternative to mall-walking while teaching them
    to get the best aerobic benefits from walking.
HOW: Through the use of special breathing techniques, variations in stride and
    posture.

-30-

Press Release

TO: MARK HOGAN, LIFESTYLE EDITOR   FOR FURTHER
INFORMATION:

IOWA CITY PRESS CITIZEN   Bernie Fanning
WALKING CLASSES FOR SENIORS   326-9477

<u>FOR RELEASE ON OR BEFORE JULY 14, PLEASE</u>

To give senior citizens the full benefit of the walking regimen that their doctors recommend, Bernie Fanning is forming special aerobic walking classes at the Fanning Dance Studio, 606 Clinton St. The classes, which will take group walking tours around the city, are medically approved for senior citizens. They begin June 20.

According to Fanning, most seniors go to the malls to walk. "Sometimes they walk alone, which can be boring and depressing. And few of them walk so that they get the full benefit of their exercise. My classes will show them how to get the most from walking."

Fanning attended several American Medical Association seminars to learn the correct techniques. His classes, which will hold about 20 people, will take a different walk through the city each lesson.

While the class members walk, they will receive instruction on proper breathing, posture, pace and stride which are medically proved to benefit circulation.

Each walk goes though a different part of the city. One features historic sites, another is for walking and window shopping. Park and garden walks are featured.

Interested people may sign up for classes by calling the Fanning Dance Studio.

-30-

Index